Warm Brothers

QUEER THEORY

AND THE

AGE OF GOETHE

Robert Tobin

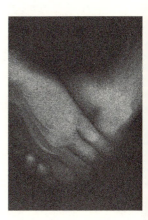

PENN

University of Pennsylvania Press

Philadelphia

Publication of this volume was assisted by a grant from Whitman College.

10 9 8 7 6 5 4 3 2 1

Published by
University of Pennsylvania Press
Philadelphia, Pennsylvania 19104-4011

Library of Congress Cataloging-in-Publication Data
Tobin, Robert Deam.
Warm brothers : queer theory and the age of Goethe / Robert D. Tobin.
p.   cm.
Includes bibliographical references and index.
ISBN 0-8122-3544-4 (alk. paper)
1. German literature — 18th century — History and criticism.   2. German
literature — 19th century — History and criticism.   3. Homosexuality in
literature.   4. Homosexuality and literature.   5. Homosexuality —
German — History.   I. Title.
PT321 .T58   2000
830.9′353 — dc21   99-058081

CONTENTS

Panik in Weimar   A. Weisgerber (München)

„Wolfgang, laſſen wir die Hände los! — der Dr. Magnus Hirſchfeld kommt!"

A. Weisgerber, "Panic in Weimar" (from *Jugend* 11.18 [Nov. 19, 1907]: 1089). Even in 1907, research in homosexuality put the Establishment on edge. The sexologist Magnus Hirschfeld, approaching from the left, provokes anxiety in Goethe and Schiller, as the original caption to the cartoon indicates: "Panic in Weimar: 'Wolfgang, let go of my hand! — Dr. Magnus Hirshfeld is coming.'"

PREFACE: PANIC IN WEIMAR

In its issue of November 19, 1907, the magazine *Youth* (*Jugend*) published a cartoon by A. Weisgerber, in which Schiller no longer wants to hold hands with Goethe in the monument to the two poets, because the sexologist and homosexual rights campaigner Hirschfeld is in the vicinity. "Wolfgang," Schiller says, "Let go of my hand! — Dr. Magnus Hirschfeld is coming!" (11.18: 1089). The title of this cartoon is "Panic in Weimar."

Although one might think that merely broaching the possibility of a sexual relationship between the two great poets of German classicism was a bold and transgressive move, the cartoon is not necessarily a progressive statement in favor of homosexual rights. James Steakley has shown that it fits into satirical campaigns against the Hohenzollern court, which was immersed in scandals involving noble favorites of Kaiser Wilhelm II like Philipp, Prince zu Eulenburg-Hertefeld, who was said to have sex with other men ("Iconography"). It also appears in the company of many somewhat bigoted, chauvinistic, and jingoistic cartoons about the German colonies, so one can see that *Jugend*, despite catering to a liberal bourgeois public, was not immune to nationalist and racial prejudices. Indeed, Hirschfeld is portrayed as a Jewish caricature, with a short physique and a long, crooked nose. While it may seem to implicate Goethe and Schiller humorously in the homophobic anxiety inspired by Hirschfeld's liberal theories, the cartoon ridicules the homosexual rights movement of its time.

One of the underlying theses of this book, however, is that the connection between authorial intent and a text is not indissoluble. Thus, this arguably anti-Semitic, homophobic cartoon also provides encouragement to the queer reader today. One of the striking points about the cartoon is its age. The fact that Germans could joke about the possibly queer sexuality of their national poets in 1907 illuminates the long tradition of the queer appropriation of literature. While right-wing academics today decry the contamination of literary studies by such allegedly sensationalist and trendy approaches to literature as gay and lesbian studies and queer theory, the cartoon reveals that serious scholars like Hirschfeld were interested in the queer sexuality of great authors long before terms like "gay and lesbian studies" and "queer theory" appeared in the American academy.

Moreover, this cartoon is merely the tip of an iceberg; Hirschfeld was only one of many German scholars in the first half of the twentieth century interested in the interplay of sexuality and textuality, of sex and culture. Far from decrying the recent fall of literary studies and its supposedly nascent interest in sexuality and the body, we should lament the retreat from such interests. After World War II, with the advent of New Criticism literary studies turned away from topics of the body and sexuality, but during the past two decades the beneficial influence of literary scholars interested in feminism and race brought back the body and allowed for a rebirth of gay and lesbian studies and the formulations of queer theory.

If one striking aspect of the cartoon from *Jugend* is its age, another is its current relevance. The year 1906 was not the only time that investigations like Hirschfeld's caused a panic in Weimar. In December 1994, Alice Kuzniar, Simon Richter, Roman Graf, Stephan Schindler, and I were part of a panel entitled "Outing Goethe" at the annual meeting of the Modern Language Association. The subject matter of the panel outraged certain critics. The *New York Post* and the *Wall Street Journal* mentioned it prominently in their annual summaries of the craziest excesses of the literary critics. The conservative cultural critic Roger Kimball not only listed the panel's title in his attack on the MLA and the association's homosexual leanings, but also specifically used a word from the title of my talk, "heterotextuality," in the headline of his article as the epitome of the nonsense coming out of the academic world today.

Subsequently, a panel I organized for the 1996 MLA called "Goethe's Masochism" also received national attention, being mentioned in National Public Radio's annual account of the outlandish doings of the professors. It is worth noting that Goethe retains this inviolable image as representative of the "nice" and "good" Enlightenment, even in an era in which German literary, cultural, and language studies are generally on the decline in the United States. Indeed, one cannot imagine that many of the listeners of National Public Radio or the readers of the *Wall Street Journal* or the *New York Post* have read much by Goethe lately, even if they are shocked by his manhandling by provocative professors. As Martin Greif writes, "attempting to show why some thinkers over the centuries have suspected the German genius of being gay is about as loaded a proposition as suggesting that Jesus and his twelve Disciples were members of the international homointern. Dare to lay a finger on Goethe and there are people out there gunning for you" (150).

In Germany, the allergic reaction to queering Goethe has been even more severe. The hue and cry was enormous in 1997 when Karl Hugo Pruys published his book *Die Liebkosungen des Tigers: eine erotische Goethe Biographie* (The Embraces of the Tiger: An Erotic Goethe Biography), in which he downplays Goethe's liaisons with women and implies the writer's interest in men. Admittedly, the book is execrable, relying on misogynist arguments to diminish the role of women in Goethe's life, providing little new information about the role of men in his life, and contributing nothing to an analysis of Goethe's texts or the history of sexuality. The book's detractors in Germany did not attack it on the basis of these faults, however. In the highly respectable weekly *Die Zeit*, the noted critic Sigrid Löffler reduced it immediately to a *Geschwuchtel*, descending to somewhat offensive vocabulary, meaning something like "faggotry," to carry her argument. The *New York Times*, which picked up on the story, quoted Werner Keller, director of the International Goethe Society in Cologne, as claiming that it didn't matter whether Goethe was homosexual or heterosexual. Again descending to invective in order to remove the question from the field, Keller declares his contempt for an era that would pose such questions. In The *New York Times*, Keller's colleague, Lothar Ehrlich of the Stiftung Weimarer Klassik (Foundation of Weimar Classicism), supports him in his dismissal of these questions. Goethe's inviolability remains constant: From *Die Zeit* to the International Goethe Society to the Stiftung Weimarer Klassik, the protectors of the German classics have reacted with extreme sensitivity to questions of sexuality and its relevance to eighteenth-century authors. Perhaps this reaction is due to the massive efforts made by the German cultural establishment to certify Goethe as the "good" German after World War II.

Whatever the reasons, queering Goethe has proven to be a provocative act; yet the more I study Goethe and his contemporaries, the more it seems to me that the entire era can and should receive a queer analysis. In this book, I analyze Wieland, Moritz, Jean Paul, Schiller, Lichtenberg, as well as Goethe and a host of lesser-known writers from the late eighteenth and early nineteenth centuries. I could easily have continued the analysis by writing entire chapters about the sentimental poet Gleim, the novelist Heinse, the *Sturm-und-Drang* writers Lenz and Klinger, the explorer and intellectual Alexander von Humboldt, the short-story writer Chamisso, the dramatists Kleist and Iffland, and the poets Hölderlin and Platen.

Too often, the conviction that these eighteenth-century German writers could not be gay has resulted in the default assumption that they must have been straight. In fact, a cursory examination of their lives suggests that they cannot be called "straight," either. Taking back the Age of Goethe from the straight gaze to which it has been subjected restores complexity to these texts and removes the oppressive burden of canonical saintliness from them. They can still speak to modern concerns, while enriching our understanding of their era.

ABBREVIATIONS

HA = *Goethes Werke: Hamburger Ausgabe in 14 Bänden.* Ed. Erich Trunz. 11th ed. Munich: Beck, 1981.

NA = Schiller, Friedrich. *Werke. Nationalausgabe.* Ed. Julius Petersen and Gerhard Fricke. Weimar: Bohlaus, 1942.

SW = Müller, Johannes. *Sämmtliche Werke.* Tübingen: Cotta, 1811–15.

WA = *Goethes Werke: Herausgegeben im Auftrage der Großherzogin Sophie von Sachsen.* Tokyo: Sansyusya, 1975. Reprint. Munich: DTV, 1987.

1

QUEERING THE
EIGHTEENTH CENTURY

To queer the eighteenth century is to look at it differently, from a new perspective informed by the sexuality and theory of a later century. Queering the eighteenth century means wrenching it from established contexts in order to read it against the grain of traditional readings and dissolving the accreted interpretations that stifle or avoid those textual passages that do not lend themselves to orthodox readings. Such passages might often suggest a queer sexuality, that is to say, a sexuality divergent from the assumptions of present-day heterosexual norms. By targeting such passages in a text, a queer analysis can produce interpretations that both resonate with the modern-day reader, while at the same time allowing for the eighteenth-century text to speak more fully than it has been able to previously.

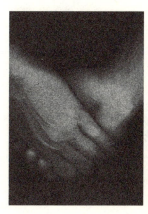

Overcomes socied stereotypes—hegemeny

QUEERING

It might still seem odd, eccentric, even queer, to use an American twentieth-century slang term like "queer," which emerges from an almost untranslatable subculture of "closeted" and "outed" "gays" and "straights," to approach a world as separated by time, culture, and language from that word as the worlds of eighteenth- and nineteenth-century German literature. Maria Kalveram and Wolfgang Popp, editors of a collection of German-language essays on the subject of homosexuality and literature, make the same point in their apology for the late appearance of their anthology: "A special problem . . . was and is that of the translation from the congress language English into German. Here it first became clear that there are linguistic problems in the appropriation of colloquial and subcultural vocabulary that are scarcely to be solved satisfactorily" (9). The reliance on a queer vocabulary to look at eighteenth-century texts seems all the more eccentric when one learns that queer theory arises from rhetorical criticism and is thus highly attuned to cultural and linguistic difference. By its own standards, then, queer theory might itself disavow any attempt it made to reach beyond the domain of modern, self-identified queers. (And indeed queer theory does disproportionately emphasize twentieth-century English and American literature.)

Yet this very attentiveness to language points in the direction of another path between modern queer theory and earlier texts: the English word "queer" is perhaps related to the German word "quer," meaning "oblique" or "slanting." By the late 1990s, the word "queer," clearly seen as related to "quer," had shown up in German academics and the gay German subculture. A 1997 conference of the Magnus-Hirschfeld-Gesellschaft on the Scientific-Humanitarian Committee was called "Queered Science" (*Verqueere Wissenschaft*). A co-host of the conference was *Queerstudien* from the cultural studies department of the Humboldt University. Following on this path of seeing queer as *quer*, a queer reading—guided perhaps by some experiences relating to the modern gay world—would, then, move against the grain of textual traditions. Rather than moving straight through literature, it would run *quer durch die Literatur*—queer through literature, obliquely through it, clear through it, all the way back through it, perversely through it. Such a reading would require readers to face multiple meanings and ambivalences; it would also allow for more perspectives, enriching these texts.

But is the queer reading, the reading against the grain, utterly ahistorical and anachronistic? One could view this project as yet another example of modern technology run amok, a grotesque colorization. Does the queer analysis ruin the classic black-and-white beauty of eighteenth-century German texts with the lurid and gaudy technicolor of the modern American? In a word, No. Reading against the grain of one's own time might in fact bring one into better alignment with another era. Queer readings, accused of being anachronistic, tend to be better informed on the history of sexuality than most interpretations, for in recent years much more work has been done, largely by gay and lesbian scholars, on the history of homosexuality than on the history of heterosexuality. Thus queer scholarship has, by and large, a highly nuanced approach to the history of sexuality.

The multiple sexualities that have become apparent as a result of historical research began to threaten to explode the categories of "gay," lesbian," and "homosexual" that had been used to analyze the history of sexuality. Even within contemporary American culture, lists that begin with "gay, lesbian, bisexual, transgendered" and end with what Judith Butler calls the "embarrassed" and "exasperated 'etc.'" (*Gender Trouble* 145) have become too unwieldy. Imagine if one needed to add "sodomite," "rake," "libertine," "molly," "invert," and "queen," plus "tribade," "dyke," and "butch" and "femme" — as well as other variants, such as "sadist" or "masochist" — to the list! In contemporary society, "queer" has come to replace these lists as an easy, perhaps even lazy way to include all those whose sexuality rubs up against the normative goals. In the same sense, it could usefully describe those sexualities that differ either from the norm of their own historical epochs or from what modern readers consider the default sexuality. "Queer" in this sense of "other," "different," or "unusual" can be much less anachronistic than the word "homosexual" when used to discuss authors and writings that appeared before 1869, when that word was first coined.

In a more rigorous vein, queer theorists like Lauren Berlant and Michael Warner usually insist that "queer" should *not* be a catch-all term to encompass a multitude of identities, but rather an anti-identitarian term. While it seems as utopian to hope to escape identity as it would be to leave discourse and power structures entirely, it is also important to recognize the contradictions within any identity, the multiple identities that any situation might impose on the individuals in that situation, and the constantly changing and self-contradictory identities of modern subjects. As Teresa de Lauretis writes in her introduction to a volume of *Differences* devoted to queer theory, queers should aim "not to adhere to any one of the given terms, not to assume their ideological liabilities, but instead to both transgress and transcend them — or at the very least problematize them." This version of queer theory thus stands for a post-identity approach to sexuality. Rather than being satisfied with distinguishing various types of homosexual from various types of heterosexual and bisexual (part of the taxonomic project of gay and lesbian studies), it looks for the homosexual in heterosexual structures and vice versa. Looking back in history, queer theory might want to know how the sexual dissident Johann Joachim Winkelmann managed to set up images from a sexually notorious culture, ancient Greece, as the standard for modern heterosexual men and women.

In summary, queer reading will usually be particularly attuned to the nuances of history, looking for subtle variations in the patterns of sexuality that now seem natural and permanent. Rather than assuming that all cultures have always sanctioned what we currently understand as "straight" sexuality, the queer reading will root around and ferret out those elements of earlier texts that transgress the boundaries of currently normative sexuality. The queer reading will be reluctant to accept any authors as clearly "straight," and will look for textual elements that resist such categorization. In so doing, it should correct the errors of those who assume an exclusively straight perspective on older literature. This queer perspective on eighteenth-century German literature, despite its appearance of anachronism, may augment and improve the accuracy of our historical view of these authors.

THE EIGHTEENTH CENTURY AND FOUCAULT

In recent decades, some scholars have begun to look at the eighteenth century, specifically in Germany, from a queer perspective. Hans Mayer began in 1981 with his book *Outsiders*, in which the art historian Winckelmann and the poet Platen figure as prominent examples of queer men who lived in the eighteenth century. As interest in gay and lesbian studies has grown in the United States, the German eighteenth century came into queer focus. In 1989, James Steakley wrote on the internalization of homophobic desire in Prussia, and Dennis Sweet considered Winckelmann again, from a decidedly anti-essentialist position. In 1990, Paul Derks published his comprehensive review of the passages from the Age of Goethe that refer to same-sex desire.

Five years later, Rainer Guldin followed in Derks's footsteps, discovering additional material suggestive of male-male love. In the same year, Heinrich Detering published a study on the productivity of the closet, suggesting that the societal mandate to keep homosexual desire secret was the force prodding many eighteenth- and nineteenth-century German authors to write. Retreating from Derks's encyclopedic inclusiveness, he concentrated on a few figures, including Winckelmann. In the United States, Alice Kuzniar's *Outing Goethe and His Age*, a collection of essays from a decidedly queer perspective by such authors as Susan Gustafson, W. Daniel Wilson, Laurence Rickels, Susanna Kord, Roman Graf, Simon Richter, and Catriona MacLeod, appeared in 1996. Chris Lorey has published a collection of essays entitled *Queering the Canon*, with an outspoken commitment to queering German literature, including that of the eighteenth century.

While there is obviously interest in developing queer perspectives on eighteenth-century German literature, even sympathetically disposed readers understand that the project is fraught with conceptual, historical, and theoretical difficulties. To begin with, one of the foundational thinkers of queer theory, Michel Foucault, seems to imply that homosexuality is barely a hundred years old, suggesting that one shouldn't look prior to the nineteenth century if one is viewing the world from a modern gay perspective. Foucault's statement that the homosexual was born in 1870 ("Westphal's famous article of 1870 can stand as its birth"; *History* 43) has traumatized many queer commentators who wish to work on texts written before the nineteenth century. On the one hand, the arguments for the social construction of homosexuality are compelling, as is the thesis that this construction took place in the nineteenth century. On the other hand, scholars specializing in the eighteenth century then wonder what to make of the evidence not only for same-sexual activity in the eighteenth century, but also for subcultural formations around that activity.

Were the members of these subcultural formations in fact only "a temporary aberration," rather than the "species" that Foucault sees in the modern homosexual (*History* 43)? Foucault's erroneous date for Westphal's article — 1870 instead of 1869 — suggests that we need not venerate his timeline. While many of these sodomites (or, as they might have preferred to be called, "warm brothers") might not have had the kind of "identity" that Foucault would see in the nineteenth-century homosexual — "a personage, a past, a case history, and a childhood . . . a type of life, a life form, and a morphology" (*History* 43) — they were able to situate themselves in subcultures that were already prefiguring the identity of the modern homosexual.

The Dutch scholar Theo van der Meer provides a useful commonsense definition of subcultures surrounding same-sex desire as "a specific form of organization of sexuality which differs from what is dominant in a culture, as a means of passing on habits, norms, and values, and as a means to identify with one another." He goes on to note that at any given time and place, there might be multiple subcultures around same-sex desire, for instance, "among soldiers, sailors, and courtiers" (286). Some of the sexual subcultures that existed in the late eighteenth century were beginning to fuse certain signifiers into a cluster that would later attach to homosexuality. This cluster included Hellenism, orientalism, the cult of friendship, and a cultivation of fashion. *Avant la lettre*, these configurations of signifiers constituted a style that would today be recognized as "gay male" (especially by modern gay men, into the construction of whose identity these signifiers have flown[1]), even though they were constructed before such a homosexual identity existed.

But if homosexuals were born in the late nineteenth century, they were begotten in the eighteenth century. Despite Foucault's dating of the birth of the homosexual to around 1870, that chronology should be read in the context of his understanding of the birth of "man" around 1800. Foucault writes that "man is only a recent invention, a figure not yet two centuries old, a new wrinkle in our knowledge" (*Order* xxiii). He concludes *The Order of Things* with the statement that "Man was constituted at the beginning of the nineteenth century" (330). The Foucauldian "homosexual" is a product of the Foucauldian "man," and in order to get at the nature of that "homosexual," one can look to eighteenth-century structures that produced "man."

"Man" appears in the shift between the classical and the modern epistemes, a shift that Foucault believes happened at "the outer limits" sometime between 1775 and 1825. More specifically, he targets the five years between 1795 and 1800 (*Order* 221) as the time of the epistemic shift. Providing corroborating evidence, the sociologist Niklas Luhmann also believes that a major shift took place around 1800, especially in matters of the heart (51).

Foucault's understanding of "man" refers to a specific construction of what it means to be human, just as his deconstruction of the author assails a specific vision of the author and his historicizing of homosexuality interrogates a specific kind of same-sex behavior. All of these specific structures — "man," "homosexual," "author" — are interrelated, and all emerge out of the eighteenth century. Although it would obviously be well beyond the scope of this book to provide an anthropology of the eighteenth century, let me lay a framework for describing the forces that gave birth to "man" around 1800 and "the homosexual" around 1870, before returning to the texts at hand.

SOCIAL-HISTORICAL BACKGROUND

To begin with, economic structures were changing fundamentally. By the end of the eighteenth century, the industrial revolution was in full swing in Great

1. Wayne Koestenbaum has described the process by which modern gay men might detect elements that went into the historical constitution of their own identity in texts: "the (male twentieth-century first-world) gay reader . . . reads resistantly for inscriptions of his condition, for texts that will confirm a social and private identity founded on a desire for other men. Reading becomes a hunt for histories that deliberately foreknow or unwittingly trace a desire felt not by author but by reader, who is most astute when searching for designs of himself" (176–77).

Britain and Holland. Its onset was easy to predict in Germany; by the 1820s, Goethe recorded its destructive ramifications quite clearly in *Wilhelm Meister's Journeyman Years* (*Wilhelm Meisters Wanderjahre*), when one character reports that "the increasing dominance of machine production torments and frightens me: it is rolling like a storm, slowly, slowly; but it is headed this way, and it will arrive and strike" (*HA* 8: 429). In a groundbreaking essay, John D'Emilio argues that such processes of capitalism and industrialization begun in the eighteenth century were vital for the establishment of modern gay identities: "Only when individuals began to make their living through wage labor, instead of as parts of an interdependent family unity, was it possible for homosexual desire to coalesce into personal identity" (8). Jeffrey Weeks has also theorized that the rise of capitalism brought about changes in society and life that produced new forms of sexuality. It is therefore perhaps no surprise that the text by Goethe with the most explicit depiction of industrialization also provides the most unabashed description of homoerotic desire — the story of the fisherman's son, with whom Wilhelm falls in love.

The progress of capitalism and industrialization furthered the rise of the bourgeoisie to hegemony. Again, this development was most pronounced in northwestern Europe. Germany's bourgeoisie was scattered and politically impotent, particularly in the east, where the great powers of Prussia and Austria retained political systems reliant on the aristocracy. Culturally, however, it was quite clear in Germany, too, that the middle classes were in command of the social agenda. Already in the eighteenth century, genres like the bourgeois tragedy and movements like *Sturm und Drang* (storm and stress) were entirely attuned to the concerns of the middle class. Plays like Lessing's *Emilia Galotti* and novels like Goethe's *Werther* depict the ideals of the bourgeoisie in opposition to those of the aristocracy. Even though an author like Goethe might eventually work for the nobility and receive a title himself, his political agenda would nonetheless still involve a coalition between progressive nobility and the bourgeoisie, which had the capital and energy to reconstruct society.

These changes in class structure had their impact on sexuality as well. On the one hand, the bourgeois mentality set loose many of the energies that have culminated two centuries later in the queer project. The bourgeois glorification of personal feelings like love not only permitted the young to defy the tradition of arranged marriage; it allowed men and women who desired members of their own sex to take those feelings seriously. Bourgeois rhetoric of rights gave them the courage to insist upon acting upon those feelings of love and desire. And, finally, bourgeois ideologies of individualism allowed for the kind of subjective interpretation that is at the core of queer reading.

At the same time, however, male-male sex objectified men in a way that struck at the heart of the middle-class ideology of the autonomous individual, promoting, as Lee Edelman suggests, bourgeois homophobia (121) and, in Eve Sedgwick's vocabulary, homosexual panic. Hence the increased persecution of sodomy documented by George S. Rousseau in England and Van der Meer and Huussen in Holland. While the rise of this particularly virulent homophobia in bourgeois circles was disastrous for many individuals, its existence suggests that homosexuality was for the first time becoming an issue important enough to merit a strong political and cultural reaction.

Currently, the documentation for the existence of German sodomitical subcultures similar to the ones in England and Holland is lacking. Perhaps this is due to the reality that German cities had not attained the density needed to develop such subcultures. There were relatively few cities in Germany in the eighteenth century that could compare in size with London, Amsterdam, Paris, or Rome. The Thirty Years' War of the seventeenth century had devastated what urban culture there was, and it took Germany about a century to recover. On the other hand, it is likely that information regarding the "warm brothers" in Germany remains to be uncovered.

One hint that the same social changes that were bringing about new sexual orders in the rest of Europe were also taking affect in Germany is the emergence of the word "family" in the German langauge. Although the Industrial Revolution and the rise of the bourgeoisie contributed to the birth of the homosexual, they gave much more publicity to their other offspring, the nuclear family. In German, "family" (*die Familie*), that seeming given in society, is actually a Latinate loan word that gained currency only in the eighteenth century. The brothers Grimm, two of the leaders of German Romanticism, describe in their monumental dictionary *Deutsches Wörterbuch* the arrival of the word "Familie" using a martial language that points to the cultural battles that prepared the way for the supremacy of this particular social structure:

Family, f., from the Lat. *familia* . . . has forcefully penetrated everywhere since the beginning of the 18. century . . . it was as unused in the 17th as in the 13th century; Frisch and Adelung [earlier 18th-century lexicographers] cannot resist it any longer . . . As beautiful and appropriate as it is in itself, it has, like innumerable other foreign words destroyed our own traditional ones and through its influence damaged many natural phrases. (vol. 3, col. 1305)

The vocabulary that the Grimms use both suggests the cultural wars that were taking place as the family was being reconceived in the eighteenth century, and locates those cultural wars in a German nationalist setting.

The Grimms go on to suggest that only the word "household" (*Haus*) offers any competition to the word "family"; they note that the mid-eighteenth-century poet and philosopher Gellert avoids the word "family" and instead uses expressions like "I greet and bless your whole household" (3: 1305). The higher mortality of earlier ages (particularly associated with childbirth) produced complicated familial structures, with second wives (the ubiquitous stepmothers of fairy tales), half-brothers and half-sisters, orphans sent off to live with distant relatives, widowed aunts and grandmothers. Such extended familial arrangements allowed one to speak of a "household" filled with more distant relatives and servants.

Moris Heyne, a later lexicographer, confirms the timeline that the Grimms propose for the origin of the word "family" and gives a sense of some of the other "traditional" and "natural" expressions that predated the word "family" in German:

Family, f. house- and blood-community (*Haus- und Geschlechtsgenossenschaft*), borrowed word from Lat. *familia*, first adopted in the early eighteenth century, and according to Frisch's documentation especially successful because of the effects of French *famille*; in the narrower and broader senses: family . . . sometimes means just wife and child alone, or includes the servants, sometimes the whole bloodline (*Geschlecht*). (1: 862)

Besides "household," some of the other phrases that "family" replaced included "bed and table community" (*Bett- und Tischgemeinschaft*). It seems almost irrefutable that, if a word like "family" is replacing a word like "house" or a phrase like "wife and child," the concept—the social entity that these words attempt to describe—will be seen in a new light. With the term "family" comes a biological bent that had not been so strong with "house," which had emphasized actual physical presence rather than blood lines. Similarly, the gradual abandonment of the phrase "wife and child" suggests an increased awareness of the possibility of a feminine subjectivity. It concedes that sometimes women might talk about their "husband and children." Luhmann therefore discusses the eighteenth-century "discovery of the woman as human" as a function of a corresponding breakdown of traditional hierarchies (127). At the same time the term "family" also includes the father in the unit, allowing for a more organic whole. With stakes that included the position of women in society and the role of fathers in the basic unit of that society, the alarmist language of the brothers Grimm becomes more understandable.

The Grimms assert that the word "family" took a long time to enter into the consciousness of the bourgeoisie: "But how long it took for the foreign word to reach the citizenry and the peasants (*Bürger und Bauer*) and be understood by them" (3: 1305). Heyne's insinuation that the French were partly responsible for the increased usage of the word has a similar implication: that the concept of "family" was perhaps a fey and decadent aristocratic introduction to German society. Nonetheless, most social historians agree that it was the bourgeoisie that achieved the medical successes (in, for instance, childbirth) that allowed the husband and wife to assume that they would live a long life together and the financial wherewithal that allowed the wife to stay at home and take care of the children.

These eighteenth-century bourgeois children were the first to have the opportunity to grow up protected from child labor or the ceremonial duties of the aristocracy even into their teenage years. As Friedrich Kittler shows, Goethe, ever the acute social observer, depicts the arrival in Germany of the nuclear family when he restructures Wilhelm Meister's family from the dysfunctional married household filled with servants and saved only by the grandmother in *Wilhelm Meister's Theatrical Mission* (*Wilhelm Meisters theatralische Sendung*; 1770s) to a nearly ideal bourgeois family, with a loving mother, a stern father, few servants, and no other relatives in *Wilhelm Meister's Apprenticeship* (*Wilhelm Meisters Lehrjahre*; 1796).

The rise of the nuclear family went hand in hand with changes in the understanding of gender. George Mosse describes the development of the modern understanding of masculinity out of the new bourgeois culture of the eighteenth century. He sees German theorists of "Bildung" like Winckelmann, Herder, and Goethe as particularly influential and articulate proponents of this new masculinity. Increasingly the father was in the public sphere, away from the family at work. The mother, in contrast, held sway in the domestic realm, removing herself from the workplace and devoting herself to the family, as Hausen demonstrates. Bourgeois motherhood was impossible for women of other classes: aristocratic women were too much in the public eye to take care of their children, while peasant and working-class women did not have the luxury of staying home and taking care of the children.

These developments cause Thomas Laqueur and Londa Schiebinger to argue that fundamental changes in the understanding of gender accompanied the rise of the bourgeois family. Prior to the eighteenth century, according to these readings, gender had been seen as a continuum in which women were merely underdeveloped men and comparable to children of both sexes —hence the ease with which certain cultures, like the ancient Greeks or the Shakespearean English, could consider women and male youths interchangeable as sexual objects. Since gender was on a continuum, it was not unheard of for women to slide into masculinity, as accounts by such authors as Montaigne show. The eighteenth century, however, saw the rise of the notion of complementary sexes, the idea that the sexes were radically different and endowed with quite incomparable biological and psychological needs. To paraphrase Foucault, the end of the eighteenth century not only brought about the birth of "man," but also the birth of "woman."

The aesthetician Friedrich Wilhelm Basileus Ramdohr makes the phenomenon very clear in 1798, when he asserts that every domestic pair always consists of someone who is "the leader, the ruler, the one who takes over word and deed" and someone who is "the one who gives in." These dichotomies run further with one partner being protecting, serious, considerate, caressing, strong, and flexible, while the other is nurturing, cheerful, pampering, weak, and offering (1: 172). It seems scarcely possible to be more thorough in one's binarisms, but Ramdohr's lists go on for several more pages. Other Germans of the era posit similar concepts of gender roles. Ernst Moritz Arndt, for instance, asserts that man is the determining partner, woman the passive and receptive one, according to Vondung.

Interestingly, however, Ramdohr does not rely on mere outward appearances in establishing his gender binarisms. He believes men can have many feminine characteristics and women can have masculine ones. Thus his notion of a domestic pair does not have to consist exclusively of one person who appears to be a man and another who appears to be a woman: "A man might live happily in domesticity with a man, a woman with a woman, or a man with a woman,—in every connection of this sort" there is always going to be one masculine type and one feminine type (1: 171). This is the era in England, according to Trumbach, of "the birth of the queen": the female in the male body. Ramdohr's reasoning suggests that the queen was arriving in the German-speaking realm as well.

Emphasizing the complementary nature of the sexes was bound to produce a new kind of heterosexism based on the alleged naturalness of the polarity of the roles assigned to men and women. At the same time it had to create a new kind of man who loved men or woman who loved women: a person who operated within this new understanding of the two polar genders, attracted to each other and circling around each other from a distance. The stage was set in northwestern Europe by the end of the eighteenth century for the birth of the modern homosexual. As Foucault writes, the homosexual was constituted "less by a type of sexual relations than by a certain quality of sexual sensibility, a certain way of inverting the masculine and the feminine in oneself" (*History* 43). Foucault's remarks rely upon the rise of the two-sex system that Laqueur describes: In order to conceive of a female soul in a male body, one needs to believe that female souls are fundamentally different from male ones, a belief that arose as the two-sex theory took hold in the eighteenth century.

QUEER EIGHTEENTH-CENTURY SUBCULTURES

The economic, cultural, and gender political factors led to the appearance of, around 1700 "in the cities of northern Europe, especially in those like London, Paris, and Amsterdam, which had populations of half a million, a minority of markedly effeminate men whose most outstanding characteristic was that they desired to have sex only with other males" (Trumbach, "Birth," 130). No German city had yet reached this size in the eighteenth century, which might explain the dearth of direct evidence of sodomitical subcultures in the German realm. A considerable body of work has arisen, however, describing English subcultures developed by this new homosexual identity. Trumbach examines the rise of something like a gay male subculture surrounding the "molly houses," where eighteenth-century English men congregated to look for sex with other men; these men also frequently cross-dressed and took on feminine personae ("London's Sapphists"). Here again the importance of new gender conceptions for the establishment of the new gay identity comes to the fore.

In his groundbreaking social history, *The Family, Sex, and Marriage in England, 1500–1800* (1977), Lawrence Stone reports that "by the early eighteenth century, homosexual clubs existed for the upper classes in London, and through the century there were well-known wealthy deviants, like William Beckford, who were never brought to book." He concludes: "What is certain is that male homosexuality was practiced and talked about more openly in the eighteenth century than at any previous time, except in the restricted court circles in the reign of James I" (337–38). From a more clearly gay-positive perspective, Alan Bray has chronicled the shifts in male-male sexuality from the age of Shakespeare to the eighteenth century. G. S. Rousseau has documented the increasing public perception of incidents of sodomy in eighteenth-century England (3–4). As he puts it, there was an "unusual degree of anxiety over the question of sodomy in the eighteenth century" in Britain, France, and Holland (109). He particularly traces the networks of sodomitically inclined friends that, along with the frequenters of the molly houses, could be said to have formed the beginnings of a gay subcultural community.

There is similar research available on France and Holland. Jacob Stockinger pursues the traces of a sodomitical presence in eighteenth-century French authors. In a Foucauldian vein, Michel Rey has documented the shift in the self-understanding of these emergent subcultures from a religious to a psychiatric identity. Theo van der Meer notes, in agreement with Rousseau's observations about England, that persecutions of sodomy in Holland accelerated dramatically after 1730. He specifically discusses sodomitical networks and subcultures in that country. Arend Huussen has documented persecutions of sodomy in Holland in the eighteenth century, and noted that officers of the law repeatedly attempted to find out "the special signs by which sodomites could be arrested and . . . the places where they met." He concludes: "From the many trials that occurred throughout the republic during the eighteenth century it is evident that there existed a kind of sodomitic or homosexual subculture, especially in the great cities, where networks of friends and clubs of men met regularly, presumably to seek sexual partners, apply their own rules of behavior, and play their specific roles" (144). It seems clear that in England and Holland one can definitely assert the presence of queer subcultures in the eighteenth century as a function of networks and organized locales.

There has been somewhat less work coming out on the presence of communities based on same-sex desire in Germany. The traces that have come to light so far are scarce. In a journal with the quaint title *Contributions Toward Reassurance and Enlightenment About Those Things That Are or Could Be Unpleasant to People* (*Beiträge zur Beruhigung und Aufklärung über dieienige Dinge, die dem Menschen unangenehm sind oder sein können*), Heinrich Detering has uncovered a rare account, published in 1789, of a man whose "sexual drive" (*Geschlechtstrieb*) was exclusively oriented toward other men. This man felt himself completely alone, but the narrator of the account (who claims not to be the person under discussion) knows of a city in which groups of sodomites had joined forces: "In a larger city, which I do not want to mention by name, an entire society of these misattuned lovers is supposed to have come together, which draws ever more into their fraternity, in order to find more nourishment for their lusts" (Detering, " 'Zur Sprache kommen,' " 276). This city might conceivably be outside of Germany; reports of the scandalous behavior of sodomites in London were mentioned in the Berlin press in January 1793 and republished in Leipzig in a book from 1796 entitled *Extraordinary Example of the Great Decay of Morals in England* (*Außerordentliches Beispiel der großen Verdorbenheit der Sitten in England*). Nonetheless, the presence of such communities was becoming recognized in Germany.

Ramdohr insists that he has made "countless observations" that document that men can produce sexual desire in other men and women in women (1:104). This is neither the result of decay nor a freak of nature, he argues: "The experiences that youths and girls whose bodies display delicately built beauty . . . awaken lustfulness and the unnamable drive in people who, based on their external characteristics, belong to the same sex as they do is so general that one cannot ascribe it to a coincidental confusion of their imagination or the rottenness or rawness of their morals" (2: 133). Steakley has—like Rey, working from a Foucauldian perspective—traced the Prussian internalization of societal constraints against same-sex behavior. From this evidence, Steakley concludes that in Berlin "a fairly continuous homosexual subculture was in place by the late eighteenth century" (170). While scholars like Paul Derks and Isabel Hull have been more cautious than their counterparts studying England, France, and Holland in referring to a specific sodomitical subculture in the eighteenth-century German-speaking world, they have also begun to document the era's interest in same-sex behavior.

At times this awareness of same-sex behavior seems close to a tolerant acceptance of diverse sexual identities. As Simon Richter observes, "individuals reputed to have liaisons with other men and boys mingled freely with men for whom sodomitical relations were out of the question" (33). Ramdohr articulates this tolerance when he declares that "drives that are based on the original layout and construction (*Bildung*) of our being, do not deserve reproach, and their struggle for union cannot be attributed to the goal of the satisfaction of an impure desire" (3:205). This notion of drives connected to our being sounds very identity-oriented, especially as it is linked with *Bildung*, one of the centerpieces of the eighteenth-century project. Thus it seems that if subcultural identities did not exist at the end of the eighteenth century in Germany, they were soon to be born.

Johann Friedel's *Letters on the Gallantries of Berlin, Collected on a Trip by an Austrian Officer* (*Briefe über die Galanterien von Berlin auf einer Reise gesammelt von einem österreichischen Offizier*, 1782) refers to the men who love other men as "warm brothers" (*warme Brüder*). According to rumor, some of the most prominent warm brothers were such historical personages as Frederick the Great, the art historian Johann Joachim Winckelmann, and the historian Johannes Müller.

An aura of homosexuality surrounded Frederick the Great even in his lifetime. In his poem *Le Palladion*, originally written in French, the king revealed himself to be acquainted with the tradition of male-male desire. The anticlerical poem deals with a man of the cloth who is trying to seduce a youth:

Wise Socrates demanded it
From Alcibaides, who was certainly
A good Greek; so behaved
Euryalus and Nisus with each other.
Am I supposed to cite more examples for you?
There is the great Caesar, who the world
Called the bridegroom of all Roman women,
And who was at the same time
         the wench of Roman men. (Campe 112)

After going through the Greek and Roman examples, alluding to Plato and Virgil among others, Frederick sacrilegiously adduces Christian tradition as well:

What do you think John did,
In order to lie at the side of Jesus?
He played his dear Ganymede. (Campe 112)

Perhaps only a king could have gotten away with such blasphemy. It is worth spending time in Frederick's biography in order to contextualize this surprising poem.

The rumors about Frederick had been particularly powerful ever since the Prussian king and Voltaire exchanged accusations of buggery. After leaving the king's court in 1752, Voltaire claimed that Frederick invited pages and cadets over for coffee, signaled the lucky one to stay with his handkerchief, and then spent a "quarter hour" with the chosen one. Voltaire added that Frederick had to take the "second role" because of a physical lack.[2]

Johann Friedel, author of the *Letters on the Gallantries of Berlin*, was also involved in this squabble. Although anti-Prussian, he did not dare to make any direct assertions about the king, and placed all the opprobrium on Voltaire: "I'm assured that these debaucheries have only been fashionable here since the time of Voltaire" (146; see also 29). But others were not so circumspect. The eighteenth-century traveler Honoré Gabriel Riquetti, the Count de Mirabeau, sent reports back to Paris seething with insinuations, particularly about the "mignons" of Frederick's brother, Prince Heinrich.[3] Heinrich, incidentally, seems to have been even more notorious for his sexual proclivities than his brother. This makes the fact that he was under consideration as a possible alternative monarch for the American colonies in the 1780s all the more intriguing (Greif 25).

To return to Frederick, Anton Friedrich Büsching makes similar accusations about the king in his biography *The Character of Frederick II* (*Character Friedrichs des Zweytens*): "He had developed early . . . a distaste for women and avoided their company. . . . Thus Frederick lost much sensual pleasure. But he regained it through consorting with men, and had retained from the history of philosophy that it was said that Socrates loved being with Alcibiades" (22). This rumor of Frederick's homosexuality spread rapidly. It is repeated almost verbatim by Johann Georg Zimmermann, the prominent physician, who as a supporter of the monarchy wanted to refute it in his book *On Frederick the Great and My Conversations with Him Shortly Before His Death* (*Über Friedrich den Großen und meine Unterredungen mit ihm kurz vor seinem Tode* 1:13). Detering's anonymous source also lists Büsching's objections to Frederick: "that he had no taste for the pleasure of women; that thereby many sensual pleasures were lost to him; that he however relaxed in the company of handsome men" (" 'Zur Sprache kommen,' " 278). Everyone uses Büsching's wording: it seems that if one was going to make insinuations like this, one wanted to make absolutely clear whom one was quoting.

Biographers noted other characteristics that could apply. As Büsching explains, the young Frederick had not enjoyed playing war games, preferring instead to read French and play the flute. To avoid his overly strict father, he ran away with a male best friend, Hans von Katte, who was subsequently executed for having seduced the prince. Assuming that the signifiers of the

2. Campe 110; Bullough 484; Steakley 167; Derks 91, 268.
3. See particularly the letters of November 4 and 7, 1786, pp. 77, 98. See also Bullough 484 and G. S. Rousseau 25.

homosexual sissy that exist today were being formulated even then, it is not surprising to read that Frederick was said to be "too generous and loving to his favorites, whom he selected from the soldiers solely on the basis of their face and body, no matter how rough they might be" (Büsching 199). These very same young men, chosen for their looks, were not allowed to consort with women: "In his domestics he could stand nothing less than spending time with women. . . . Whether the king only wanted to prevent negligence and unfaithfulness in his service with this prohibition, or whether he had some other reason, I dare not surmise" (Büsching 200–201). Büsching's dark and pointed nonspeculations about the possible reasons for the king's behavior with his manservants are about as clear as one could be in this time period. A final ornamental insinuation by Büsching comes in the form of repeated comparisons between Frederick and the Emperor Hadrian, about whom Büsching observes that he composed poetry for his favorites, the most famous being Antinous, long a symbol of homosexual desire (24, 37).

In a chapter entitled "On Frederick's Alleged Greek Taste in Love," the physician Johann Georg Zimmermann, who attended Frederick the Great in his last days, quotes Büsching's lines in order to refute them, as he considered them libelous. Later in the chapter, Zimmermann again concedes the frequency of the gossip about Frederick: "It was rumored: 'He had really loved many of his pages, many an Antinous, many a beautiful youth, not as Socrates actually loved the beautiful Alcibiades—but rather as the Jesuits, according to his own story, so often loved their beautiful pupils'" (*Fragmente* 85–86). Eighteenth-century readers like Zimmermann understood that the references to misogyny, excessive male bonding, and Socrates amounted to libel, for which reason he went to the king's defense (Derks 60). Just as he tried to save Socrates from his reputation as a pederast (while getting in a jibe at the Jesuits—not surprising for an eighteenth-century Protestant), Zimmermann excused Frederick's behavior with a rather elaborate tale involving a venereal disease that required an operation on the king's private parts. The operation, referred to as "a ghastly cut" ("*ein grausamer Schnitt!*" 70), led to a deformation of the genitals that supposedly made the king too self-conscious to court women. Zimmermann seemed to think that this story would placate any people suspicious of the king's sexuality. While it might not allay such suspicions, it accords with Voltaire's insinuation that a physical lack forced the king to play the passive role in his encounters with his soldiers.

Of all the possibly "warm" eighteenth-century German historical figures studied in recent years, Johann Joachim Winckelmann has attracted the most attention. The first extensive study in the current wave of gay studies to look at Winckelmann intensively is Hans Mayer's *Outsiders*. Paul Derks has a lengthy chapter on Winckelmann in his book (*Die Schande*), and Heinrich Detering revisits the subject in his study (*Das offene Geheimnis*). Dennis Sweet offers a gay-friendly reading that is, however, opposed to a "homosexualization" of Winckelmann. Considered by many the founder of art history as a discipline, Winckelmann made no secret of his admiration for male beauty, either in his art criticism or in his own life. He took a position working for the papacy in Rome, becoming, as Derks puts it, the first German to live, think, and act as a homosexual (183).

Winckelmann's behavior was noted by contemporaries such as Casanova, who recalls stumbling into the art professor's chambers and observing him retire quickly with a young man who was hastily adjusting his disordered clothes. Casanova pretended he hadn't seen anything, but Winckelmann smilingly broached the subject. He denied he was a pederast but asserted his need to study pederastic desires in order to get into the classical mindset (197–98). Ramdohr noted in 1798 that "it has already been said often that the blessed Winckelmann had obscurely felt the influence of the physical sexual symptoms in his enthusiastic dependence on delicate male beauty. Compare the way in which he writes to his beautiful youthful friend or represents the beauty of youthful male statues with the way in which he expresses himself about a masculine figure of a more mature age" (2:134). Indeed, Goethe took considerable flak for praising precisely Winckelmann's proclivity for young men, being accused by the newly religious German Romantics of endorsing immoral behavior (Derks 211–31).

It can be argued that Winckelmann's example made the eighteenth-century world of art connoisseurship comfortable for the many men interested sexually in other men who frequented it. G. S. Rousseau suggests that art connoisseurs in Italy were beginning to acquire a sodomitical reputation in the eighteenth century (as does, incidentally, Susan Sontag in her historical novel *The Volcano Lover*). However, as Ramdohr reminds his readers, "the physical sexual sympathy that accompanies the enthusiasm for youthful male beauty cannot be held against the art lover, in whom it is most frequently found. It is in no way shameful, for they are often not aware themselves of this accompanying effect" (2:133). Not only is Ramdohr providing evidence for the linkage of queer desire and a specific kind of art appreciation, he is also excusing that desire as an unconscious and unavoidable reaction to the presence of male beauty.

At the same time, Winckelmann managed, as Goethe argues, to insert his own queer desire into the center of what would become the modern ideal of classical art. Mosse demonstrates the paradox that the homosexual—in this case, Winckelmann—was profoundly instrumental in basing the modern masculine ideal on a culture—Greece, which was perceived at the time as sexually suspect: "Winckelmann's own homosexuality is not irrelevant in this regard; whatever the evolution of the male stereotype, a homoerotic sensibility stood at the start of an image that was to inform the ideals of normative masculinity such as the clean-cut Englishman or the all-American boy" (32). Same-sex desire, specifically male-male desire, turns out, if these speculations are correct, to be not only the defining margin of many institutions, but also the originary center as well. The queer perspective on German literature targets issues of central importance.

In what might be construed as an early example of queer appropriation, Winckelmann quickly became a role model for a subsequent queer figure, the Swiss historian Johannes Müller. In Müller's preface to the *General Overview of the Federal Republic in Switzerland* (*Allgemeine Aussicht über die Bundesrepublik im Schweizerland*), Winckelmann—along with Cicero, Tacitus, Horace and Montesquieu—is one of the great men whom the lonely Müller conjures up as he hopes for a friend: "If nature is to reassert her rights, she must send him [the lonely author] a man . . . such a man would destroy the evil work of chance through his spirit and the power of friendship" (*Allgemeine Aussicht* 27–28). Repeatedly, as Jacques Derrida has noted in his theoretical treatment of friendship, the friend is addressed in terms of the rarity of friendship: "O my friends, there is no friend" (*Politics of Friendship* 1). This stands in contradiction to the democratizing aspect of friendship ("All men are brothers"), a discussion to which Müller also contributes. I shall return to the ambivalences surrounding the concept of friendship shortly, but for now let us examine how it developed in Müller's life.

In a letter to his family, Müller gives an example of how such a meeting of two friends might occur:

It was the coming together of two people determined by eternity to be together, and I can't say which of the two felt it first and most warmly; just as unable am I to say whether I thought in this moment especially about his extraordinary charm, which wins all hearts for him, or about the rich and fine culture of his mind, about his many fields of knowledge, about his noble, honorable, emotive, and rich heart . . . but the beautiful harmony of the whole tore me away, I felt that I was his, and he mine, before I knew what and how it happened. I had never hoped that I would find another— and such a!—friend, who would fill the daily needs of my soul. (January 28, 1797; *SW* 6:123)

Müller's admiration for the "beautiful harmony of the whole" is reminiscent of Winckelmann's ideal of classical beauty. In light of Derrida's observations about friendship, it is noteworthy that this friend is a rarity—Müller had never hoped to find another. While modern-day academic readers might dismiss this writing as merely an example of the cult of friendship, Müller himself felt the need to defend himself against the charge that he has somehow behaved inappropriately. A few weeks later he wrote:

Previously, I had poured out my heart to you regarding my friend and then it occurred to me that you, used to feeling more quietly, might find my youthful fire (for I feel that I am not more than 25 now!) silly, that you might *discuss* the tender bloom that delights my heart with a "word of wisdom" . . . and that worried me particularly because I would have been guilty myself: for Ch. [the friend], although Italian, and although 13 years younger, and although poet, and although he loves me uncommonly, would not have written so, and disapproved of the letter when I showed him it. (March 4, 1797; *SW* 6:127)

Müller's anxieties that the letter would be discussed, and the reluctance of his friend to join in his effusive celebration of friendship, suggest that his case was not so clearly a case of innocent friendship.

In general, Müller was a passionate devotee of the cult of friendship, that eighteenth-century German tradition of extremely effusive and intimate friendships: "The thought of friendship, which so few really grasp, often uplifts my heart," he wrote in 1802 to a certain "N," citing David's love of Jonathan that surpassed the love of women (*SW* 17:261). He wrote to the poet Johannes Wilhelm Ludwig Gleim, the high priest of the sentimental cult of friendship, that he would never disavow his love of his friends: "I am so proud of whatever I said about my deep love for you. . . . I won't hide it" (August 4, 1802; *SW* 17:204). Again, it is intriguing that Müller was so defensive about his devotion to friendship. Despite the claims of many modern readers that the rhetoric of friendship is meaningless, a closer look shows that such extreme statements of same-sex love were critiqued as excessive by the end of the eighteenth century.

Müller's letters to Karl Victor von Bonstetten, reprinted by Friederike Brün, "the Danish muse," are monuments of the cult of friendship. The Swiss scholar Bonstetten was something of a muse himself, having entranced not only Müller but also the English poet Thomas Gray, author of "Elegy Written in a Country Churchyard" (Greif 214). The letters between Müller and Bonstetten depict, according to Müller's relative and editor, "a friendship of the strictest, purest virtue," which was "in every other respect identical to

activity in Romans I, chapter 27 (December 9, 1800; *SW* 6:421–22). One wonders how such a principled man even came across these texts. But Müller read widely: A subsequent letter, from February 29, 1801, cites *Justine* specifically and alludes quite clearly to *The Philosophy of the Bedroom* (*SW* 6:438).

Regardless of what Müller actually did in his private life, he soon became a symbol of male-male desire for German intellectuals in the early nineteenth century. Karl Friedrich Graf Reinhard writes to Goethe that the "red thread" that united the historian's work is the love of men for each other. Although his history of the Swiss Federation is not explicitly homosexual, its emphasis on the bonding together of free men may be the "red thread" that, according to Reinhard, would link this text to his published letters (cited in Derks 343). Derrida meditates extensively on the political dimensions of friendship as a "homo-fraternal" institution, uniting all men together in a democratic bond (*Politics of Friendship* 306). The convicted sodomite Franz Desgouttes reports in his diaries that he gave Müller's four-volume history of Switzerland to the lover whom he subsequently murdered, suggesting that by this time (January 12, 1817) the historian had become part of a queer canon (Hössli 3:182). On a more uplifting note, the poet August von Platen, whose poems and diaries are imbued with expressions of male-male love, also mentions reading Müller in 1817 (97).

Further suggesting that the glowing descriptions of his friends and students were not "of the strictest virtue" in the late eighteenth-century sense, Müller fell into ignominy and disgrace as a result of his homosexuality in the so-called Batthiany affair, which lasted from June 19, 1802, to March 24, 1803. One of his pupils, a young Fritz von Hartenberg, mulcted Müller by inventing an epistolary lover who allegedly wrote under the pen-name "Count von Batthiany." Using letters supposedly from the lover, the young man convinced Müller to give him considerable amounts of cash, as loans supposedly guaranteed by the lover. When it finally became clear that there was no lover, Müller was broke and embarrassed. He was compelled to leave Vienna because of the scandal. Goethe, incidentally, was apparently one of the prominent figures who tried to help Müller by hiring him in Weimar.

One of the most significant aspects of the Batthiany affair is that both Müller and his student understood that there was a certain code by which sodomites could recognize each other. The love of Greece, the desire for a good friend, the absence of a wife—a whole series of signifiers from Batthiany's letters to Müller suggest that there was a sodomitical subcultural rhetoric to which both Müller and his pupil Hartenberg, as well as others at this time in the German-speaking realm, had access. Müller and his pupil,

that friendship that produced the best and greatest things in a
4:ix). This "in every other respect" suggests that the ancient f
not "of the strictest purest virtue." Whether we believe the ed
letters represented the "purest virtue," their publication was k
that required a certain smoothing of feathers (as the previous
to Gleim of August 4, 1802, shows) and simultaneously an ac
be celebrated in the eyes of others.

Of particular interest is the notion that these letters could l
a culture of male-male bonding from one generation to the ne:
felt that the letters would serve as a wonderful model to youth
1805; SW 17:253–56), and Johannes Müller himself had the exp
"a noble youth" introduced himself to him in Berlin on account
lished letters (letter to the family, March 12, 1804; SW 7:119–20
that published letters could provide a kind of intellectual capi
ing an eternal stream of young male friends was frequent in c
circles of the era, as Richter has elegantly shown in his essay "Win
Progeny."

Müller's eros was definitely of the pedagogical sort. Like Wi
he delighted in his many contacts with young men, who gave hi
the future: "I know many of the hopeful among the German y
therefore have hope myself" (August 12, 1806; SW 17:411). Urging
process his reading, he suggests that if one doesn't want to write
an essay à la Montaigne about something that one has just read, o
at least discuss the material with "a blossoming youth or an interes
(June 1802; SW 7:26). His letters to such luminaries as Herder, Wie
Nicolai are filled with references to his young male students. Wiela
about "a youth from the Steyermark, full of spirit, fire, courage,
agathos in the physical and moral sense . . . he speaks Turkish th
speak German, and reads Persian as we read Greek" (May 18, 1796; S
Müller writes weepily to Herder about the death of "a youth full of ta
of virtue, charming and blossoming" (October 6, 1795; SW 17:24). To
family, he describes "one of the best, purest, liveliest youths that I e
(November 22, 1799; SW 6:344), a "very charming, wise youth" (Feb
1802; SW 7:4), and "an excellent youth of heart and mind, unders
and charm" (September 17, 1803; SW 7:88).

Naturally, one could interpret these effusions over his male s
as innocent, an interpretation upon which Müller and his editor p
would insist most vehemently. In a letter in which he denounces the v
of the Marquis de Sade, Müller even cites Paul's condemnation of sa

his pupil's virtuosic manipulation of the warm signifiers of friendship, Ramdohr's observations, Winckelmann's lifestyle, and the rumors around Frederick the Great all hint that something was happening in the semantic field around male-male desire in late eighteenth-century Germany. These examples suggest that certain signs — like inversion of gender identity, art history, friendship, Switzerland, and the Greek, Roman, and biblical traditions — were coalescing around a queer proto-identity. They suggest that there is something like a queer eighteenth century that both is grounded in historical fact and speaks to today's readership.

2

WARM SIGNIFIERS

Eighteenth-Century Codes
of Male-Male Desire

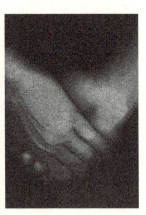

Whether individuals like Frederick the Great, Johann
Joachim Winckelmann, and Johannes von Müller were involved in queer subcultures and what kind of identity grew
out of such subcultures is properly a historical question
that asks what really happened between the individuals in
question and what sort of identity they really had. Queer
theory generally does not discuss this historical question
about what happened in the eighteenth-century boudoirs;
instead, looking at two texts from around 1800, it ana-
lyzes the rhetoric that surrounded whatever sexuality or
proto-sexuality was "there."

That rhetoric surrounding textuality can be said to
have a history, producing what one might call a genealogy of signifiers. In *The Genealogy of Morals*, Friedrich
Nietzsche elucidates how many "meanings" the term
"punishment" has accrued in our society:

Punishment as a means of rendering harmless . . . as recompense
to the injured party for the harm done . . . as the isolation of a
disturbance of equilibrium . . . as a means of inspiring fear . . .
as a kind of repayment . . . as the expulsion of a degenerate
element . . . as a festival . . . as the making of a memory . . .
as payment of a fee . . . as a compromise with revenge . . . as a
declaration of war. (80–81)

In terms of the history of sexuality, a similar list can be
devised around the varied "meanings" of such specific

acts as, say, sodomy. Clearly, those who are interested in tracking the social construction of sexuality would see that the meanings of an act like the "active" anal penetration of another male have varied through time and geography, from an indication of social superiority in ancient Greece to proof of power in modern penal society and to proof of homosexuality in modern civic society. Conversely, a man's being "passively" penetrated has had a multitude of meanings over time as well, from an indication of social inferiority in ancient Greece to evidence for lack of manliness in many circles, including prison culture, and to proof of homosexuality in modern civic society. The same physical act therefore can be associated with a variety of meanings. These meanings change with time, but—thwarting any neat and tidy analysis—as new meanings accrete to a certain act, the older meanings often remain, either undercover or quite prominently co-present.

Nietzsche's insight on the archeology of meaning is valuable for modern discussions of sexuality, because many of those discussions have a tendency to assume a much too simple relationship between cause and effect. A typical, overly simplistic view of the history of homosexuality would begin as follows: persecution of homosexuals created the closet, which generated ironic, campy strategies of resistance as well as modern gay identity. So far, so good, but the next step in this argument is problematic: removal of persecution will result in the disappearance of the closet and eventually cause the demise of ironic, campy, queer subcultures. Following Nietzsche, one would argue that this subculture and its signifiers are now present and will find their own justification even if the original justification loses its urgency. Social constructionists who argue that today's homosexual will disappear in the near future because the circumstances of the homosexual's birth no longer obtain are seriously underestimating the staying power of signifiers.

Commenting on shifting patterns of love, the sociologist Niklas Luhmann cogently restates Nietzsche's argument on the accretion of meaning around socially significant institutions like punishment: "in evolutionary transformations of this sort, the verbal clothing, the phrases, the proverbs, and the statements of experience may be handed on; but they change their meaning, their selectivity, their ability to package experiences and open new perspectives" (9). Looking at the semiotics of same-sex desire in the eighteenth century, we will find many of the signifiers that we still use today to describe queer culture, even if the signifieds have changed. This is because, as Luhmann argues, love is only possible when it can rely on the traditional semantics of literature and language (47). This means, he asserts, that "love is a literarily pre-formed, downright pre-scribed feeling" (53). The signs of this feeling will be in place before the sensation itself exists. Luhmann explicitly considers heterosexual love when he makes these assertions, but they also apply to queer love as well.

While Nietzsche's analysis obviously transfers easily from one physical act (like punishment) to another (like sodomy), it can also transfer to less concrete signifiers. Punishment and anal sex become, for the purpose of this analysis, signifiers referring back to a host of historically evolving signifieds. The signifier, rather than the signified, has the primary position: it is not the case that because one needs to express one's lack of masculinity, one enjoys passive anal sex, but rather the case that because one enjoys passive anal sex, one expresses one's lack of masculinity. Nietzsche's analysis can also be useful in looking at signifiers like cross-dressing, or feminine behavior in men, or a fondness for opera, that today often connote homosexuality, although they perhaps meant something else in an earlier context. Here again, the primacy of the signifier is paramount: it is not that because one is homosexual (the signified), one likes opera (the signifier of homosexuality), but rather—to follow Wayne Koestenbaum in *The Queen's Throat* and put it strongly—that, because one likes opera, one becomes homosexual.

THE *LETTERS* AND *KYLLENION*

The *Letters on the Gallantries of Berlin, Collected on a Trip by an Austrian Officer* (*Briefe über die Galanterien von Berlin auf einer Reise gesammelt von einem österreichischen Offizier*), published in 1782 and attributed to Johann Friedel (1755–1789), and *A Year in Arcadia: Kyllenion* (*Ein Jahr in Arkadien: Kyllenion*) published by August, Duke of Sachsen-Gotha and Altenburg (1772–1822), in 1805, both suggest that there was a queer style even before there was a homosexual content. The *Letters* and *Kyllenion* can help determine what signifiers were eddying around the "warm" elements of German society in the late eighteenth century, signifiers that later came to mean "homosexuality."

Addressing both a "factual" and a "fictional" text together blurs the distinction between the two categories and shows the power of the signifier independent of any kind of signified, whether that signified be an alleged fact of life in Berlin or a fantasy of a fictional life elsewhere. Analyzing relatively minor works—not just the large projects of canonical authors—allows the reader to see how the textile of signification consists of a multitude of signifying threads. In the genealogy of these "warm" signifiers of sodomy and other same-sex practices, it can be seen that these incipient subcultures adopted many of the signifiers and conventional markers that still characterize large segments of the queer population.

The *Letters* are comprised of twenty-nine communications written by an Austrian officer to a friend about the perversions of Berlin. Of most interest here are the letter writer's observations, in his fifteenth and seventeenth letters, on "warm brothers" (*warme Brüder*) and "pederasty" (*Knabenliebe*). The letter writer claims to have stumbled upon large groups of "warm brothers" and even organized male prostitution: "You will find here houses which exist under the honorable name of boy tobacco shops (*Knabentabagie*) in which young men of fourteen, fifteen and more years of age come in order to pass the time. . . . You will find procurers and procuresses who wander about on the streets and look for children, as well as grown-up youths, attract them to such houses and make their profit thereby" (Friedel 142–43). The *Letters* have only limited value as historical documents, as the collection was published anonymously and with malicious intent. However, even if Friedel exaggerates or invents what he has seen (and one must say that "warmth" could well be like smoke: where one finds it, one also finds the fire of reality), it is still revealing to note what kinds of signifiers he uses to label even an imaginary queer society.

Quite a different text is August von Sachsen-Gotha's *Year in Arcadia*. Sachsen-Gotha was a duchy that at the end of the eighteenth century unsuccessfully attempted to compete with nearby Weimar as a cultural center. The ruling family was in other respects, however, not entirely unsuccessful: August was the grandfather of Prince Albert, consort of Queen Victoria, and thus one of the progenitors of the mightiest monarchs of the nineteenth century. Despite his progeny, August was by all accounts a queer fellow who scandalized the local gentry by cross-dressing. Goethe found him somewhat repugnant: "I must not forget the ruling Duke, August of Gotha, who liked to present himself as problematic and to be pleasant and repulsive in a certain soft way [*unter einer gewissen weichlichen Form, angenehm und widerwärtig*]" (*HA* 11:827).

Sachsen-Gotha's novel is one of the earliest homoerotic novels in the German tradition. It tells the story of "Alexis the splendid, and Julanthiskos, the no less delightful" (106). Alexis is the local nobleman who lives in a beautiful palace; Julanthiskos is his hail-fellow-well-met shepherd. They see each other at a dance, appreciate each other's beauty, and even dance with each other. Julanthiskos is completely smitten with the prince, but Alexis, in the whirl of his social life, only toys with the shepherd boy's affections. After other romances are brought to a conclusion, Julanthiskos chances upon his beloved Alexis, lying wounded in the forest: "thus Julanthiskos found him wounded and spattered with blood. . . . The youths were finally discovered by the slaves of Alexis, as they slumbered mouth on mouth on the soft moss of one of the Kyllenian caves" (79). The rest is history: "Alexis, the saved, was no longer ungrateful, and Julanthiskos, the finder, was no longer unhappy" (79). The two go on to live happily together, like all the other lovers in the story.

SODOM

The two accounts—the allegedly factual *Letters* cynically exposing the mercenary aspects of love and critical of the "warm brothers," and the fictional novel romantically glorifying the ideal aspects of love and sentimentally attached to the "warm brothers"—share a number of rhetorical traits in describing the behavior of the same-sex couples. To begin with, neither of them uses the term "sodomite." The discourse of Sodom and Gomorra, which has religious origins and, in the eighteenth century, increasingly legalistic applications, was not one that the Duke, who seems to portray male-male desire quite sympathetically, would wish to utilize. Unlike the early twentieth-century author Proust or the late twentieth-century entertainers the Village People, he rejects rather than embraces the disgrace of Sodom and Gomorra. Perhaps surprisingly—because he is more critical of these perverse sexual practices—Friedel also avoids the discourse of Sodom in his depiction of the "warm brothers." His only reference to the "vice of Sodom und Gomorra" comes early on in the book (36) when he is describing the general moral decay of Berlin, not the specific sinfulness of the warm brothers. In so doing, he follows the understanding of the story of Sodom and Gomorra found in the Biblical books of Isaiah and Jeremiah, which emphasizes the general arrogance and lack of charity of the Sodomites rather than their sexual behavior.

It is important to note that neither Friedel nor Sachsen-Gotha use the vocabulary of sodomy, because—following Foucault's *History of Sexuality*—many historians assume that the vocabulary of sodomy is appropriate for the discussion of same-sex activity prior to the development of the terms "homosexual" and "homosexuality." In fact, however, the rhetoric of sodomy was not something that was universally applied to same-sex desire. In particular, those whose lives were closest to the world of same-sex desire avoided the term.

MISOGYNY

In the more unappetizing parts of his book *Outsiders*, Hans Mayer argues that misogyny is a fundamental part of the "typology of homosexual literature" (264–65, 278). Like his use of "Sodom" as a metonymy for homosexuality, however, his insistence on misogyny as a signifier of homosexuality is misplaced in the eighteenth century. Although, as we saw in the case of Frederick II, misogyny did sometimes figure in the constellation of signifiers around eighteenth-century male queerness, many other queer male eighteenth-century writers were explicitly pro-feminist. Rather, it was the critics of queerness who were actually misogynist. In the *Letters*, the letter writer is very concerned lest Laura, the girlfriend of the man to whom he is writing, read any of the reports about the "warm brothers": "And even if your Laura banishes me to the witches on Blocksberg, I cannot do elsewise. You must not let her read today's letter either. . . . What use would it be to the girl to be so familiar with the secrets of the warm [*mit den Geheimnissen der Warmen so bekannt zu werden*]?" (144). The male "homosexuality" depicted in the *Letters* serves to bolster the male homosociality between the two correspondents. By excluding women from observing male-male desire, they can maintain their sense of a privileged patriarchy while also protecting the heterosexual male subject from ever being in the object position. According to the letter writer, women don't need to know that men are sometimes the objects of desire.

In contrast, *A Year in Arcadia* places the two male lovers in the context of a society with many articulate women who are involved in their own love affairs. In fact, one of the remarkable and utopian aspects of *A Year in Arcadia* is the extent to which this homoeroticism merges so sensibly with the rest of society. Both Alexis and Julanthiskos confide their interest in the other to sympathetic female friends, who encourage the relationship—first Julanthiskos to his beautiful cousin Nikrion, and then Alexis to Myris. Sachsen-Gotha presents a positive assessment of the situation that the *Letters* found so potentially dangerous. Indeed, if the *Letters* worry that sodomy could endanger patriarchy, *A Year in Arcadia* actually plays with the idea, by allowing Julanthiskos to complain bitterly about the pride and selfishness of men to his women friends (65).

Rejecting the possible Biblical frame of reference of Sodom, both authors instead use a rhetoric immersed in allusions to the classical world. Like the discourse of Sodom, the discourse of Greco-Roman antiquity can be directed both at specific sodomitical subcultures and at eighteenth-century culture in general. *A Year in Arcadia* is set in Greece and filled with references to Greek culture. More surprisingly, perhaps, the *Letters* also are rife with allusions to Greek culture. At the beginning of the first letter, Berlin is described as "Frederick's Athens" (13). Given the rumors about Frederick and the sexual associations of ancient Greece, such an appellation is certainly suspicious! Even the letters that are not concerned with the "warm brothers" are filled with references to Zeus (28), Adonis (81), Agathon (98), and even Ganymede (192) and Alcibiades (42), who is specifically named as a pederast. In 1836, a few decades after Friedel and Sachsen-Gotha published their respective works, Heinrich Hössli would write an extensive two-volume apology for male-male love, *Eros: The Male Love of the Greeks* [*Eros: Die Männerliebe der Griechen*], in which he provides a remarkably similar list of the names that comprised the world of Greek male love: "Hyacinth, Plutus, Adonis, Ganymede, Diocles, Narcissus, Pelop, Cadmus, and a thousand others" (1:260).

Overall, the presence of Greek referents both within and without the sodomitical subculture suggests two things. On the one hand, it was difficult to discern who the real sodomites were because of an irritating tendency of the signifiers to shift—as we shall see, sometimes sodomites appropriate the signifiers of nonsodomites and, even more confusingly, sometimes the nonsodomites reappropriate those signifiers. In this case, the "meaning" of Greek referents was unstable—it could mean sodomy or it could mean culture. Secondly, this confusion suggests that the sodomitical subculture might indeed be much broader than anyone—now or then—had suspected; perhaps even those Greek referents that seem legitimate are directly linked to sodomites.

However, some of the Greek referents deal specifically and unambiguously with same-sex desire. *Kyllenion* blossoms with references to Narcissus, the beautiful youth who fell in love with his own handsome image, and Hyacinth, the young man who died as a result of the jealousy of his two lovers, Apollo and Zephyr. Crompton documents that Byron's letters contain other instances of early nineteenth-century use of "Hyacinth" as a code word for homosexuality (127–29, 141–42). Julanthiskos spends time near Hyacinth's grave, and he is rarely more than a page or two away from the heavy scent of hyacinth blossoms.

Certain readers understood the connection that Sachsen-Gotha was making between the Greek and same-sex desire: Friedrich Jacobi, whose own letters were so roundly criticized for their effusive declarations of same-sex love, was concerned that the story was "Greek through and through" (Derks, afterword to Sachsen-Gotha, 135). In his afterword, Derks also mentions Friedrich Jacobs, a classicist from the same Gotha over which August ruled, who writes about the Duke's novel that *sed omni in istro libro Graeca sunt* [everything in this book is Greek] and remarks that this "Grecian nature" has been legitimately criticized (156–57). Jacobs himself also wrote an essay on the "love of men" (*Männerliebe*), which was published in 1829.

Friedel also makes use of the rhetoric of classical antiquity to describe same-sex behavior in Berlin. The warm brothers are "Socratic lovers" (*sokratische Liebhaber*) and even "Socratic escorts" (*sokratische Gesellschafter*; 138). The clients of the brothel are compared to Zeus and the prostitutes to Ganymede (143, 145). The epistolary narrator has an entire classical history for this kind of desire:

It is true that the Greeks and the Romans set the example for these gentlemen. If one looks at it seriously, this debauchery found its first birth in the Greek gymnasia. Ovid assures us that Orpheus was already sullying himself with this vice; and in Anakreon's times, all men were already completely given to unnatural pederasty [*unnatürliche Knabenliebe*]. Plato and Socrates, along with their whole school, drew upon themselves precisely this reproach. Alcibiades himself, so loved by all women, wasn't ashamed to disgrace youths openly. Greece's poets certainly sang as much of beautiful youths as of beautiful maids. (141)

Although the vocabulary of "debauchery," "sullying," "unnatural," "reproach," "ashamed," and "disgrace" is overwhelming negative, the fact that the activity takes place in Greek culture allows it to be discussed and grants it a certain legitimacy. Subsequent writers in the nineteenth (and, indeed, even today) would remove such negative vocabulary, but retain the rest of the speech in order to defend homosexuality.

In 1789, an anonymous apologist for homosexuality published a "Report on a Strange Deviation of the Human Drive" ("Nachricht von einer seltsamen Irrung eines menschlichen Triebes"), an account of a lonely individual who loved members of his own sex in the *Contributions to Reassurance and Enlightenment*. Like Friedel, the author also concludes by citing the classics: "This unnatural tendency of men is apparently very old and seems to have gotten its start thousands of years ago. *Socrates* has been charged with an inappropriate love of Alcibiades; *Virgil* and *Horace* are supposed to have been boy-lovers (*Knabenliebhaber*)" (Detering, " 'zur Sprache kommen,' " 277) The author of the article then goes on to mention Corydon from Virgil's Second Eclogue, a text that Gide, among others, would use at the beginning of the twentieth century to defend homosexuality.

It is noteworthy that this classicizing rhetoric is already so clearly in place, even before clear documentation of a highly self-conscious homosexual subculture or identity. Nor do these works stand alone in eighteenth-century German culture: we find echoes of their thought in more serious histories of Greek culture by classicists of late eighteenth-century Germany. As Derks demonstrates, classicists from the mid-eighteenth century, like Johann Matthias Gessner and Moses Mendelssohn, defended Socrates from the charge of pederasty (61). As we move through the latter half of the eighteenth century, though, Johann Georg Hamann and Johann Gottfried Herder already accept that Greek men regularly practiced and discussed sex with each other and that passages that seemed queer were indeed so. Arguing along the same lines, Wilhelm von Humboldt wrote a lengthy treatise on the subject in 1806, which was not published until 1896.

One of the most thorough of the published essays on same-sex desire among the Greeks is "Observations on the Male Love of the Greeks, along with an Excerpt from the Symposium of Plato" ("Betrachtungen über die Männerliebe der Griechen, nebst einem Auszuge aus dem Gemahle des Plato"), which Christoph Meiners, professor in Göttingen, included in his *Various Philosophical Writings* (*Vermischte philosophische Schriften*) of 1775. Like many classicists, Meiners was troubled by the seeming contradiction between the status of the Greeks as "the most enlightened nation of the ancient world" (*die aufgeklärteste Nation der alten Welt*; 63) and their obvious propensity for male-male love. To a certain extent, he was sure that this male-male love remained "platonic," in the sense of spiritual, and not physical, love: "It is not possible therefore that this love of the soul could, in all states and all eras, be merely a mask for unnatural vice. It was—if one doesn't want to present all writers as liars and the greatest men as worthless hypocrites— pure, irreproachable love of the soul" (1:81–82). Present-day social constructionists will appreciate Meiners's insistence that love cannot have been the same in all times and places. Queer literary scholars looking to provide new readings of historical figures will be intrigued to see that Meiners fears that *all* writers and *the greatest* men might come under suspicion if the purity of their love isn't reaffirmed.

Meiners knew, however, that he couldn't explain away all the same-sex love of the ancient Greek as "pure love of the soul." He had two theories to explain the presence of the vice of male-male sexuality in such a young and cultivated country. On the one hand, like many critics of homosexuality, he connected this male-male love with the oppression of women in ancient Greece. He surmised that Greek men loved women less because women stayed at home, were less educated, and were considered "creatures of a lower rank, of less dignity, almost as creatures of another sort" (72–73). Meiners even goes so far as to assert that "pederasty [*Knabenliebe*] was connected by the Greeks and Romans, as in the Orient, with the most bitter hatred of the female sex" (88–89). The idea that the misogyny of the Greeks produced the high incidence of male-male sexual acts seems to have been a common belief in Europe around this time. Ramdohr agrees that the women of ancient Greece were not educated enough to compete with men as partners in love. He adds the belief that male-male desire originally emerged from the intense male bonds between warriors: "its first origin is to be found in the heroic brotherhood [*Heldenverbrüderungen*] of those first benefactors of human civilization" (2:144). Incidentally, in "A Defense of Poetry," Shelley also discusses the "emancipation of women from a great part of the degrading restraints of antiquity" and writes that "the freedom of women produced the poetry of sexual love," as he compares medieval and modern poetry with that of the ancients (510).

However, as Sachsen-Gotha's *Kyllenion* shows by its generous treatment of women characters, those who were somewhat more open to male-male desire tended to reject the explanation that ancient Greek men loved men because their women were so oppressed that they were unattractive partners. Wilhelm von Humboldt took issue with Meiners's understanding of Greek sexuality as a product of the misogyny the era. He is not convinced, to begin with, that things were that bad for Greek women; nor does he find it surprising that, at the beginning of time, when women were closer to their "natural" calling as guardians of the family, that Greek men would associate amongst themselves (see MacLeod, "The 'Third Sex'"). A few decades later, in his apology for the male love of the Greeks, Hössli would also vigorously reject the notion that they were misogynist (2:215).

Meiners's other explanation for the prominence of ancient Greek same-sex activity is more specifically located. Like Friedel, he suspects the gymnasia, in which one could easily develop a taste for the "most beautiful living bodies" (86). He singles out the gymnastic exercises, "in which the most beautiful youths exposed all the charms of the body without covering to the desirous eye" (82). The general glorification of the body by Greek philosophy led, thought Meiners, to sexual excesses by offering too much temptation. Again, not all classicists agreed with Meiners. As its title indicates, the author of "Gymnasia as Wet Nurses and Procuresses of Pederasty" ("Gymnasien als Säugammen und Kupplerinnen der Knabenliebe," *Jenaer Literatur Zeitung*, vol. 4, 1803) seems also to have been of the opinion that gymnasia were sexually dangerous. Ramdohr agrees that the gymnasia encouraged pederasty, but asserts that ultimately the pederastic traditions predated the pedagogic ones—indeed, he claims that gymnastics grew out of "the rape of youths" (*Knabenraub*; 2:132). Friedrich Jacobs disagrees with the theory that the gymnasia were responsible for the sexual debauches of the Greeks, saying that they were "very far indeed from being schools of shamelessness [*Schulen den Schaamlosigkeit*]" (quoted in Derks, *Schande*, 83).

Ample evidence suggests that for the eighteenth century the terms "Greek," "platonic," and "Socratic" signified some sort of same-sex desire. Derks cites passages from Hamann, Herder, and Friedrich Schlegel all commenting on Greek love (57–78). According to Schenk, for instance, the writer Heinse understands Socrates "not only as the man with the high ethics and the enlightened pedagogue, but primarily as the lover of beautiful youths [*der Liebhaber schöner Jünglinge*]" (Wangenheim 91). Kotzebue, in a scurrilous attack on the opponents of the physician Johann Georg Zimmermann, attributed to the anthropologist Adolf Freiherr von Knigge, has one of his characters demonstrate "Greek love" to another (*Doktor Bahrdt* 30). Despite the disagreement on the exact explanations for ancient Greek sodomy, it is clear that many eighteenth-century thinkers assumed that ancient Greece provided the model for understanding sexual relations between men. Joan DeJean, indeed, argues that much of our modern conception of sexuality was informed by this classicist understanding of ancient Greek sexuality rather than by the more traditionally cited medical and legal traditions.

ORIENTALISM

In addition to ancient Greek allusions, the *Letters* and the novel both make use of orientalist discourses to describe same-sex relationships. The overlap is not surprising, for in the eighteenth- and nineteenth-century European imagination Greece became part of the Orient and the Orient developed certain classically Greek traits. Greece was in fact far to the east and south for many Europeans, and during much of the eighteenth century part of the Ottoman empire; the Orient in turn was seen as a place where one could perhaps find some remnants of classical civilization—and classical sexuality (see Aldrich and Hyam). As noted above, Meiners, in his explanation for Greek sexuality, explicitly compares the Greeks with the Orient. Hössli, in his defense of male-male love, mixes—liberally and without much explanation—Turkish, Persian, and Arab poetry in with his Greek citations.

In the *Letters*, the author observes, "Whatever one can fault the Persian, the Moslem, and the Italian for in terms of pederasty [*Knabenliebe*], you will find in these debaucheries" (138). The novel *Kyllenion*, which takes place in an idyllic Greece, an Arcadia, points even more to the orientalist discourses that were to develop around homosexuality. Arcadia was the point where Greece led directly into escapist fantasies of exotic locales. As Aldrich, for instance, has shown, those who felt the need to escape the oppression of the bourgeois family fantasized about sexual Arcadias that were not located in the past, but in the colonies somewhere. In the German literary tradition, one can find an "orientalization" of homosexuality from Platen's ghazals to Mann's *Tod in Venedig*. Once again, as in the case of the Greek allusions, same-sex desire avails itself of a set of signifiers that would remain in place even after that same-sex desire had begun to manifest itself differently.

FRIENDSHIP

The discourse of friendship is another rhetorical feature that both authors employ to portray same-sex desire. This romantic discourse used between friends is one of the most difficult hurdles in analysis of the sexuality implicit in these eighteenth-century texts because it consists of exclamations that sound like declarations of love between members of the same sex. In a footnote, Luhmann decides to leave aside "the difficult question of homosexuality as a secret mortgage on the concept of friendship" (147). It may come as a relief to know that determining the boundaries between an intense, but asexual friendship and an erotic relationship was also confusing for those who lived in the eighteenth century. Ramdohr actually tries to establish a "semiotics, system of signs, for distinguishing friendship from sexual intimacy" [*Semiotik, Zeichenlehre, zu Unterscheidung der Freundschaft von der Geschlechtszärtlichkeit*] (1:229). In an interview, Foucault observes that the cult of friendship died in the move from the eighteenth to the nineteenth century precisely because of the inability to agree on this system of signs, which would have reduced anxieties about sex between men (Gallagher and Wilson 58).

As we have seen in the discussion of the historian Johannes von Müller, who fell in love with a series of male youths, the eighteenth-century cult of friendship recurrently blurs the distinctions that modern society draws between gays and straights. Throughout the eighteenth century members of the same sex were able to say and write things to each other under the rubric of "sentimental friendship" that sound incredibly queer today. Gleim, for instance, could write a love poem to Jacobi, expressing his desire to be his girl:

I would really like to be a girl:
He would marry me;
He wouldn't lack friends,
Nor love, nor wine:
I would really like to be his girl!

[Ich möchte wohl ein Mädchen sein;
Er sollte sich mit mir vermählen;
An Freunden sollt' es ihm nicht fehlen,
An Liebe nicht, und nicht an Wein:
Ich möchte wohl sein Mädchen sein!] (cited in Dietrich 30)

Jacobi in turn could write to Jean Paul that friends should love each other as wives love their husbands (cited in Dietrich 33). Lenz writes to Goethe that he wanted to be his wife, as does Kleist to Pfuel (see Graf and Pfeiffer). Whether these declarations of love are always only declarations of friendship is a bit doubtful, for, as Luhmann argues, the exclusivity that would be inherent in the desire to be married was one of the features that distinguished (heterosexual) romantic love from (homosocial) friendship. That is to say, one could be friends with several people, but one could be in love with only one person. By the mid-nineteenth century, in any case, the distinction between friendship and love would become much firmer. For instance, by 1836 it is very clear to Heinrich Hössli that the Greek love was quite distinct from romantic friendship. Greek love is clearly corporeal and physical, whereas friendship is a matter of the soul; the devotees of Greek love are not also in love with mistresses; Greek love always consists of unequal partners (a lover and a beloved), whereas friendship obtains between equals (Hössli 2:219–23). In the nineteenth century such romantic statements between men become impossible, although, as Faderman documents, sentimental friendship among women lasted to the beginning of the twentieth century.

Curiously, as Luhmann points out, precisely when the rhetoric of male-male friendship becomes ever more distinct from that of heterosexual love, heterosexual love attempts to take on the characteristics of male-male friendship. Throughout the late eighteenth century husbands were encouraged to be friends with their wives, to be as close to their wives as they had been to their intimate male friends (102). The effusive rhetoric of friendship was not modeled on that of romantic love, but rather romantic love took on the semiotics of friendship.

Traditionally, interpreters of these texts have assumed that such expressions of friendship are to be read within the context of firm heterosexuality. Sedgwick sarcastically describes this tendency in her list of tactics used by heterosexist or homophobic readers to disregard the discourse of sentimental friendship: "Passionate language of same-sex attraction was extremely common during whatever period is under discussion — and therefore must have been completely meaningless" (*Epistemology* 52). Clearly either this language did have a meaning that became somehow offensive or disconcerting in later eras, or the language's meaning changed in ways that meant many people no longer felt comfortable using the terminology. Either way — a change in the attitude of society toward the meaning of the language, or a change in the meaning of the language — presents modern readers with a historical conundrum that requires thought, not glossing over.

It seems that even in its own era friendship was always suspicious. The scandal provoked by the publication of the letters between Gleim and Jacobi or between Müller and Bonstetten demonstrates that the cult of friendship was never completely unproblematic. Anna Luise Karsch's critique of the effusive *Letters of Misters Gleim and Jacobi* (*Briefe von den Herren Gleim und Jacobi*) shows that the language of the friendship cult was provocative even in its own day: "There are too many kisses in this work to avoid slander, suspicion, and mockery. I understand that such love is possible, I know that one can love that way; yet the more I know this, the more it disturbs me that you disapproved of my equally platonic, pure, and perhaps more upstanding love" (cited by Simon Richter 36). Despite running against the grain of contemporary orthodox criticism, a queer reading can actually be true to history, for in fact the discourse of friendship between members of the same sex frequently provoked concern even during its own heyday.

The classical Greek tradition was one site where the boundary between friendship and love was anxiously contested. While some early eighteenth-century classicists had seen Greek expressions of love between men other as mere friendship, the late eighteenth century was increasingly certain that there was something more than friendship at stake in these classical texts. Exemplifying this second line of reasoning, Ramdohr states clearly: "It therefore cannot be maintained that the love of youths [*Liebe zu den Lieblingen*], as custom approved it in the era of the Socratic school, was friendship. It was rather a tenderness [*Zärtlichkeit*] built on sexual sympathy [*Geschlechtssympathie*] and even bodily drives [*körperliche Triebe*]" (3:151). He goes on to make clear that the Greeks already distinguished quite clearly between friendship and love: "Nowhere does one find by Xenophon or Plato . . . a confusion between love and friendship" (3:152). If the Greeks distinguished between love and friendship, they probably did not mean friendship when they said love. A few decades later Hössli uses the same argument to deny emphatically that Greek love between men was friendship alone.

Derrida refers repeatedly to the androcentric structures of friendship, which he sees as based exclusively on a fraternal model. Derrida claims that the traditional view is that women can neither become friends with men nor develop friendship amongst themselves, because "this double exclusion of the feminine in this philosophical paradigm would then confer on friendship the essential and essentially sublime figure of virile homosexuality" (*Politics of Friendship* 279). Although Derrida is otherwise reticent about the sexual ambiguity of friendship, he clearly sees it—somewhat ominously—as fundamentally sexual in nature.

Robert Luftig has demonstrated that the presumption has always been that friendship between men and women had an erotic base. If a man and a woman in an eighteenth-century novel hugged, kissed, expressed their love for each other, and declared that they wanted to live together for ever and ever, would anyone assume that they were "just friends"? On the other hand, traditional commentators typically assure readers that two men or two women who behaved in such a fashion with each other were "just friends." The calcified presumption of heterosexuality prevents critics from thinking of male-female friendships in a non-physical way, while homophobia prevents them from viewing same-sex friendships as physical. Ironically, queer commentary would have us give Anna Luise Karsch's proposal to Gleim a try: read more sexuality into friendship between members of the same sex and less into friendship between members of different sexes. Here especially the queer reading can do its duty and shake up the reading experience.

In *Kyllenion*, Sachsen-Gotha does not observe a rigorous boundary between nonerotic and erotic friendships. Thus it seems that all of his pairs are friends intellectually, emotionally, and physically. It would be difficult to distinguish between the friendship that obtains between the men and women and the friendship between Julanthiskos and Alexis. Only the most heterosexist reader could assume that in *Kyllenion* the male-female couples have a sexual friendship and the same-sex couple does not.

In contrast to Sachsen-Gotha's narrator, the epistolary narrator of the *Letters* is very interested in distinguishing between friendship and sex. He reports to his friend that when he met the warm brothers, he at first thought that he was witnessing the most admirable friendship: "I considered all these acts for pure friendship, for true masculine sympathy of the soul. And observing from the side, I admired the small circle of cordial friends" (138). He only later discovers to his horror that the cult of friendship, the "true love of the soul," could in fact be, as the classicist Meiners fears, a mask for more specifically sexual behavior. The discourse of friendship not only confuses modern readers of eighteenth-century texts; it also mixed things up for the eighteenth century and considerably thereafter.

FASHION

As part of my objective in this chapter is to suggest that the signifiers of homosexuality may already have moved into place before the signified homosexuality itself emerges, it is fitting that I close with a final discourse that was used to identify the warm, a discourse that itself has always stressed style over content: the discourse of the fop, later to become the dandy. The epistolary narrator of the *Letters* reports that the sodomites had a certain clothing code that enabled them to identify each other:

The first zeal went so far that the young men who dedicated themselves to pederasty [*Päderastie*] differentiated themselves from others by visible signs in clothing. Thus, for a long time a youth with a broad pigtail, heavily powdered back, and a thick neck scarf was signaling that he belonged to the society of the warm [*die Gesellschaft der Warmen*]. (146)

Though doubt has been cast on the historical accuracy of the *Letters*, the description of clothing as signifier is valid. According to Van der Meer, Dutch authorities prosecuting sodomites in the eighteenth century were very interested in learning their clothing codes (288). By the end of the nineteenth century ornaments like red ties or green carnations were signals of male homosexuality throughout Europe and North America. Quite possibly, such codes were also present in Berlin by the end of the eighteenth century. Attention to a certain dress code (rather than, say, a specific taste in food or some other conceivable signifier of sexuality) was being established in the rhetoric around same-sex behavior at this point in time.

If the *Letters* present the sodomite as a creature of a certain style, *A Year in Arcadia* enacts that stylishness. Sachsen-Gotha's idyll is purple prose with a vengeance. It begins with "purple swans" upon which one might ride, surrounded by the scent of orange blossoms; it is replete with "purple sap," "purple leaves," "purple plums," a "purple-locked godhead," "the departing purple of the blessing Phoebus," "purple wool," "purple clothing"; it closes with "purple curtains" bedecking the crystal gates. Perhaps the purple harks back to the hyacinth, a signifier of male-male desire because the flower is named after Apollo's male lover who was killed by Zephyr, the West Wind, as Apollo and the youth were throwing the discus. In any case, the whole image is lush and rich, anticipating the decadent writings of the fin de siècle.

Critics frequently saw the novel as completely burdened and encumbered by its stylistics. In a letter about the book to his brother, Wilhelm Grimm is typical when he refers to the "idyll belabored with the most horribly bombastic verbiage" and "cluttered with word-clang" (quoted by Derks, afterword to Sachsen-Gotha, 152). Subsequent nineteenth-century readers saw in it nothing but "pure affectedness and fustian," calling it "pompous" and "overly opulent" (Derks, afterword to Sachsen-Gotha, 158). The literary depiction of male-male love is denigrated as overly concerned with style to the point of ridiculousness, an image that has persisted to this day, particularly with respect to effeminate homosexuals: one thinks of the dandy Ronald Firbank or the queens in "La Cage aux Folles."

But there have been those who applauded the style-conscious homosexual. Thomas Mann, for instance, argues that Platen's scrupulous adherence to the complex forms of the ghazal has to do with his homoerotic desire, which according to Mann must be formalistic rather than content-oriented (*Leiden*). He would presumably find it fitting that according to Derks in his afterword to *Kyllenion*, the novel strictly follows the traditions of the idyll (136). In both its negative and positive evaluations, then, *Kyllenion* enacts a link between the sodomite and the lover of the signifier. Derrida finds this connection in Plato's discussions of writing as well—that the reliance on writing, on the signifier, is a "perversion . . . substituting the passive . . . for the active," something that he links specifically with homosexuality at a number of points (*Disseminations* 108).

Once style is freed of content, however, it naturally becomes hard to make it stick to a particularly sexual nature. This leads to a fluidity of the chains of signification, as the warm brothers of the eighteenth century become linked with various discourses that permeate other aspects of their society in general (classicism, orientalism, friendship, fashion), and then as those now "warm" discourses are reappropriated by other aspects of that society. Similar developments take place in the twentieth century when, for instance, the rock star Madonna appropriates the type of dancing known as vogueing from gay men of color who, in order to dance this way, have appropriated the clothing of presumably straight women, which was in all probability designed by gay men, and so on.

In Berlin, according to the *Letters*, this chain of reappropriation created problems for the "warm brothers," problems familiar today to those who witness straight society's ravenous appetite for queer fashion. After describing the dress code of the warm brothers in Berlin, the Viennese reporter informs his reader that very quickly society in general took pleasure "in the thick pigtails and heavily powdered backs and such as a new fashion," which meant that warm suitors were occasionally disappointed in their efforts (146). Subcultural fashions have been co-opted by the dominant paradigm.

Kyllenion also gives an example of the queer chains of appropriation. Sachsen-Gotha makes use of Goethe's famous poem from *Wilhelm Meister's Apprenticeship* that begins, "Do you know the country . . . where the lemons bloom" (*Kennst du das Land . . . wo die Zitronen blühen*), with his own variation, "Do you know the beach, the magic mirror of prehistory, where eternal lilies of innocence bloom?" (*Kennst du den Strand, der Vorzeit Zauberspiegel, wo ewige Unschulds-Lilien blühn?*) The poem continues:

Whither, my dear, whither?
Over embers, over yearnings,
Over kisses, over attractions
Your bold sense drives you
Toward a forbidden heaven.

[Lieblicher, wohin, wohin?
Über Gluthen, über Sehnen,
Über Küsse, über Reize
Treibet dich dein kühner Sinn,
Nach verbotnem Himmel hin.] (17)

Although Goethe's Mignon poem definitively states "thither" rather than asking, like Sachsen-Gotha, "whither?" it seems to have the same journey in mind, filled with caves in which dragons dwell and crashing boulders and raging torrents.

The presence of this homage to Goethe in *Kyllenion* represents an intriguing appropriation of the figure of Mignon who, although wasting away with heterosexual desire for Wilhelm, is characterized by a complicated enough gender identity and sexual orientation that it makes perfect sense for Sachsen-Gotha to give her a prominent position in his novel of homoerotic desire. The general understanding of Mignon as "yearning" incarnate makes her an ideal figure for appropriation by those who yearned without hope for others of the same sex. Goethe himself appropriated a bit of sodomitical lore when he named his character Mignon, for, in the eighteenth century, that word could have the meaning of male homosexual prostitute or favorite and was used to describe the courtiers around the French king Henri III. A tangled chain of rhetoric emerges as the queer Sachsen-Gotha borrows from the canonical Goethe who filches from the libertine royals.

The utility of the Mignon figure for queer appropriation makes itself evident again in modern queer German film. The first example of that genre of film, Rosa von Praunheim's *It's Not the Homosexual Who's Perverse, but the Situation in which He Lives* (*Nicht der Homosexuelle ist pervers, sondern die Situation, in der er lebt*; 1971), features a number of older gay men listening to a musical setting of the poem "*Kennst Du das Land.*" Praunheim is critiquing gay culture that has based itself for so long on the appropriation of high art. The characters listening to the music are not held up as role models; indeed, the film demands that the audience reject this way of life. But while Praunheim objects to the use of Mignon as a prop for gay culture, his film demonstrates the historical importance of Goethe's figure in the construction of gay identity in Germany. The first East German film to deal openly with issues of gay desire, Heiner Carrow's film *Coming Out* (1989) also features a young student who later turns out to be gay, reading "Do You Know the Country" to an inattentive classroom. Carrow is less critical than Praunheim of the tradition that has developed around this poem. He in fact seems to be endorsing the understanding of Mignon's yearning as analogous to the unfulfilled desire of East German gays.

In his *Logic of Sense*, Gilles Deleuze devotes a chapter to two endless series, one on the level of the signifier (such as words) and one on the level of the signified (such as things; 23–26). As is so often the case, sexuality seems to provide a good example for the critical study of language. One can imagine one chronological series about sexual relations between members of the same sex: a couple of the links in this series would include the sodomite and the homosexual. At the same time one can imagine another chronological series, one that links the discourses identifying those sexual relations between members of the same sex. The links in this rhetorical series might not correspond exactly to the links in the other historical series. Thus the discourses that Friedel and Sachsen-Gotha use to define the warm brothers—the discourses of classicism, orientalism, friendship, and fashion—remain in place even after the birth of the "homosexual" in 1869 and continue to resonate. One could even say that these discourses provide the historical, cultural, and literary continuity that allows modern gay and lesbian readers to connect with those texts from the past that seem to have been formative of our cultural legacy.

3

JEAN PAUL'S ORIENTAL

HOMOSEXUALITIES

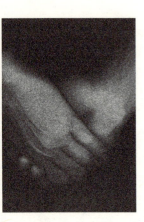

In the works of Johann Friedel and August von Sachsen-Gotha, one of the eighteenth-century German discourses that structures modern homosexuality is orientalism. One of the most positive reviews of Sachsen-Gotha's novel came from the novelist Jean Paul. Goethe, in his own orientalist project *The West-Eastern Divan* (*West-Östlicher Divan*), grants the novelist Jean Paul a certain preeminence among orientalist poets: "A man who has penetrated the breadth, height, and depth of the Orient will find that no German author has approached the Eastern poets and other authors more than Jean Paul" (*HA* 2:184). Given that according to Goethe, "the tender feeling for the beauty of the growing boy" could not be missing from an orientalist work like the *Divan* (*HA* 2:202), it is not surprising that another reader of Jean Paul, the composer Robert Schumann, notes the constant doubling of male protagonists in the novelist's works: each of Jean Paul's novels seems to feature a pair of male best friends (Ortheil 145).[1] As perceptive members of Jean Paul's huge early nineteenth-century audience, Goethe and Schumann may have been pointing to two facets of the same phenomenon: the orientalization of intense, erotic male bonding, and the homosexualization of the non-European male.

Jean Paul, nom de plume for Johann Paul Friedrich

1. This doubling corresponds to Schumann's own self-understanding as a combination of "Eusebius" and "Florestan." For more on Schumann and Jean Paul, see Siegel.

Richter (1763–1825), wrote lengthy, elaborately plotted novels filled with long-lost or hitherto unsuspected identical twins, hidden chambers, lifelike automatons, cataleptic princesses, and drunken geniuses. Although he was immensely popular in his own era, and at the same time remained well regarded by subsequent generations of German authors, intellectuals, and scholars, he has faded into obscurity today, especially in the United States. This obscurity is unfortunate, for Jean Paul has an important role to play in the development of love, romance, and sexuality in Germany and the Western world. Luhmann associates him above all with the triumph of that aspect of romantic love that glorified "love for love's sake" (75), although the phrase was actually first used prominently by another author, Christoph Martin Wieland, who will interest us in the next chapter.

While Jean Paul may be the novelist of romantic love, he has another claim to fame. He coined the word *Freundesliebe*, "love of friends," a term that was to gain favor among early twentieth-century German homosexuals (Dietrich 34). Thus Jean Paul became the object of St. Ch. Waldecke's analysis in the early twentieth-century militant homosexual magazine *The Exceptional* (*Der Eigene*). The interest of Waldecke, whose real name was Ewald Tscheck, is not completely unfounded, for there is biographical justification for looking at Jean Paul from a queer perspective. Jean Paul mentions an early memory of a childhood crush on a fellow schoolboy: "I remember namely also that a poor schoolboy loved me very much and I him" (cited in Pietzcker, *Einführung*, 127). As a young man, he seems to have identified intellectual life with masculinity and desired to have a platonic sort of intercourse with other men (Pietzcker 94, 114). His antagonism toward religion was its rigid sensuality, the way it turned every earthly pleasure into a sin. An example of such an earthly pleasure turns out to be wrestling with a school chum, "not out of animosity, but in innocent playfulness" (cited in Pietzcker, *Einführung*, 100). The problem with religion therefore becomes its refusal to let Jean Paul have playful physical contact with his male friends. Jean Paul's flirtation with the death of God in his famous "Speech of the Dead Christ from the Firmament that There is no God" (*Rede des toten Christus vom Weltgebäude herab, dass kein Gott sei*) suggests a desire to rid himself of this proscriptive influence, even if he was unwilling to embrace atheism unreservedly.

Jean Paul's relationships with women have the signs of a man uncomfortable with heterosexuality (Pietzcker 118–21). When he finally married, at age thirty-seven, he informed his friends that what he wanted was a woman who would make his food (cited in Ortheil 88). Passion remained reserved for friends like Christian Otto, his "eternal beloved" (*ewig Geliebter*; cited in

Ortheil 80). To another friend he writes, "love must have something physical, a twig, down to which it flies. Send me this twig" (cited in Waldecke 169). The metaphor of the physical twig is suggestive, to say the least. His Jewish friend Emmanuel Samuel (who later changed his name to Emmanuel Osmund and is sometimes referred to as such) Jean Paul addresses as "my good warm dear black-eyed Emmanuel" (cited in Waldecke 169). Given the usage of the word in Friedel's *Gallantries of Berlin*, one wonders how innocently "warm" is meant. Much more blatant is another letter to "my ever more dear Emmanuel, with whom I'm confident I would get along, even if I had had myself copulated with him [*wenn ich mich mit ihm hätte kopulieren lassen*]" (cited in Waldecke 169).

On a more fundamental level, the queer reader might be intrigued by Jean Paul's self-construction—his decision to write under the name Jean Paul rather than his given German name Johann Paul Friedrich Richter. This new identity is a literary masking that resonates with Mishima's *Confessions of a Mask*, along with thousands of other sources; the mask is a staple of queer identity. The choice to take a French name at a time when many Germans would have regarded France as effete and even effeminate is intriguing. At one point Jean Paul writes that "the history of mankind may appear, indeed, only the long disguise of a masquerade," something that Schumann picked up on and transmitted through such pieces as the *Papillons* (Siegel 17).

Jean Paul's novel *Siebenkäs*, published in 1796, provides a rich text for an analysis of the links between the fantasy of same-sex desire and orientalism. Its full title is *Pieces of Flowers, Fruits, and Thorns, or Marriage, Death and Wedding of the Public Defender F. St. Siebenkäs (Blumen-, Frucht- und Dornenstücke oder Ehestand, Tod und Hochzeit des Armenadvokaten F. St. Siebenkäs)*. As the title adumbrates, the novel begins with Siebenkäs married to Lenette. With the help of his best friend, Leibgeber, Siebenkäs escapes the marriage by faking his own death. While Lenette subsequently marries the schoolteacher, Siebenkäs assumes Leibgeber's identity and weds one of Leibgeber's friends, Natalie. Leibgeber's very name translates as "body giver," thus for Siebenkäs he seems to offer the opportunity to acquire corporeality. Leibgeber suggests the possibility of giving body to German fantasies surrounding male-male desire and orientalism.

While most romantic novels glorify marriage, *Siebenkäs* is in part an exercise in misogamy. Reversing the traditional narrative structure, the entire plot relies on the conceit that Siebenkäs must escape the literally sterile and life-destroying marriage that begins the novel. Lenette feels guilty and self-conscious about her infertility when Siebenkäs puts flowers originally meant for her on the freshly dug grave of a woman who has died in childbirth (639). After she marries the schoolteacher, Lenette herself dies in childbirth, along with her baby girl (858). Metaphorically, this lethal marriage stifles creativity, art, and writing: "Marriage builds over the poetic world a rind of the real" (851). These and other images of death and sterility surrounding bourgeois marriages and liaisons suggest, along with the novel's countless digressions on the differences between men and women, Jean Paul's efforts to fashion a new program of relationships between the sexes.

In contrast to the sterile bourgeois marriage stands the relationship between Siebenkäs and Leibgeber. The two happen to look exactly like each other; the most interesting homosocial tension is between them and the two are frequently referred to as "beloveds" (Geliebte; 711, 713, 775, 825). Admittedly, this may be a convention of the era, but "beloved" is the same word used to describe Natalie, whom Siebenkäs eventually marries, and critics rarely suggest that Siebenkäs and Natalie are "just friends," as we would expect after the analysis of friendship in the previous two chapters. Indeed, if kissing is any measure, Siebenkäs's relationship with his beloved Leibgeber is much more physical than his relationship with Natalie. Throughout the novel, Siebenkäs wants to kiss Leibgeber (480), but must be satisfied with quick pecks (493). Eventually, things heat up between them: "they lay clasping each other on the high tide of life, like two shipwrecked brothers, who swim in the cold waves, embracing and embraced, and who hold nothing more than the heart, of which they are dying" (713). With the trope "embracing and embraced" (umschlingend und umschlungen), Jean Paul is probably making reference to Goethe's poem "Ganymed," where the same idea appears with the same combination of verb forms, although slightly different vocabulary: "encompassing and encompassed" (umfassend umfaßt). "Ganymed," being about the male youth who appeals to Zeus, lends itself easily to a queer reading. Later, in his fake deathbed scene, Siebenkäs finally gets a good long kiss out of Leibgeber: "He tore him to his mouth and kissed in silence" (818). The construction of desire between the two men and its eventual satisfaction is one of the structuring principles of Jean Paul's novel.

Other images of male-male love saturate the text. A so-called "dream within a dream" ends with an image of bloody warriors bonding sensually together:

Finally the smoke parted in billows above two bloody people who lay in each other's wounded arms. It was two sublime friends who had sacrificed everything for each other, themselves first of all, but not their fatherland. "Lay your wound on mine, beloved!—Now we can reconcile again. You sacrificed me to the fatherland, and I you.—Give me your heart again, before it bleeds to death.—Ach, we can die only with each other." (648)

The image of two wounded men in each other's arms connects the passage to Leibgeber and Siebenkäs in Bayreuth, "embracing and embraced," "dying" of their hearts. Indeed, death seems to suffuse the same-sex relationships as much as the heterosexual ones, for Siebenkäs kisses Leibgeber most passionately when he is on his deathbed.

These passages substantiate many of the theses that Derrida outlines in his book *Politics of Friendship*. For Derrida, as for Jean Paul, the mettle of friendship is always tested by death—it is only in death that one understands how deeply one has loved. Derrida, working with the ideas of the German thinker Carl Schmitt, finds that the classic scene of friendship is the battle to the death between friends, a vision with which Jean Paul seems entirely comfortable, as the passages just cited indicate. The tensions and releases provided by this "homo-fraternal" model of friendship provide the basis of modern democratic politics, according to Derrida. Jean Paul also links friendship with nationality tellingly. On the one hand the love of the men transcends their nationality; on the other hand, they are ultimately loyal to their national backgrounds.

In his book, *The Case of California*, Laurence Rickels, whose analysis of the cult of adolescence circles ceaselessly around the group identification that results when brothers bond against the father figure, sets the stage for provocative interpretations of friendship in Jean Paul. Jean Paul's famous vision of the death of God certainly invites a Freudian interpretation, along the lines of *Totem and Taboo*, in which Jean Paul's male characters unite as brothers against their father and are simultaneously guilt-stricken because of their rebellion.

Several personal interjections from the narrator suggest the importance of the issue of same-sex friendship for Jean Paul. In an inserted section called "First Breakfast" (*Erstes Frühstück*), the narrator commiserates with Viktor, a character from *Hesperus*, another novel by Jean Paul, who has lost a number of male friends. The passage concludes with an appeal to one of the deceased friends: "But come now to your Victor and to your brother, JP" (766). The close male-male relationship between Viktor and Flamin in *Hesperus* is said to be based on the relationship between Christian Otto and Jean Paul (Ortheil 51–53). It is therefore not too surprising that Otto in fact appears later in the novel. When Leibgeber and Siebenkäs part for the last time, the narrator as author Jean Paul breaks down and addresses his own real friend: "And why does my heart break so violently in two, why couldn't I dry my eyes long before I came to this separation? O . . . my good Christian . . . what tortures us on that hill is the thought: 'Ach, how much I would have loved you, good heart, had I known in advance of your departure' " (840). The narrator is alluding, apparently, to the death of two young men, Johann Adam Lorenz and Christian Adam von Oertahl, whom both Otto and Jean Paul had known and loved (986). Finally, however, the narrator pulls himself together and explains the moral of the story to Otto: "No, my Christian, something better remains left for us, a warmer, more faithful, more beautiful love for every soul that we haven't yet lost" (840). Links between friendship and death abound here, as Derrida suggests would be the case: it is only in death that the friendship becomes clear.

An additional narrative break takes place at the beginning of the fourth volume of the novel, when Jean Paul requests that a mysterious man who had written to him please identify himself. It concludes with the wish that if this man is lonely "a good person will send a letter full of love" to him, like the one he had sent to Jean Paul (769). In a later edition, Jean Paul reveals that this person was none other than the poet Gleim, who in fact sent money to Jean Paul when the author was in need (Ortheil 87). This compellation refers the reader to Gleim, who is omnipresent in the homoerotic history of eighteenth-century German literature. He was the enthusiastic architect in the cult of friendship; there was even a temple to friendship (*Freundschafts-tempel*) in his house in Halberstadt (Derks 587). As we saw in Chapter 1, Gleim corresponded with the historian Johannes Müller, specifically about accusations of sodomy, and as we shall see in Chapter 4, he discussed "Greek love" with Wieland in his letters. His presence in Jean Paul's writing is therefore significant.

These repeated breaks in the narrative flow, in which Jean Paul interrupts his narration in order to interject matters that normally belong to the private personal sphere, are unique and significant, for the only issues that cause Jean Paul to interrupt his narrative concern his relationships with other men. They suggest the day-to-day urgency of the issue of male-male friendship for the author and his readers.

Of course, it is conceivable to regard the depiction of male-male friendship within the plot of the novel and in the narrative breaks as "pure," that is to say asexual, friendship. Regardless of the nature of Jean Paul's personal interest in the subject, however, *Siebenkäs* provides some insights into the late eighteenth-century reconfiguration of the boundary between an increasingly homophobic homosociality and a developing sense of homosexuality. To begin with, the narrator attempts to recover as much homosociality as possible within the matrimonial state. He asserts that women enjoy their role as the glue cementing the bonds between men, and wish their male friends to have many other male friends: "the friendship or love that a girl has for a boy grows before our eyes due to the friendship that she perceives between him and his friends" (777). Men do not, however, appreciate women more if the women have more same-sex friendships: "The same electric charge or magnetic armor of our love is rarely granted to us lovers by the friendship that we notice between our [female] beloved and her friend" (777). Tellingly, the narrator refers to the women in the singular, as though all the men shared one girlfriend. Although the narrator continues with some critical remarks directed toward his own gender, the rhetoric of the one female lover shared by all the men conforms easily to Luce Irigaray's understanding of "hom(m)osexuality" that bonds men together through women. Indeed, in the novel Siebenkäs and the schoolteacher develop a stronger relationship through their competition for Lenette, because men competing for a woman will forgive "a [male] rival more easily than an unfaithful woman" (530). Women are said to be the opposite in that they will forgive a philandering husband rather than a female rival, which allows for maximum male homosociality because the men can bond under almost any circumstance, while it provokes extreme female isolation in the matrimonial situation, as they relate only to their husbands.

In this respect, Jean Paul seems to be anticipating the trivialization of friendship between women found in Karl Pockels's *Attempt at a Characterization of the Female Sex* (*Versuch einer Charakteristik des weiblichen Geschlechtes*; esp. 2:168–232). This would be the tradition upon which Derrida is relying when he asserts that friendship is an exclusively male prerogative. Incidentally, his argument stands in opposition to Ramdohr, who believes that women like to chat with their girlfriends about their love, so "love seems to damage the bonds of friendship less among the delicate sex" (2:312). In contrast, according to Ramdohr, "the male friend of a man in love is certainly not a happy friend" (2:312).

As evidence of the kind of behavior between the genders that Pockels and Jean Paul believe they can find, Lenette is sympathetic to a threesome involving her, Siebenkäs, and the schoolteacher Stiefel, whom she likes and with whom she apparently has an affair. After Siebenkäs's death, she marries the schoolteacher. Siebenkäs, as mentioned before, does not mind the development of this relationship, and discovers he can bond more easily with the man because of his ex-wife's new marriage. The schoolteacher does not mind either, but finds that "his love for the woman puts not chains, but wings, on his love for the man" (636). This relationship reaches its apex on Siebenkäs's deathbed, when, as Lenette kisses him, he reaches out for the teacher's hand: "and now he held together on his depressed breast the two things nearest heaven on earth, friendship and love" (809). Here, interestingly, the narrator does distinguish between friendship and love. Yet, with all the "love" going on between men in this novel, one wonders for whom Siebenkäs feels love and for whom he feels friendship. A heterosexist reading would assume that friendship aligned with the male-male relationship and love with the male-female one, but the novel does not necessarily support such a conclusion.

However, even with this establishment of a great deal of leeway for male homosociality within the heterosexual marriage, Siebenkäs is unhappy. The novel suggests that one way to rejuvenate infertile heterosexuality is the threesome, consisting of two men and one woman. When preparing to die, Siebenkäs dreams blissfully of walking the bosky allée from his house to his grave, resting on the way at every mossy bank "between his friend and his wife, in each hand a beloved" (792). However, when Siebenkäs attempts to draw Lenette into his "manfully quiet embrace" (480) with Leibgeber, the menage à trois turns into a mirage: "In his increasing giddiness, the spouse wanted to draw his [female] beloved into the embrace of his [male] beloved, in order to expand the high bond; but bride and friend remained separate from each other and embraced him alone" (480). Both friend and bride are referred to as the "beloved," indicating their parallel status in the eyes of the narrator and Siebenkäs. But while Siebenkäs thinks he can bring a man into his marriage, his beloveds know this is impossible, as evidenced by the other failed triangular constellations consisting of two men and one woman — the schoolteacher, Siebenkäs, and Lenette, and Leibgeber, Siebenkäs, and Natalie.

As none of the threesomes work out, Siebenkäs settles on another solution: androgyny. While he aims his misogyny at Lenette who has all the "typically" feminine faults, he loves Natalie for her masculinity. When he first meets her, he sees "a feminine head that was sawed off the neck of the Vatican Apollo and softened by only eight or ten feminine traits and with a smaller forehead" (712). Since Winckelmann, the Vatican Apollo had been the standard for male beauty. In addition to her boyish good looks, Natalie's "masculine cheerfulness" (721) and her "manly enthusiasm" (732) thrill Siebenkäs. Siebenkäs himself has always been somewhat androgynous. In one scene, he sees himself as a northwestern Native-American woman (502). At another point, the narrator describes him as lounging around the house in his wife's robes, "in the demi-negligee of an Amazon . . . like a hermaphrodite" (512).

Jean Paul's references to North America points to the exoticism that always couches Siebenkäs's attempts to escape his first marriage. The possible destinations are as numerous as they are exotic: Morocco, Tahiti, Siam, the West Indies, Northwest America, India, Arabia, Algiers, Egypt, Turkey, China, Siberia, and Constantinople are some of the alternatives to small-town life in Germany that appear throughout this novel. All of these destinations qualify as what Edward Said calls "the free-floating Orient" (119) — everything that in the late eighteenth century Europe was poised to conquer and colonize. It is worth recalling here that, as Said notes, "from 1815 to 1914 European direct colonial dominion expanded from about 35 percent of the earth's surface to about 85 percent of it" (41). The Orient is thus a term for everything that in this era required differentiation from Europe, and against which Europe could identify itself. Said writes: "Orientalism is never far from what Dennis Hays has called the idea of Europe, a collective notion identifying 'us' Europeans as against all 'those' non-Europeans" (7).

The Orient has been associated with "an excessive 'freedom of intercourse' " since the beginnings of orientalism (Said 167). In Flaubert, for instance, Said sees "an almost uniform association between the Orient and sex" (188, see also 190); for the orientalist Lane, "everything about the Orient . . . exuded dangerous sex" (Said 167); analyzing a text written in 1974 (which is to say, considerably after the heyday of orientalist fantasies), Said notes, "the association between the Orient and sex is remarkably persistent" (309). Although, as Boone suggests, Said almost actively represses homosexuality in his discussion of the sexuality of the Orient, he does nevertheless call it "a living tableau of queerness" (103; see also Bakshi).

This "Orient" overlaps exactly with the nineteenth-century British explorer Richard Burton's "sotadic zone," in which he alleged homosexuality and pederasty were especially prevalent. The zone centered on the equator, reaching as far north as Italy in the European realm, expanding further north in East Asia in order to encompass China and Japan, and engulfing the entire New World. The sotadic zone was the Orient, in the sense of everything that Europe was not. Small wonder then that European homosexuals, like Burton himself, flocked to the colonies. Nor is it surprising that Jean Paul locates his most extreme fantasies of a solution for the problem of male homosociality far away from Europe. In the Orient he situates male homosexuality.

As the nineteenth-century English sexologist Havelock Ellis notes, "the peoples of every country have always been eager to associate sexual perversions with some other country than their own" (*Sexual Inversion* 4). The particular tendency of Europe to identify the non-Europeans with sodomy and other sexual deviance can perhaps be dated back to the discovery of the New World, when the alleged sodomitical practices of the natives were used to justify the conquest of the Americas. Jonathan Goldberg has extensively demonstrated the early sixteenth-century consensus on the perversion of the natives (177–222). Hernán Cortes's first letter from Mexico sweepingly declares that the natives "are all sodomites," and Gonzalo Fernandez de Ovideo concurs (Goldberg 193). Piedro de Ciezo reports in 1553 that the natives "practiced the unspeakable and horrible sin of sodomy, committing it openly and in public without fear of God or personal shame" (Goldberg 185). Gloria Flaherty refers to other explorers who found the natives of the Americas to be addicted to the vice: Samuel Purchas (1577–1626) was concerned about the "women-men" of California and Peru who dressed as females and satisfied the "sodomitical lusts" of other men (*Shamanism* 35), and Martin Sauer, writing in the late eighteenth century, reported that Alaskans kept boys as "objects of unnatural affection" and that mothers were "happy to see them taken by the chiefs, to gratify their unnatural desires" (*Shamanism* 93). In certain West Indian tribes, every sixth boy was said to become a bisexual, transgendered berdache (see Flaherty, "Sex").

The Near East is actually the area of the world that early writers most frequently associate with the word "Orient." Louis Crompton notes that as early as 1688 explorers of the Ottoman empire and Egypt were "remarkably communicative on the subject of homosexuality" (112; see also Rousseau 26). The connection between the Near East and sodomy remained strong throughout the nineteenth century. Ellis, perhaps looking at the same society that Flaubert enjoyed in the middle of the nineteenth century, asserts that the Egyptians do not regard sodomy as punishable or reprehensible (*Sexual Inversion* 4). Indeed, throughout the first half of the twentieth century, many European homosexuals, from Oscar Wilde and André Gide to Joe Orton, regarded North Africa as a playground full of potential sexual partners.

The northern shores of the Mediterranean also developed a queer reputation. As early as 1376, the English parliament accused the Italian merchants of having brought sodomy to the island (Guldin 51). Aldrich, Mitter, and Rousseau have all documented the endless fascination that Italy exerted on the homosexuals of northern Europe. Again, Ellis corroborates from a medical perspective that the assumption of Italian sodomy remained constant at least until the end of the nineteenth century (*Sexual Inversion* 58). Authors like Hans Christian Andersen, who in his diaries is keenly aware of the presence of male prostitution in southern Italy, and Thomas Mann, who wrote such canonically homosexual stories as *Death in Venice* (*Tod in Venedig*), provide further evidence of a literary sort for the durability of the assumption of Italian homosexuality.

In addition, the Far East was also frequently associated with sodomy. Again the history of this tradition is quite old. The first reports from the Jesuits in China emphasized the presence of male prostitution and homosexuality in that country. Matteo Ricci writes at the beginning of the seventeenth century:

But that which may be most descried in this area, and which most reveals the wretchedness of these people, is that, not only is natural lust given free rein, but also the unnatural and perverse, which is forbidden neither by law nor custom and considered no cause for shame. Thus it is a subject for public discourse and is universally practiced without hindrance. In some cities where this practice is most prevalent, as in this Court, the main court, there are public streets filled with young men made up like prostitutes and likewise with people who buy these young men and teach them to play, sing and dance; and dressed very erotically and daubed with rouge like women, they entice men into this nefarious vice. (cited in Guy 70)

In 1696, almost a century later, Louis Le Comte refers to a certain Prince Ki, who filled a pool with wine "so that he might bathe in it with three hundred youths in a lascivious manner" (cited in Guy 75). Siberia was frequently seen as another a hotbed of sodomy: John Perry along with Catherine the Great considered sodomy one of the archaic practices to be eliminated from the new Russian possessions in Siberia (Flaherty, *Shamanism* 25, 118).

Starting particularly in the late eighteenth century, the Germans absorbed and repeated all of these sexual clichés about the Orient, strengthening them in the process. In 1768, in a text published in Berlin for Frederick the Great, Cornelius de Pauw emphasized the high incidence of homosexuality and effeminacy among Native American men (Zantop 305, 307). Discussing the link between ancient Greece and the modern Orient, Christoph Meiners, in his 1775 study on Greek love, asserts that erotic male-male friendships were to be found "among all warlike primitives in America" (83). In 1796, Johann Valentin Müller discusses the deleterious influences of sodomy among the Greeks, Romans, and "the Orientals of today" (135). In 1798, the aesthetician Friedrich Wilhelm Basilius Ramdohr cites the frequency of sodomy among the "rough" southern peoples as proof that it must be natural (3: 137). Just as Goethe and Platen are aware that the poetry of the Near East is pederastic, Hössli cites extensively from Turkish, Persian, and Arabic literature in his apology for male-male love.

The German beliefs about Italian sodomy are almost worth a chapter for themselves. Johann Georg Krünitz, the encyclopedia writer with a medical training, opined in an entry on pederasty (*Knabenschänderei*) in 1784:

Pederasty [*Päderastie*] is more common in Naples than in any other city in Italy. Climate and leisure encourage this unfortunate practice . . .

Lord Tilney, who died in 1784, was a great pederast [*ein großer Päderast*] and for that reason made Naples his home for 25 years. To avoid a criminal trial that threatened him in England because of his favorite passion, which no race hates more than the English, he left his homeland forever and lived from his 18,000 pounds Sterling with the splendor of a great lord. He was usually in Florence in the summer and in Naples in the winter, where he threw splendid parties and satisfied his passions until his death. (Campe 119)

In 1798, Ramdohr reconfirmed that sexual sympathy for male favorites was "so common today in Italy" (3:190).

The Germans went on to codify and promote these stereotypes, reinforcing them with the mechanics of such varied nineteenth-century disciplines as classics and sexology. The classicist Friedrich Jacobs, who sympathetically reviewed the accomplishments of Sachsen-Gotha, reports in a footnote to his essay on "male love" (published in 1829) that sodomy was quite common among Moslems, Aleutians, and the residents of Lima, Peru (212). In 1879, the sexologist Gustav Jaeger put together the reports of an anonymous source who claimed to have known 1,000 homosexuals from three continents in the previous twenty years. According to this source, "there never was and there still is not an Asian, of whatever tribe, who will not put up with and practice homosexuality, passively and actively [*Homosexualismus, passiv und dann aktiv*]" (84). Similarly, according to this report, "almost all Nubians are born homosexuals [*geborene Homosexuelle*]" (89). Jaeger suppressed this information for a while, but when he finally did publish it in 1899, he lent its sweeping assertions about homosexuality and the Orient the seriousness of the medical profession. Edward Westermarck, who admittedly wrote in English, first published in Germany in 1908 the chapter about homosexuality in his book on the history and development of morals. He repeated almost all of these assertions: many native tribes of the Americas and the Bering Sea encourage homosexuality, Africans and Asians also practice the vice, and the Chinese even have homosexual bordellos.

It is worth noting that the biography of one of the great figures of German classicism, the scientist and explorer Alexander von Humboldt, links indications of queer sexuality with a penchant for non-European travels. From 1799 to 1804, he traveled to the Amazon with A. J. A. Bonpland, who was alleged to be his intimate. He explored the Amazon, the Orinoco, and the Peruvian Andes. Upon returning to Europe, he still felt estranged from his homeland and lived in Paris, where he wrote up his findings. Later in life he explored Russia and Siberia. When he died, he named his valet Seifert his sole heir, further fostering suspicions about his sexuality. Whether these suspicions are founded or not, they suggest a link between sexual nonconformity and a desire to leave Europe.

Jean Paul avidly and accurately reproduces this identification of the non-European as homosexual and vice versa in *Siebenkäs*. Anthropological travel literature informs the novel to a great degree. It alludes to Count Stolberg's description of his trip to Switzerland, Italy, and Sicily (537, 962) as well as Nicolai's travel journals (605, 968), and cites Moritz's journey to England (547), Johann Meersmann's travels through the British Isles (623), and Jean Baptiste Labat's voyages to Italy (680). Fictionalized travel accounts like *A Sentimental Journal* by Laurence Sterne, who had a lifelong influence on Jean Paul, are also alluded to in the novel. Jean Paul's childhood favorite (Ortheil 20) *Robinson Crusoe* by Daniel Defoe is not to be missed either (555). Defoe's novel is particularly interesting because it locates the male-bonding of Crusoe and Friday on an exotic isle. The narrator quotes the memoirs of the diplomat and traveler Georg Heinrich von Langsdorff (502), who is, incidentally, Jacobs's and Westermarck's source for the claim that same-sex behavior is common among the Aleutians. Much of this travel literature is specifically about travel to exotic locales beyond Western Europe: Besides the writings of Townson and Fortis, the novel mentions Uno de Troilius's journal of a trip to Iceland (520) and alludes to Louis Le Comte's memories and observations of his trip to China (742), in which the anecdote about Prince Ki's three hundred boys bathing in wine appears.

As we have seen in the previous chapter, one of the possible discursive links between the Orient and homosexuality is the story of Sodom. While Friedel and Sachsen-Gotha do not make use of this link, *Siebenkäs* alludes twice to "apples of Sodom," a fabled fruit said to grow in the area of the Dead Sea that looked "ravishingly delicious" on the vine but "dissolved into dust" when it was picked (Poubelle 7). In one passage, Leibgeber gives this appellation to a letter in which he had questioned the value of procreation at length, only to reaffirm it because it had created his male friend—heterosexuality justified because it produces new lovers (700). Later, the narrator calls the writings of Rosa von Venner, one of Siebenkäs's slimy adversaries in the novel, "an apple of Sodom in paradise" (737).

The presence of this second "apple of Sodom in paradise" points to another traditional linkage between homosexuality and the Orient, this one positive: the notion of a homo-utopia, an Arcadia, where sexuality was freer. As noted earlier Jean Paul, almost alone among his contemporaries, praised Sachsen-Gotha's *Year in Arcadia: Kyllenion*, an early text in this tradition.

Tahiti was considered by many eighteenth- and nineteenth-century Europeans and Americans to be an idyllic paradise. The Tahitians and their island "paradise" had come to the attention of Germans in 1777 through Georg Forster's *Journey Around the World* (*Reise um die Welt*), which relates Forster's travels with his father on Captain Cook's voyage around the world. Cook had noted the open sexuality of the natives of Tahiti in 1769; Diderot is one of the first, but certainly not the last, to use the Tahitians as examples of a natural and non-repressed view of sexuality (Porter 120). In the next century, the Pacific Islands quickly developed an image of free sexuality (Hyam 50, 104–5; see also Austen). Numa Praetorius, the pseudonym for Eugen Wilhelm, reports in the *Yearbook of Sexual Intermediary Types* (*Das Jahrbuch für sexuelle Zwischenstufen*) that the Tahitians practice a kind of societally sanctioned same-sex union: "In Tahiti, bonds of love [*Liebesbündnisse*] are cemented between men who even belong to different and enemy tribes; they are recognized by both sides in such a way that each member of the couple can enter the area of the enemy tribe without danger" (148). In 1911, Berthold Schidlof reports that pederasty is a "national custom" (*Volkssitte*) among the residents of another South Pacific island, New Caledonia. Specifically about the Tahitians, Schidlof writes that

Tahiti or Otahiti had a class of men who dressed in women's clothes, took up women's occupations, submitted to the same restrictions as women regarding food and such, and—like women—attempted to win the approval of men. They preferred those men over all others who lived together with them and renounced all dealings with women. (121–22)

Although these so-called "Mahhus" or "Mahoos" preferred men who renounced women, they themselves interacted well with women. Westermarck also refers to the "Mahus" who "adapt the clothing, posture and manners of women and display the fantastic queerness and coquetry of the vainest women. They move mainly in the society of women and women seek them out" (250). These reports must come from the same tradition upon which Jean Paul draws. Himself a part of the continuation of this tradition, the narrator of *Siebenkäs* explains in the opening pages of the novel that Leibgeber and Siebenkäs had exchanged names at university, "imitating the Tahitians, who exchange names as well as hearts with their beloveds" (474).

In addition to Sodom and Tahiti, the Balkans show up as a locus of homosexuality in *Siebenkäs*. Crompton documents assertions by such eighteenth-century intellectuals as Gibbon, Vaudencourt, and Pouqueville alleging that the Romanians and the Albanians both were susceptible to homosexuality (133–35; for a reference to Bulgarians, see Curtis). Ellis reports on the same-sex proclivities of both the Albanians and the Bulgarians (*Sexual Inversion* 4, 9). Westermarck asserts that it is "a general custom" in some areas of Albania "that most guys over sixteen have their 'lovers' [*Lieblinge*] who are between twelve and seventeen" (253). For his part, Jean Paul cites the most recent information available to him, Alberto Fortis, who asserts in a volume published in 1778 that

Friendship, that among us is so subject to change on the slightest motives, is lasting among the Morlacchi. They have even made it a kind of religious point, and tie the sacred bond at the foot of the altar. The Sclavonian ritual contains a particular benediction for the solemn union of two male or two female friends in the presence of the congregation. (56–57)

Intriguingly, Fortis suggests the comparability of the short-lived friendship of modern northern Europeans and the marriage-like vows of Balkan friendships, implying that friendship could flow naturally to lifelong nuptials. Fortis, incidentally, is the last source who claims to be an eyewitness to the tradition of same-sex unions going back to antiquity that John Boswell discusses in his book *Same-Sex Unions* (265–67).

One of the reasons for the links in the European imagination between the Balkans and homosexuality is undoubtedly the area's proximity to Greece. In the eighteenth century, besides being the Orient from a northern European perspective, Greece and Italy had a historical tradition that allowed for a respectable discussion of homosexuality and pederasty. According to Said, the Germans particularly tended to view the Orient in "classical terms" (19, see also 79, 168). Like many eighteenth-century observers, Jean Paul sees the ancient world and the colonized world as comparable. He asserts, for instance, that in both societies only a limited number of citizens were truly free: "Were there not even in free Athens and Rome—certainly in the West Indies—more servants than freemen?" (500). Just as he emphasizes the sexual elements of exotic countries far removed geographically, Jean Paul also cites the homosexual referents to antiquity: Lycurgus, who was known in Jean Paul's time as the framer of laws allowing male-male relationships (654); Hyacinth (765), who will return repeatedly in German eighteenth-century literature as a marker of male homosexuality; Zephyr, who killed Hyacinth out of jealousy (657); and the notoriously decadent Roman emperor Heliogabolus (718), who dressed as a woman, scoured the empire for the most amply endowed men, and told them to call him their queen. Socrates and Plato, whose names were among the most frequently used bywords for homosexuality in eighteenth-century German culture, surface frequently in Jean Paul's novel, usually in passages relating to gender, love, and passion (494, 630–34, 792). Far from classical serenity and control, Jean Paul's Greek antiquity becomes a signifier of erotics and a venue for the discussion of unruly passions. It is thus an important discourse running parallel to the orientalist discourse, strengthening the homoerotic charge of the entire novel.

Siebenkäs is abuzz with all the benefits of the globalist impulse that has informed the interest in travel literature. Exotic products pepper the novel. The purveyors of these products, the various East India companies, appear frequently as symbols of prosperity (465, 561, 797). The narrator finds the voice of the Moroccan ambassador in Vienna better than opera (462). In this context it is conceivable that one of the possibilities offered by the colonialist drive was the satisfaction of same-sex urges.

One of the countless allusions to the Orient makes clearer the (homo-) erotic stakes of the colonialist spirit in the novel. In his "apple of Sodom," a letter discussing whether he would procreate were he Adam, Leibgeber refers to (and rejects) the notion that "the entire earth as a European possession in the India of the universe" belongs to him as the first human (531). He implies that even if Europe conquers the entire earth (including, presumably, all of India), the universe will still represent some unfathomable Orient, endlessly mysterious and inscrutable. Textually, Leibgeber links the question of European expansion with procreation, on the verge of deciding against both— until he decides that procreation is worth it, because it has produced his bosom buddy Siebenkäs. By extension, colonialism is also worth it—because it allows for homosexuality.

Interrelationships between the characters of the novel reinforce the eroticism of orientalism while revealing how polymorphous and protean that exotic identity is. In the foreword, the narrator imagines showing his book, which is described as "a flowering, glowing Orient" (*ein blühendes glimmendes Morgenland*; 463), to the shopkeeper's daughter, who is said to represent the reading public in contrast to her father, the purchasing public. Thus the book itself becomes the equivalent of all the colonial treasures being offered to Europe at the end of the eighteenth century, while the reader is the beloved of the author. The erotic drive of the author for the reader is to be satisfied by the orientalist offering.

If, in the foreword, the Orient is a love offering from the writer to the public, in the main body of the novel it becomes itself the object of desire, when Siebenkäs compares his Occident to Natalie's Orient (784). Herein Jean Paul anticipates Goethe's *West-Eastern Divan*, in which East and West are in an erotic interchange. More important for this chapter, however, he continues to see the Orient as the object (in this case of desire) to the Western subject. But Siebenkäs does not always see himself as the exploiting, globalist West. Sometimes he identifies himself as the exploited Orient, just as he sometimes identifies with women. With his first wife Lenette, he takes on the characteristics of northwestern Native Americans when he declares that he must wear wooden plates in his lips in response to Lenette's reproach that he is inappropriately amorous when she is dressed in her Sunday best (502). Significantly, the sexologist Westermarck specifically mentions "the tribes of the Northwest of the United States" as being particularly prone to innate sexual inversion (*angeborene Verkehrtheit*; 255).

Europe, in this case embodied in Siebenkäs's wife Lenette, sees itself as religious and sexually controlled, while the sexually irrepressible is identified with the natives. Said has noted the persistent orientalist belief that European scholars have been able to exhibit sexual self-control as they observe the morally decadent Orient (147, 162–63). At the beginning of orientalism, Siebenkäs seemingly already uses the orientalist trope quite adroitly. What he wants—Natalie—he sees as a kind of oriental fruit to be picked and savored. But unable to express sexuality as a good European, he must imagine himself oriental when attempting to express his desires.

Particularly in conjunction with his beloved Leibgeber, Siebenkäs becomes oriental. Leibgeber compares Siebenkäs with an African slave when trying to put a good face on his friend's scheme to fake his death: "you have killed yourself like a Negro slave in order to come . . . into liberty" (833). Leibgeber also claims to be Africa: He complains that he remains to the most famous people of all time "an unknown inner Africa . . . an invisible darkness, a miserable *je ne sais quoi*" (699). Leibgeber is the character most frequently associated with ancient Greece as well (Siebenkäs said he would have "to be a Socrates" if he were going to impersonate Leibgeber), but given the linkages between the Orient and antiquity, it's not surprising that he can also be dark Africa. Significantly, this identification with all that is not modern Europe is also associated with inscrutability. Leibgeber's self-understanding as a "*je ne sais quoi*" connects with his desire to live without a name, or at least with a constantly changing one (495). This ineffability is famously connected with the love that dare not speak its name.

Whether ancient Greece, the Balkans, Tahiti, or Sodom were in fact ever centers of homosexuality (and the scholars Aldrich and Hyam tend to read these accounts of the homosexuality in the Orient too uncritically), what matters is that people talked about them as centers of homosexuality. As Alice Kuzniar notes, Jean Paul is often more about the distance between language and its subject than language's accurate portrayal of that subject. His particular genius is the analysis of discourses, particularly those that have an effect on sexuality. In his foreword, the narrator indicates that the poet is distinct from the philosopher and the politician because he uses language appropriate neither for business, theology, administration, government, or medicine.[2] Although the character Siebenkäs, who is also a novelist, may not use these discourses in the conventional way, he is highly sensitive to their nuances, calling for a translation of Klopstock's lengthy epic *The Messiah* not only into Latin (so that academics can read it), but also into legal style for students of law, a prosaic style for merchants at the fair, and Yiddish for the Jews.[3]

Jean Paul refers humorously to his ability to use society's discourses when he tells his own mother that his writing is neither theological nor medical, but satirical (cited by Pietzcker 112). Satire, according to Siebenkäs, who in his spare time is writing a "satirical" book (503), is that which travesties, rather than imitates, human foolishness (660). Jean Paul has to explain this concept to his mother, just as Siebenkäs cannot hope that his wife, Lenette, will understand "the malicious satire" with which he and Leibgeber "correctly imitate bourgeois habits, but for the fun of it" (483), because "every male reader—and no female reader—understands" satire (660). Jean Paul's misogyny points in the direction of his acute awareness of gender difference and his unhappiness with the developing "compulsory heterosexuality"; his

2. Specifically, in Jean Paul's vocabulary: "*Handel und Wandel . . . Synodalschreiben . . . General-Reglements . . . Reichshofratsconclusis . . . medizinischen Bedenken und Krankheitsgeschichten*," 457.

3. In a review, Siebenkäs writes: "*Rezensent gesteht gern, daß er immer große Bedenklichkeiten darüber gehabt, daß man Klopstocks Messiade nur in zwei Rechtschreibungen geliefert . . . daß aber weder an eine lateinische Ausgabe für Schulleute . . . noch an eine im Kurialstil für die Juristen, noch an eine im planen prosaischen für die Meßkünstler oder an eine im Judendeutsch für das Judentum gedacht worden*" (579).

discussion of satire reveals his understanding of a proto-drag, proto-camp sensibility that understands discourses and expertly imitates them in order to travesty them.

When the narrator contemplates the intimacy between Siebenkäs and Leibgeber, he puts their relationship in a tradition of male friendships that had inspired him as a youth: "But why am I constantly supposed to repress the old feeling welling up in me that you have so strongly reawakened and with which earlier in my youth the friendship of a Swift, an Arbuthnot, and a Pope in their letters furtively, as it were, but powerfully penetrated and enlivened me?" (495). The effusive correspondence among Pope, Arbuthnot, and Swift, published in 1737, was celebrated throughout the eighteenth century as the product of exemplary friendship (956). The narrator assumes that others in the future depend on such published letters for inspiration: "And won't many others, like me, have warmed themselves and gotten courage from the moving peaceful loving of these manly hearts for each other [. . .]?" (495).[4] As Johannes Müller and his readers too had hoped, male-male sexuality becomes by this account a discursive tradition.

Jean Paul's awareness of the confining nature of orientalizing discourses in particular is evident in his sensitivity to the situation of Jews. Jews are also the Orient, a kind of fifth column of non-Christian, Semitic difference within the Occident. Johann Kasper Lavater asserts that the Jews carry the "sign of their fatherland, the Orient, throughout the world" (cited in Gilman, *The Case of Sigmund Freud*, 28). Gilman has shown how the same fantasies that the "Oriental" man was effeminate and homosexual applied to Jewish men; as Marjorie Garber shows, the very borderline status of the Jews as Orient within the Occident, as disrupter of the binarism Orient/Occident, also connected them to homosexuals, who similarly disrupt the boundaries between male/female (*Vested Interests* 80, 226).

References to Jews, frequently sympathetic, occur repeatedly in *Siebenkäs* (528, 594, 654). Jean Paul was well acquainted with the situation of the Jews in Germany because one of his best friends was Emmanuel Samuel, who was of Jewish extraction. On April 3, 1795, as he was finishing *Siebenkäs*, he wrote that he was concerned that he had read "more about than by Jews" (cited in Och 129). Asked to elaborate, he responds: "I regret that I know the oppressed [*die Unterdrückten*] almost exclusively from the mouth of the

---

4. *Sich ermannen*, with the root *Mann*, in English "man," is the German word that I have translated as "get courage." Its emphasis on manliness points out that Jean Paul sees this male-male relationship almost as a right of initiation into full manhood.

oppressors [*Unterdrücker*]" (April 15, 1797; cited in Och 129). Jean Paul then generalizes that it is very difficult for one people to speak about another: "For the fine spirit of every people—especially such a dissimilar people—vaporizes, like every spirit, in every depiction; and . . . its life spirit can only be purely condensed and collected from its history and the life and writings of the people themselves" (April 15, 1797; cited in Och 129). In *Siebenkäs*, the lesson to be drawn from these insights is that European accounts of the sexual freedom of the Orient might be quite different from the reality of life for people in lands Europe considers exotic.

Not everyone has been so perceptive however. Large advertisements in gay magazines promoting sex tourism in Thailand, the furor over Robert Mapplethorpe's photographs of African-American male nudes, the lurid attacks in the presidential campaign of 1992 against the funding by the National Endowment for the Humanities of Marlon Riggs's film *Tongues Untied*, and the tremendous crossover success of the black transvestite singer RuPaul are just a few examples that show that among whites in the United States, erotics and exoticism, when played together in a homosexual mode, strike a chord rich in excitement, dread, anxiety, and anticipation. Indeed, few have been able to keep a hold of the slippery union of homosexuality and orientalism.

The assumption of oriental homosexuality was probably originally intended to cast aspersion on the native peoples of the Orient, but had the unintended effect of creating an Arcadia, a possible utopia, for gays in Europe—the understanding of Berlin's subculture as "Eldorado" comes to mind (see the museum catalog *El Dorado: Homosexual Women and Men in Berlin, 1850–1950* [*Eldorado: homosexuelle Frauen und Männer in Berlin, 1850–1950*]). But such well-intentioned and emancipatory homosexual utopian thinking both condemns the Euro-American homosexual to eternal foreignness in his or her homeland and proves objectifying and oppressive for people from those countries styled as more free sexually. Modern African-American gay thinkers and artists like Audre Lorde, Marlon Riggs, and Kobena Mercer have discussed the burden of fulfilling the white man's or woman's sexual fantasies in ways that Jean Paul's letters to Emmanuel Samuel suggest he might have understood.

Jean Paul's novel *Siebenkäs* suggests the significance of orientalism in the modern development of male homosociality into the twins of homophobia and homosexuality. Orientalism was, according to Said, being articulated in its modern form around the end of the eighteenth century (3, 41–42). It was intricately connected to those discourses more commonly assumed to have played a role in the construction of sexuality, like medicine: Europe anxiously awaited discoveries about medical phenomena from its explorers (Flaherty, *Shamanism*, 9).

Because of its liminal status in the West in the eighteenth century, Germany was particularly keen on establishing its presence on the occidental side of the divide between Orient and Occident, and thus was especially involved in the exploratory effort. Describing the inferior intelligence of the dark races, Benjamin Franklin included the Germans, along with the Swedes, in the same category as the Africans (Flaherty, *Shamanism* 157). Marshall Berman talks about eighteenth-century Germany as the first "third world" nation, on the one hand determined to prove it was as advanced as its "first world" (Western Europe), and on the other hand insisting that its own Germanic culture was worth preserving against the influences of global civilization.

If German orientalist thinking was commonplace in the eighteenth century, its sexual theorizing proved extremely long lived. German sexologists from the middle of the nineteenth century passed on orientalist notions as they codified concepts like homosexuality. Literature of the time, like Jean Paul's *Siebenkäs*, recorded and thereby helped transmit these discourses. These sexological notions have taken a thousand paths—for instance psychoanalysis and film—that have led into our own society. In other words, *Siebenkäs* suggests that there is a way from Jean Paul to still potent modern orientalist fantasies.

4

LITERARY CURES IN
WIELAND AND MORITZ

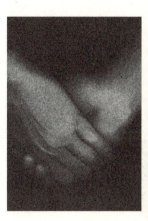

Because the terms "homosexuality" and "heterosexuality" have strong roots in the sexological, psychiatric, and ultimately medical discourses of the nineteenth-century German-speaking realm, medicine is an obvious point of departure for a study of the discursive origins of modern sexuality. Of interest here will be both the connections between medicine and sexuality as well as the literary nature of medicine and sexuality and their interrelationship. The characteristic contribution of Germany to eighteenth-century literature, the Bildungsroman, carefully recorded the medical discourses of its era and revealed their fundamental, literary ambivalence.

The eighteenth century witnessed the rise of medicine both in society and in literature, particularly that form of literature that saw itself as the mirror of society, the novel. In particular the eighteenth-century novel began to depict the intersection of medicine and the new familial and sexual structures that were developing in society, including early characterizations—and pathologizations—of same-sex desire. In English literature a British physician, Tobias Smollett, produced one of the first "medico-moral" narratives of a homosexual subculture in *Roderick Random* (G. S. Rousseau 25).

The German eighteenth-century contribution to the history of the novel, the Bildungsroman or the novel of development, also devoted particular attention to the importance of medicine. Indeed, one could say that the histories of *Bildung* (development or education) and *Heilung* (healing) were closely intertwined. At the same time, George Mosse demonstrates that the notion of *Bildung* is central to the emerging concept of masculinity. Where gender is involved, so is sexuality: the Bildungsroman is thus a place to look for the nexus of medicine, gender, and sexuality.

Because of the nature of literature, the depiction of its relationship with medicine and sexuality will be ambivalent. To begin with, medicine is bound to produce both positive and negative reactions, reactions that have to do with the dialectic of Enlightenment. For Max Horkheimer and Theodor Adorno, the progress of medicine clearly fulfills the dialectical conditions described in their writing: on the level of common sense, it has obviously positive effects by healing human suffering due to illness and increasing the quality and length of life, but on another level medicine has also become a means of concentrating societal power, which has resulted in new categorizations — for instance, those surrounding sexuality and the family (237–40). This ambivalence is palpable in the eighteenth-century accounts of the medicalization of sexuality.

MEDICINE

The most important theoretical development in eighteenth-century German medicine was its adoption of a new approach to the mind-body problem. Early eighteenth-century physicians such as Hermann Boerhaave and Friedrich Hoffmann used a Cartesian philosophy distinguishing mind and body to articulate a mechanistic medicine concerned only with the physical functioning of the body, while delegating emotional, mental, and spiritual problems to others (Rothschuh). Starting with Georg Ernst Stahl, however, the medical community in eighteenth-century Germany began to reject this strict separation between physical and mental realms: Stahl wrote as early as 1695 that "a system of healing that does not take the constitution of the soul into account and that does not know the world of feeling is useless" (37). Stahl's beliefs gradually took root in the medical community, until by the middle of the eighteenth century medical authorities agreed that, as the Berlin physician Ernst Anton Nicolai put it, "body and soul are in the most exact harmony, and a sickness in the body produces . . . a sickness of the soul and this in return a sickness of the body in every instance" (49). By the second half of the century, this stance on the mind-body problem spread from medicine back to philosophy when Immanuel Kant, in a pre-critical essay, supported Stahl and his disciples: "I am convinced that Stahl, who likes to explain animal changes organically, is often closer to the truth than Hofmann, Boerhaave, et al." (939). As the century drew to a close, the medical beliefs of Stahl and his disciples concerning the unity of mind and body had permeated society and become commonplace in literature and anthropology as well as philosophy and medicine.

Calling themselves "philosophical" or "moral physicians," these medical experts used their new belief in mind-body unity to treat problems formerly reserved for philosophers or the clergy. Regarding philosophy and questions of the mind, the radical physician Julian Offray de La Mettrie, who had spent considerable time at Frederick the Great's court in Berlin, wrote that "experience and observation should therefore be our only guides here. Both are to be found throughout the records of the physicians who are philosophers, and not in the works of the philosophers who are not physicians" (88). The same skepticism greeted religion, as most physicians agreed with Moritz, who cautioned in his "Proposal for a Journal of Experiential Psychology" (1783) that, despite their work with problems of the soul in the past, religious figures could not adequately perform the tasks of psychologists because their outlook was too tainted by superstition (*Journal* 1.1).

Medicine's belief in mind-body unity, with its concomitant expansion into psychological fields formerly considered philosophical or religious, allowed it new approaches to gender and sexuality. Concerning gender, Laqueur postulates that a "radical eighteenth-century reinterpretation of the female body in relation to the male" took place, largely emerging from a medical tradition (4). "In the late seventeenth and eighteenth centuries," he explains, "science fleshed out, in terms acceptable to the new epistemology, the categories 'male' and 'female' as opposite and incommensurable biological sexes" (154). In the discipline of pathology, the genders came to be associated with specific illnesses. In the 1780s the English physician Thomas Arnold, whose works were avidly translated into German, emphasized the connections between menstruation and madness, particularly hysteria (2: 180–200). Increasingly, hysteria became gender-specific—that is, applicable only to women—whereas while men were afflicted with hypochondria (Foucault, *Wahnsinn*, 268). In general, women were considered especially likely to go mad, partly because of biological facts such as menstruation and partly because of social constraints that, for instance, prevented them from getting adequate movement and exercise (Zimmermann, *Erfahrung*, 600, 733).

If males and females were essentially different in body and mind, then their sexuality would obviously differ as well. Medical thought on male sexuality emerged in part from the context of a phallocentric glorification of semen. The Swiss physician Simon-André Tissot asserted in 1771 that "Semen . . . is so noble that, as Galen notes, the loss of half an ounce does more damage than when one draws forty ounces of blood" (8). He cites Aristotle to show that semen was one of the most salubrious fluids, as it contained everything necessary for human reproduction: "Aristotle considered secreted semen one of the most nutritious liquids because it contains within itself the power to create a being such as the one out of which it was ejaculated" (46). A patriarchal bias clearly informs much of this medical thinking.

The view of female sexuality seems couched in much more negative terms. According to Laqueur, this was the era that saw the banishment of the female orgasm "to the borderlands of physiology, a signifier without a signified." Women were thought to be either "passionless" or in extraordinary control of their sex drives (150). So powerful were these beliefs that many physicians ignored female sexuality entirely, even while they devoted increasing attention to deviations from the norm of male sexuality (Faderman 34). When physicians bothered to concern themselves with female sexuality, they severely censured those women who defied these theories by exhibiting too strong a sex drive in the form of masturbation, nymphomania, or same-sex desire.

Lesbianism in particular came under attack from eighteenth-century medical authorities—actually more specifically than male-male sexuality. Johann Valentin Müller, the important eighteenth-century forensic physician, wrote in 1796 about sodomy between women:

Besides the sort [of sodomy] in which they use certain machines *ad imitationem Penis*, there are also female personages in whom the clitoris reaches an unusual size so that it can also take the place of the male member in the degree of its stiffness. In the olden times, one called such women tribades or fricatrixes, "rubbers," because they allowed themselves to be used by immoral ladies for coitus. . . . one called this bestial pleasure lesbian love, after the famous lesbian poet Sappho, whose fiery and irritable temperament drove her to the extravagant indulgence in this passion, and she betrayed the unnatural passion of a tribade all too much in her delicately suffering verses. (214–15)[1]

Much is made of the absence of a continuous language to describe and define gay men and the fact that men who engage in sexual acts with other men have gone under a variety of names, including "warm brothers," sodomites,

1. See Faderman, Greenberg 374ff., and Laqueur 53 for more on tribades. Tissot refers interested readers to a 1730 dissertation on the subject by a certain T. Tronchin.

urnings, homosexuals, gays, and queers. It is therefore notable that the vocabulary of lesbianism and the tradition of Sappho was already firmly in place in the eighteenth century, in a way that requires much less linguistic archaeology than the language of male same-sex behavior.

A generation before Müller, in 1771, Tissot was already making some of the same charges, raging against female masturbation and particularly "the feminine disgrace which happens with the clitoris [*Küzler*]" (39):

Nature tends to play sometimes, and creates female personages of a sort who, because of the size of their clitoris and out of ignorance about its proper usage, fall into an abuse and want to play the man. Stimulated, they stimulate others and attempt to create hereby for themselves the pleasure of true intercourse. This sort of female personage hates men and is their enemy; they were not unknown to the ancients, who called them "tribades" (lewd women who perform shameful acts with their own sort) and divided them into various categories; writers also did not silently ignore these appellations and they attributed the establishment of this order to the young Sappho. (39–40)

It is interesting that these women are said both "to play the man," that is, to substitute for him, and to be antagonistic toward men. They are a clear threat to men, which might explain the relative openness of the medical discussion of female-female sexuality compared to the discussion of male-male sexuality. Sexual acts between men also threatened men of course, but, so to speak, from within the masculine realm itself. This male threat was handled with silence, while the female threat could be taken on more directly.

The clearly sustained medical perspective on female-female sexual behavior does not have a counterpart in the realm of male-male sexuality. Male-male sexuality is also beginning to be medicalized at this point, but more obliquely, less stridently. Interestingly, the same phenomenon—the pathologization of female homosexuality preceding that of male homosexuality—takes place in the mid-nineteenth century. Carl Westphal's groundbreaking and paradigm-changing article on contrary sexual feelings (1869) takes as its starting point a woman: "N has apparently suffered since she was eight from the mania of loving women and, in addition to joking and kissing, also masturbating with them" (73). It seems quite plausible that the discourse around male homosexuality emerges from anxieties about female sexuality.

Women who tried to engage in too much sex with men could also become health problems—for men, because of the preciousness of semen. Typically the issue of allegedly excessive female sexuality is seen as primarily a problem for men's health; since all of the physicians writing on the subject were men, male sexuality (although not male homosexuality) received more medical attention. One of the major concerns of the entire era was male masturbation, about which Tissot wrote an entire treatise. Goethe's physician Christoph Wilhelm Hufeland (240), who went on to great honors and fame in Berlin, and Johann Georg Zimmermann, physician to Frederick the Great (*Erfahrung* 615), agrees with Tissot on the dangers of masturbation (see also Greenberg 364). Johann Valentin Müller, who was incidentally opposed to a counterproductive repression of masturbation, provides a list of symptoms of self-abuse that includes items such as difficulties in learning how to duel and dance. These symptoms clearly relate to the gender ideals of the time, dueling and dancing being skills that men should be able to carry out in a specifically masculine way. Medicine is thus interested here in treating gender as it takes on the sexual problem of masturbation.

Masturbation came to be seen by German physicians such as Johann Valentin Müller as a "precursor of same-sex love" (Greenberg 367), pointing to another area of sexuality that came increasingly under medical supervision. Already in 1688 Paulus Zacchia, a founder of forensic medicine, includes a chapter on pederasty, in which he asserts that medicine has the duty to help locate men who violate male youths, since the violation of males youths was the certainly the worst offense against decency (reprinted in Hohmann 205–9). Significantly, Zacchia not only draws medicine into the surveillance of sexuality, but does so in order to protect male privilege or patriarchy.

Detering's anonymous "Report on a Strange Deviation of the Human Drive" in *The Contributions Toward Reassurance and Enlightenment* from 1789 sees a more specific justification for medical observation of same-sex behavior: "Would that psychologists, physicians, and students of nature considered it worth the trouble not to overlook completely a subject on which the lifelong happiness of a person depends and which, were it to spread more widely, would necessarily interest the state!" (Detering, "'Zur Sprache kommen,'" 271). The eighteenth century was an era in which appeals to individual happiness were still possible in public policy statements, as the opening sentence of the American Declaration of Independence similarly demonstrates. Indeed, the ambivalences of eighteenth-century medical discourses would lay the groundwork not only for the persecution of homosexuality, but also for the claims of homosexuals for their own rights to happiness.

Even in the eighteenth century, however, appeals to happiness had less effect on the state than other attempts at persuasion. Ramdohr concedes that sex between members of the same gender is problematic because of "its disadvantageousness with regard to the population of the state, its ruinousness with regard to the well being of the individuals, and the hindrances . . . that such excesses [cause] for the happiness of marriage" (3:138). The forensic physician Johann Valentin Müller heeds the call to pay more attention to the phenomenon of same-sex desire and devotes an entire chapter of his treatise on forensic medicine from 1796 to sodomy. He includes a quote from Johann David Michaelis justifying the death penalty for sodomites because of the danger that their behavior presents to the state. Sodomites, it is argued, get sexual satisfaction on the cheap, so to speak, which entices young men to satisfy their biological urges without the price of supporting an entire family. If this behavior were to spread, there would soon be no one willing to pay for the social or economic consequences of sex and reproduction.

In a survey conducted between 1791 and 1794, H. B. Wagnitz reports that insane asylums are among the institutions incarcerating sodomites (Wagnitz 2.2:14). Wagnitz's numbers are small (0.5 percent of inmates), but they indicate institutional medicine's rising interest in the formerly religious category of sexual deviance.

The desire to conserve semen also contributed to more general warnings against immoderation in intercourse. Arnold writes that "of all origins of madness, . . . none are more efficient and stubborn than excessive intercourse [*Übermaß im Beyschlaf*]" (2:128). Noting the particular link between brain and genitals, Hufeland states that "nothing in the world can blunt the most beautiful mental gifts so extensively and so irreparably as this [sexual] excess" (241). Zimmermann, who also sees "a strange linkage between the ideas of [religious] enthusiasts and their sexual parts" (*Einsamkeit* 2:132), felt that excessive copulation led to melancholy and hypochondria, particularly for men (*Erfahrung* 600).

While excessive expenditures of semen were a health problem for eighteenth-century physicians, ascetic retention of semen was also dangerous. In his assessment of the medical consequences of celibacy, Zimmermann argues that the repression of the passions in the cloisters results in an explosion of irrational acts, including suicides, unnatural emissions during religious services, castration, love-madness, and pederasty (*Einsamkeit* 2:232–33). To a certain extent, anticlericalism motivates Zimmermann, just as it permeates Denis Diderot's novella *La religieuse*, in which a woman forced into the convent by her family must submit to the amorous advances of a lecherous mother superior. According to Laqueur, this anticlerical pattern can also be found in the writings of the English radical (and, incidentally, avid translator of German) Thomas Carlyle, who saw masturbation as "born of the cloister" (229).

Most of all, however, eighteenth-century physicians concentrated on promoting a safe compromise between waste and ascetic retention of semen: the sensible, moderate usage of semen prevalent in a monogamous, heterosexual relationship. Unfailingly and tirelessly the new philosophical and moral physicians propounded the health benefits of a moderate level of intercourse. For Arnold, moderation in intercourse (along with moderation in eating, sleeping, and working) was the first rule for the prevention of insanity (2:351). Zimmermann concluded his four volumes on the pros and cons of solitude with the compromise solution of living in solitude with one's spouse (*Einsamkeit* 4:178–80). The newly emergent bourgeois family, characterized by its exclusion of distant relatives and large numbers of servants and by its removal from the workplace (Hausen), becomes in the medical writings of the time a catalyst and determinant of physical and mental health.

Nonetheless, forms of sexuality and family that differed from this norm could be seen not only as a poison, but also as an antidote leading toward monogamous heterosexuality in a bourgeois marriage, for, according to the most progressive medicine of the time, every disease contained its cure. Coming out of the tradition of reform physicians who emphasized the mind-body unity, Samuel Hahnemann developed the foundations of homeopathic medicine, which attempted to use the causes of disorders to cure those disorders (Hahnemann 133; Schwanitz). Especially in matters of mental health, progressive physicians in the eighteenth century believed in using madness to combat madness and bring about sanity. The "pious fraud," usually some sort of deception by which a caretaker would play along with the insanity of his or her ward and trick that person into sanity, was a frequently used form of therapy (Diener).

Although the physicians of the era were almost always male, one of the era's most famous cases of a "pious fraud" was Ernestine Christiane Reiske's treatment of her maid, who tortured herself with groundless self-reproaches. Reiske reported the case herself in the 1785 issue of Moritz's *Journal* (3.3:30). Moritz subsequently discussed it in the 1786 issue of the *Journal* (4.1:40), as did Immanuel Mauchart in the *General Repertory* (*Allgemeines Repertorium*) of 1792 (2:21, 50). Londa Schiebinger writes on Dorothea Erxleben, one of the only female physicians trained academically before the twentieth century (250). Thus there were some women physicians in the eighteenth century, but the medical discourse remained dominated by men.

In his innovative *Journal of Experiential Psychology* (*Das Magazin für Erfahrungsseelenkunde*, 1783–1792), often considered the first magazine ever devoted to psychology, Moritz discusses the cure of a young man suffering from a pathological obsession with the theater, which was endangering his happiness and well-being. Rather than forbidding the patient to attend the theater, which according to the progressive eighteenth century belief would have backfired, Moritz encourages him to dedicate himself to the theater and visit it daily. Even when the patient himself began to doubt the sanity of his theatrical visits, Moritz encouraged him to persevere in his theatrical ambitions, which had the desired result that the patient decided not to attend the theater any longer and to go back to his parents, after which he was "completely cured of his fantasy" (*Journal* 3.1 [1785] 121–25). Mauchart, who eventually published the *General Repertory*, also revisited the subject in the *Journal* in 1789 (7.3:115).

LITERATURE

The mention of Moritz and his *Journal* is appropriate here, for the authors of the canonical Bildungsromans of the eighteenth century—specifically, Christoph Martin Wieland and Karl Philipp Moritz—all use their era's new medicinal language to discuss the gender roles, sexuality, and familial structures of their characters. At the same time, their novels provide the chance for readers to comment upon this new system of signification—literature can engender a discussion of the nascent discourses. Particularly, the novels capture the ambivalences in the homeopathic approach to medicine, according to which deviant sexuality could be seen as both a cause and also as a cure of sickness.

In particular, the Bildungsroman itself is the subject of highly polarized debates. Perhaps the same instincts that call forth ambivalent responses to medicine have provoked the radically opposed interpretations of the classical Bildungsroman, interpretations that describe the genre sometimes as a triumph of humanism and other times as a dismal portrait of society's everdiminishing humanity. Not coincidentally, issues of family and gender are often a focal point for these interpretations: It is either said that the protagonist heroically navigates the passage from childhood through adolescence to well-adjusted participation in an adult family or that certain characters of the novel, particularly women, suffer at the hands of the novel's familial structures. Thus, the ambivalent response to the Bildungsroman is rooted in the novels' portrayal of gender and sexuality, a portrayal that is inflected medically.

Two of the first Bildungsromans, both taken from the canon of eighteenth-century German literature, exhibit medical discourses on sexuality. At the same time, they take an ironic distance from that discourse. Christoph Martin Wieland's *Agathon* (first published 1766) dutifully reports that medicine brands nonbourgeois family structures as pathological, but does not seem to take such diagnoses too seriously. Karl Philipp Moritz's *Anton Reiser* (1785–90) also views nonbourgeois families as pathological, but has a strong sense of the tragedy, rather than the punitive nature, of such pathologies.

CHRISTOPH MARTIN WIELAND

Wieland's *Agathon* contains much of the vocabulary of its era's medical debates, not surprisingly, as Wieland (1733–1813) was well versed in the medical discourses of his era. He engaged in a lengthy dispute by correspondence with his friend Zimmermann, eventually coming over to the medical belief in mind-body unity (Schings, "Der anthropologische Roman"). The mind-body problem thus receives prominent billing in *Agathon* (418, 503, 705, 830). The first edition of the novel begins and ends with references to physicians and illness. The book's very first paragraph points out that an archival account of a historical personage would conclude by revealing the medical detail of the cause of that figure's death (375). Wieland creates a medical frame for the novel by concluding it with an allusion to another physician, *Don Quixote*'s "Doctor Peter Rezio von Aguero." As humorously ironical as this allusion turns out to be, it nonetheless helps medicine frame the novel and thereby establish the context of its questions. At the same time, it distinguishes the novel from the medical case study, and thus allows for a distanced look at the medical discourses he employs in the story.

In part because he was a prolific translator of classical texts, Wieland was well aware of a great variety of sexual practices. Caroline Böhmer Schlegel Schelling, born Michaelis and daughter of the man who defended the death penalty for sodomy, described Wieland as "immoral" in a letter to Ludwig Ferdinand Huber on November 22, 1799 (cited in Derks). The poet of friendship, Johann Wilhelm Ludwig Gleim, wrote to Wieland in 1774 that the reproach was circulating in literary circles that it was from Wieland that German youth first heard about "Greek love," that is, homosexuality, and thus started keeping "Ganymedes" (cited in Derks 234). Luhmann, it should be noted, dismisses the suggestion that Wieland was in fact responsible for the introduction of a taste for male youth to German men out of hand (146). Peculiarly, given his current reputation as a stuffy classic, Wieland not only shows up in the reading list of Franz Desgouttes, the sodomite who killed his lover and inspired Heinrich Hössli to write his apology for male-male love, but is even listed as a bad influence on the poor man! Reading *Agathon* allegedly led Desgouttes to "sensual excesses" (*sinnliche Ausschweifungen*; Hössli, *Eros* 3:159). In any case, Derks writes that "Wieland was probably the first [writer] in German literature to make homosexuality a thematic subject of a poem" (234).

The poem in question is "Juno and Ganymede," published anonymously in 1765 as part of the *Comical Stories* (*Comische Erzählungen*) and filled with humorous and lascivious passages of a rococo sort, insinuating a knowledge of nonheterosexual practices. In the ballad, Juno and Zeus fight about the god's new predilection for the boy Ganymede. As Zeus defends himself, he ridicules the claim that "platonic love" is without sexuality:

In this light you must see the love
That draws me to Ganymede.
His beautiful spirit, his virtuous disposition,
The grace that ornaments his brow,
The innocence that looks out of his eyes;
These, not his blond hair, not his rosy cheeks,
Are, believe me, the charms with which he entrapped me.
You see that here the body plays no role at all.
At least in this kind of love
Nothing physical is intended.
The truly beautiful is only felt by understanding
And never produces base drives.

[In diesem Licht müßt ihr die Liebe sehen
Die mich zu Ganymeden zieht.
Sein schöner Geist, sein tugendlich Gemüt,
Die Grazien, die seine Stirne schmücken,
Die Unschuld, die ihm aus den Augen sieht;
Dies, nicht sein blondes Haar, nicht seine Rosenwangen,
Ist, glaube mir, der Reiz wodurch er mich gefangen.
Du siehst, daß hier der Leib gar keine Rolle spielt.
Zum mindsten wird bei dieser Art von Liebe
Nichts körperliches abgezielt.

Das wahre Schöne wird nur vom Verstand gefühlt,
Und zeuget nie gemeine Triebe.] (Wieland 4:131)

Juno asks dryly whether such ethereal spirits tend to kiss. Zeus responds, "Why . . . should that not be possible?" [*"Warum,"* spricht Zeus, *"soll das nicht möglich sein?"*]:

The souls, lady, the souls are that which
Pour out in such a kiss.

[Die Seelen, Frau, die Seelen sind's, die sich
In einem solchen Kuß ergießen.] (Wieland 4:131)

Eventually, Juno holds her husband to his word, and tells him that he can have the boy's mind, if she can take his body. Wieland's poem seems to be a well-adjusted and humorous take on the foibles of sexuality.

Wieland's *Novella Without a Title* (*Novelle ohne Titel*), published in 1805, also sympathetically follows the development of a woman, Galora, raised as a man, who then falls in love with another man. Galora doesn't get the man, but at least discovers her true sex and uses her love to return to her natural femininity. Wieland titillates his readers with the possibility that this desire could end in same-sex love and thereby shows a certain openness to non-traditional families (for more on this story, see Lehnert).

In another work from the second half of his life, *The End of Peregrine's Life* (*Das Lebensende des Peregrinos*; 1791), Wieland again treats the subject of same-sex desire. The philosopher Peregrine is charged with having violated a fourteen-year-old youth. Although Greek precedents are cited — Jupiter and Ganymede, Socrates and Xenophon — and the blackmailing father is discredited, Peregrine must pay for his actions. Derks argues that the novel is clearly on the side of family values and that Wieland in his old age had lost his liberality (243-46), but readers who retained that sense of liberality could interpret the story as a protest against such values. All the arguments in favor of a liberal position on male-male sexuality are presented. Even if they don't convince the characters within the novel, Wieland may have intended them to convince the reader.

In *Agathon*, in any case, Wieland lets a tolerant light shine through on many forms of sexuality. The narrator alludes to his era's understanding of ancient Greek sexuality when he casually asserts that "it has long been made clear that the Greeks had completely different notions of love from modern Europeans" (1:683-84). Wieland here shows his openness to the kind of classical studies that his contemporaries Hamann, Herder, Humboldt, and

Meiners were undertaking—the kind of studies mentioned in Chapter 2. He also alludes without censure to the episode in which Critobulus kisses Alcibiades' beautiful son, merely pointing out that it is "our" custom to kiss beautiful girls, not boys: "'O unhappy one!' he [Socrates] said to the young Xenophon, who could not understand that it was a dangerous thing to kiss a beautiful boy, or—to speak in accordance with our customs—a beautiful girl" (1:665; see also 1:659). In his understanding of sexual desire as a matter of custom, Wieland does not seem to entertain any speculation that there could be something like an innate homosexual drive, but he does not seem particularly judgmental of this custom either.

In contrast to this tolerant spirit, however, Wieland's *Agathon* incorporates aspects of eighteenth-century medical anthropology, which censured forms of sexuality outside the bourgeois family. Within the first pages of the novel, Agathon's childhood sweetheart Psyche tells the story of her kidnapping by pirates while she was dressed in a boy's clothing. When the ship's captain calls her "Ganymede" and tries to seduce her, Psyche calls his passion "disgusting" and "absurd" (*ekelhaft* [395] and *unsinnig* [396]). Significantly, it is not the forceful seduction, but rather the homosexual desire itself that Psyche reacts against.

Psyche's tale anticipates Agathon's own "Ganymedic" experience. As a youth he had dreamed of being, like Ganymede, loved by divinities (555). His Neoplatonic interpretations of the myth, assuming a purely mental love, are dashed when a priest disguised as Apollo attempts to seduce him. The priest cynically argues that everything attributed to the gods consists merely of traps to ensnare women and naive boys: "He drew the conclusion: that everything that was said of the gods was the invention of clever minds to draw women and gullible boys into their nets" (1:559). Fortunately for the reader's sense of poetic justice, the priest attempts to seduce one gullible boy too many—a relative of a superior, for which reason he disappears from Delphi (560). Once again, the passage rejects not the unethical means of satisfying this passion, but the pederastic passion itself—this time as "immoral" (*unsittlich*; 559).

It is appropriate that the priest dresses up as Apollo—the mythic figure who was known for his homosexual leanings, most famously because of his affair with Hyacinth, which in Ovid's version ends tragically when the god's discus fatally strikes the beautiful youth. Through the name "Hyacinth" Danae is linked to the homosexuality that the novel finds disgusting, absurd, and immoral, because her lover before she meets Agathon is called "Hyacinthus" (473). Indeed, her cynical and worldly friend Hippias refers to "your

Hyacinths" as a general category of Danae's lovers. As the lover of Hyacinths, Danae can even be equated with the bisexual Apollo, making clear that the novel posits Agathon moving from one morally questionable expression of sexuality to another.

Linking the aggressively heterosexual woman Danae with the male homosexual sea captains and priests is not as ridiculous as it may seem at first glance, for Danae differs from the healthy norm as much as they do. As tolerantly as Wieland's narrator regards the different mores of Greek society, and as positively as he portrays Danae, he nonetheless concludes her story with her decision to pursue a life of solitude outside of Tarentine doing penance for her lifestyle before she met Agathon. Eighteenth-century bourgeois society would certainly agree that Agathon cannot remain in the love nest with Danae, "for you certainly will not want an Agathon to waste his whole life, like a *veneris passerculus* (let your lover translate that for you!), making love on the bosom of the tender Danae?" (1:671). The narrator acknowledges that the reader will likely believe that Danae's excessive sexuality is a concern that could interest the medical establishment, which saw inordinate intercourse as damaging for the man and an indication of something wrong in the woman. At the same time, his assumption that the reader will have a lover who can translate *veneris passerculis* once again ironizes this all-too-moralistic medical perspective. (For those of you without lovers to translate the Latin, a *veneris passerculus* is "a little sparrow of Venus.")

Although Wieland implies that male homosexuality and excessive female heterosexuality are wrong in a number of ways, he stops short of bringing Agathon into a conventional family approximating bourgeois norms. Instead, he ironizes the process by referring to Sancho and "Doctor Peter Rezio von Aguero," "an all-too-scrupulous physician" who objects to so many forms of food that the residents of Barataria waste away, malnourished. In this case, the best thing to do would be to follow Sancho's example, and rid oneself of the doctor (852)! While the novel's fictional editor mentions medicine at the novel's beginning as part of an argument establishing the historical truth of his work, Doctor Rezio's story obviously lampoons medicine and reason; moreover, the allusion to *Don Quixote* removes the novel from the empirical world to the literary one. Wieland's depiction of gender roles, familial structures, and sexual identities recognizes the belief of his contemporaries that certain deviations from bourgeois norms are unhealthy — yet in the absence of a positive solution to these problems, he suggests that the reader chose his or her poison and ignore the medical advice.

Moritz (1756–1793), a friend of influential physicians such as the Berliner Marcus Herz (Lothar Müller 48), had connections with the medical world of his time that are even better documented than Wieland's. Indeed, nowadays Moritz's activities as the editor of the *Journal* receive as much attention as his novels. Not that comparisons between his psychological and novelistic work are even necessary, for it is clear in *Anton Reiser*, subtitled a "psychological novel," that Moritz's two interests converge on the same raw material: the study of the soul and its sicknesses. Much more so than in *Agathon*, sickness is one of *Anton Reiser*'s recurrent themes (17, 30, 61, 76, 93, 225). While *Agathon* begins and ends on an open, ironical note, *Anton Reiser* presents a much bleaker image of essentially irresolvable familial problems. If *Agathon* regards skeptically the medical claim to know what is healthy, *Anton Reiser* underscores the seriousness and perhaps the injustice or tragedy of such a diagnosis.

Moritz's work in medicine and psychology show his awareness of non-heterosexual inclinations, particularly the remarkably sensitive letters he published in his *Journal*.[2] The first letter was published in 1791, and was the account of a friend, "a certain -g," who had mysteriously deep feelings of friendship for other men. When he met "a young Herr von * *," these feelings became even more intense. After the noble friend left, "-g" was plunged into depression and despair.

Interestingly, this apparent male-male love attraction occurred at a university. In his *Venus Urania* of 1798, Ramdohr also reports an account of a love affair between two students that was inexplicable to both of them because it took place between men (2: 104–6). As it is today, the university seems to have been a setting in which young people made sexual discoveries about themselves. In Ramdohr's account, the two young men actually have a physical encounter, which they perceive as disastrous, but in Moritz's the letter writer assures his reader that "pederasty [*ta paidixa*] certainly was not at the root of this desire."

At the same time, the letter writer concedes that "feelings of friendship do not manifest themselves this way either." The precariousness of the

---

2. "Aus einem Brief," *Magazin* 8.1 (1791), and under the rubric "Seelenheilenkunde" in *Magazin* 8.2 (1791). For a less sensitive reference to "the disgusting suspicion of pederasty" (*der abscheuliche Verdacht der Knabenschänderei*), see "Auszug aus dem Leben H. Cardus," *Magazin* 6.1 (1788): 79.

boundary between friendship and something else, something more like pederasty, is of great concern in this letter. For the young man in question, "the feelings of friendship, of which he always spoke with a certain respect and with a dignified seriousness, were all the more holy." This use of friendship to explain deeper feelings is one of the signs of homosexuality that developed before homosexuality itself was named and conceptualized.

The letter has other signifiers of same-sex desire. The youth "-g" is primarily characterized by "a certain cold contempt," pointing to the trope of the inwardly insecure homosexual who covers up his anxieties with cynical, supercilious, and haughty behavior. In general, "-g" attempts to deny his bodily and emotional urges, which is also a tried and true method of getting by for gays: "For his healthy reason did not let itself be bribed easily by his warm bloom, nor his head by his heart." Despite the era's belief in mind-body unity, the denial of the physical and the unhappiness with one's own body and its emotions are tropes that appear frequently throughout the late eighteenth-century German sodomitical world and continues through much of subsequent gay history.

At the university, this denial of the physical resulted in an intellectualization of the friendship, which manifested itself in an appreciation of Shakespeare's sonnets: "It was remarkable that -g fell with a kind of mania upon Shakespeare's sonnets, which he directed to his young friend, and knew them all by heart in a short time." Shakespeare's position in the gay canon was already developing in late eighteenth-century Germany. The Elizabethan playwright was already functioning as a shibboleth that allowed men who loved other men to test each other; "von * *" clearly passed the test: "He told me that no one had ever understood the sonnets as well as he, and he pressed my hand and tears filled his eyes." Like Klopstock for Werther and Charlotte, Shakespeare gives these men a way of communing with each other.

Moritz's *Journal* was also providing men who were interested in other men with an opportunity to interact and share experiences and advice. The letter from the first issue of 1791 provoked a response that appeared in the second issue, in which a man reported that he had developed an "immoderate desire" to be with another man. When another friend suggested that the object of desire might be strolling with a pretty girl, the letter writer was distraught and plunged into depression. Subsequently he was able to modulate this passion into a more acceptable friendship. Even though the letter writer wants to prove that such same-sex desire can be healed, the presence of such medical documents as his letter has a necessarily ambivalent function of both controlling same-sex desire and normalizing or naturalizing it.

In general, reports about male-male desire tended to be written in the third person, even if they were actually autobiographical. Detering therefore assumes that both the 1789 letter to the *Contributions Toward the Reassurance and Enlightenment* and the 1798 account in Ramdohr could well be autobiographical; Derks also believes that the passage in Ramdohr's *Venus Urania* could easily be autobiographical (383). It is known that many of the contributions to the *Journal* were published anonymously by Moritz himself and were actually autobiographical. Apparently, the letters about male-male love in the *Journal* are not generally thought to be by Moritz. However, Moritz's student, close friend, long-time roommate, and subsequent biographer was a man whose last name ended in "-g": Karl Friedrich Klischnig.

The relationship between these two men was so close that in 1794, after Moritz died, Klischnig had to deny charges of "Greek Love" explicitly:

This *jealousy of friendship* [*Eifersucht der Freundschaft*] had manifested itself so intensely several times that a friend once said to us in warning:
"*People, if I didn't know you better, you could lead me to believe that more than friendship, that Greek love [griechische Liebe], ruled between you!*" (109)

Once again same-sex desire threatens to explode the boundaries of socially acceptable friendship. Alluding to this passage, Mark Boulby asserts that "there is no evidence of perversion, although the ménage with Klischnig did lead to gossip in Berlin" (73). Was there really "no evidence of perversion"?

In general, once Moritz moved to Frederick the Great's Berlin, which Moritz thought of as "Eldorado" (Klischnig 27, 153), he seems to have known certain pedagogues and intellectuals whose names are associated with eighteenth-century same-sex subcultures. Moritz discovered and promoted the writings of Jean Paul, for instance. Among his earliest friends was the clergyman Carl Friedrich Bahrdt, after whom Kotzebue named his polemic against the forces arrayed against the physican Johann Georg Zimmermann, *Doktor Bahrdt with the Iron Forehead. Or: The German Union against Zimmermann* (*Doktor Bahrdt mit der eisernen Stirn. Oder: die deutsche Union gegen Zimmermann*). In Kotzebue's farce, sexual acts take place in Bahrdt's garden between two men whom Moritz knew quite well professionally and personally—the librarian Johann Erich Biester, and the director of the Friedrich-Werdersche Gymnasium Friedrich Gedike, both editors of the *Berlin Monthly* (*Berlinische Monatsschrift*): "There the good Biester and the well-raised Gedike demonstrated what Greek love [*griechische Liebe*] is" (32). The sexual politics of this feud between Kotzebue and the anti-Zimmermann forces are fascinating. The one side is insistent on its straightness: Kotzebue peppers his polemic with homophobic attacks and Zimmermann, whom he is defending, denied the King's homosexuality. The other side is accused of sodomy; in addition to Biester and Gedike, Anton Friedrich Büsching, the historian who hinted at Frederick the Great's homosexuality and whom Moritz got to know quite early, is also associated with many of these men (Klischnig 53). The aphorist Georg Christoph Lichtenberg also plays a role in this farce, for which reason we will return to it in a later chapter.

Another of Moritz's friends was a certain Johann Georg Zierlein, a professor of Hebrew and Greek. Moritz asked Zierlein why he never married, and the professor responded that he was a "weak person" and feared that he "would not be able to satisfy a woman" (Klischnig 55). Zierlein also relates a rather ungraceful story of a poor sickly innkeeper whose wife insists that they have sex. The innkeeper accuses his wife of being the death of him. At the end of the story, Zierlein tells Moritz: "And you too, my colleague, can only look inward and say: 'God be merciful to me, sinner'" (55). Zierlein, at least, seemed to think that Moritz was guilty of some failing having to do with male-female relations, and Klischnig must have had some fascination or concern with aberrant sexuality in order to print the anecdote.

Klischnig's account of his life with Moritz sounds quite romantic. At certain points, they seem to have spent every moment together, reading, writing, and amusing each other: "We spent some beautiful moonlit summer nights in the garden, walking or resting in the high grass on the shore of the small little river that bordered it" (73). Of course such descriptions do not prove homosexuality, but it is telling that immediately after denying the presence of Greek love in their relationship, Klischnig then comments skeptically: "It's an eternal shame that a purely *platonic love* rarely lasts. Only too soon the body demands its rights and destroys the most beautiful dreams of the *soul*" (110). Jürgen Peters quotes the same passage and says that Klischnig has made "the mistake of the unpracticed liar—he talks too much" (25). Admittedly, Klischnig is by this point talking about a relationship that Moritz had with a woman, but as the passage immediately follows Klischnig's analysis of his relationship with Moritz, it almost seems like an admission that a purely non-physical relationship would have been next to impossible.

Four pages after denying that the relationship with Moritz was anything more than friendship, Klischnig presents his reader with a series of "hieroglyphs," aphorisms taken from Moritz's novel *Andreas Hartknopf* that he expressly wants the reader to *interpret*. They have to do with friendship and love: "*More tender* bonds connect to the beloved woman, *stronger* ones to the friend, upon whom one relies in bad weather and storms" (Klischnig 114).

Returning to the question of the relative strengths of male-female friendship the question that so preoccupied Ramdohr, Pockels, and others in the eighteenth century—Moritz argues that the beloved woman is indeed a presence in one's life, but the beloved male friend a stronger one. Another aphorism emphasizes the permanence of friendship, which "is higher than tenderness, more permanent than love, strong like virtue and powerful like understanding" (Klischnig 114). A subsequent fragment seems to drop the rigid distinction between loving someone and being their friend, or at least it seems to imply that the verb "to love" is appropriate for friends: "The greatest sorrow is . . . that they [lovers] cannot be for the beloved object what they would desperately desire to be for it" (Klischnig 114). Since Klischnig asks that his readers interpret these hieroglyphics, one can question what Moritz could have wanted to be for the objects of his love and who those objects were. In the context of Klischnig's narration, it makes sense that Moritz wanted to give his friend everything, to break the boundaries of friendship, to be that lover that society would not let him become.

It may well be that Moritz and Klischnig never did break the boundaries of friendship, that the rumors of "Greek love" as a kind of societal censor did in fact keep them in line. Both Klischnig and Moritz did eventually take wives as well. But, like many of his contemporaries—notably Lichtenberg but also including Goethe—Moritz married a young girl from a poor background: "He finally hit upon the idea to take a very poor girl for himself and make himself a lady out of her. He was encouraged in this intention upon hearing from a good friend that very pretty children could be found among the young girls at the French orphanage" (Klischnig 143). Moritz did not marry one of the girls from the orphanage, but did (at the age of thirty-five) marry the fifteen-year-old Christiane Friederike Matzdorff, the daughter of a lottery collector. This pattern of marrying women who were inferior in age, social standing, and education, while socializing intensely and intimately with men who were on a more equal footing in all of these categories seems to demonstrate a high degree of homosocial relations among eighteenth-century German intellectuals.

Possibly this propensity to choose children as marriage partners, which Moritz as well as Lichtenberg did, can lend itself to a queer interpretation. In any case, it is clear from Klischnig's account that Moritz was looking more for a student than for a lover: "To educate a beautiful youthful girl gradually just as he wanted, to make her receptive to all his ideas and then to harvest her deep gratitude, which would naturally soon become love—this thought entranced him" (Klischnig 143). Such a relationship is more pedagogical than loving, for at first the girl does not experience any love at all. Whatever this relationship is, it is certainly not in accordance with the heterosexual ideal that is present today. At the very least this should discourage modern readers from assuming a default heterosexuality when thinking about eighteenth-century sexuality.

In any case, Moritz's hopes for an easy ascension through gratitude to love were soon dashed. Karl Philipp almost immediately wanted to break off the relationship, while his wife Christiane had an affair. Henriette Herz, the wife of the famous doctor Marcus Herz, claims that when Karl Philipp presented his wife to her, he said, "Haven't I done something stupid?" (Boulby 246). Herz goes on to relate a wild story of Christiane's lover and nightly chases in which revolvers play a role. As Karl Philipp's health worsened, Christiane had some pity and tended him upon his death bed. In any case, it does not sound as though this particular heterosexual relationship was any good for Moritz, or his wife.

For those who prefer to consider only the text and not gossip about the biographical details of the author, Moritz has always presented a problem, because his most famous work, *Anton Reiser*, is largely autobiographical, at least in its inspiration. Here too certain critics have noticed a queer tendency. Lothar Müller writes, "the silence about the nature of the hero's sexual drives can be interpreted as an either conscious or unconscious coding of the homosexual orientation of the author" (291). Let us look at the novel to see how it depicts same-sex desire psychologically, medically, and textually.

The narrator claims that Anton Reiser, in the eponymous novel, had only very "dark and confused concepts" about "certain things," which were clarified when he looked at a book on anatomy (218). Further clarifications about sexual matters came in the context of lessons on the Sixth Commandment: "He had heard at catechism in the seminary about all sorts of sins of which he could never form a clear concept, like sodomy [*Sodomiterei*], silent sins and the vice of self-abuse, which were all named in the explanation of the Sixth Commandment" (132). As Moritz presents this sexual enlightenment, sexuality is closely related to text: Reiser found out about it through reading, and in particular through studying traditional textual prohibitions.

One pedagogic consequence of Moritz's account of his experience would be the tolerant eighteenth-century notion that lifting prohibitions would be likely to decrease transgressions. This would be very much in accord with Moritz's own psychology as witnessed, for example, by his treatment of theater mania, in which he allowed the patient to watch the plays that were responsible for his illness. Again this homeopathic approach, so

[*eine unmoralische Neigung gegen sein Geschlecht*]" (quoted in Derks 436). In another police report from March 31, 1809, it is stated: "I was assured that he was devoted to sodomy [*Sodomie*], that it was quite astonishing that a person who was devoted to this vice could complete the kind of moral plays that he writes" (quoted in Derks 436). The descriptions of Iffland in *Anton Reiser* invoke the gay stereotypes that were emerging even before gay identity had been conceptualized. For instance, Iffland is witty and quick of mind, but has no depth: "Iffland thought much more quickly and therefore had wit and presence of mind, but no patience to spend a long time on a subject. . . . [Reiser] lost every time against Iffland whenever it was a matter of wit and liveliness, but he always won as soon as it was matter of practicing the actual power of thought on a subject" (153). Although this passage seems to be setting up a distinction between the quick-witted queeny Iffland and the slow but thorough and straight Reiser, other moments in the paragraph suggest that Moritz sees many similarities between the two. To begin with, the narrator asserts that "Reiser's fate had many similarities with his [Iffland's] up until a certain time point" (153). And he concludes the Iffland passage with the testimony, "Reiser loved him however and would then already have liked to have had closer contact with him" (153).

Reiser loves his teachers as well as his fellow students. At one point, he writes: "Now his feeling for friendship also received nourishment. He loved some of his teachers in the actual sense and felt a yearning for their companionship—in particular his friendship manifested itself for one of them named R. . . ." (113). Although Moritz uses the vocabulary of friendship here, he also explicitly says that Reiser loved "in the actual sense" of the word, suggesting that this love was not just a substitute term for friendship. The fact that it was concentrated on a particular teacher further suggests it was a kind of sexual crush. Reiser explains his dependence on his teachers' opinions of him in a similar way: "The thought of incurring a punishment from the men whom he loved and honored as his teachers was unbearable to Reiser and he wished for nothing more ardently than to achieve in turn their love and respect" (154). In another place, Moritz writes that it "was so pleasant to him that his teacher now knew for himself how much he loved him" (158). In his essay on Schiller's *Don Carlos*, Friedrich Kittler argues that this kind of intense pedagogical eros was part of the educational reforms of the eighteenth century. It too helped form modern notions of homosexuality.

Clearly, Reiser's enthusiasm for his fellow youths and his teachers owes much to his era's friendship cults (Meyer-Krentler). In particular, Reiser explicitly refers to models from the literature of the Sturm und Drang. As Fou-

typical for the eighteenth century, is highly ambivalent. In the case of same-sex behavior, it could result in a lifting of punitive measures; at the same time, if the justification is to be believed, the lifting of the prohibition woulc only serve to diminish the amount of same-sex behavior.

Anton claims he had no idea what words like sodomy actually mean and had to resolve to resist all evil urges: "Fortunately Reiser didn't under stand what was actually meant with this and didn't dare to ask further ques tions about the subject. Instead he resolved firmly to fight valiantly against al evil desires [*böse Lüste*] — in whatever form they might appear — should the awaken in him" (132). Reiser's pleas of ignorance regarding these practice reveal, however, that Moritz knew and thought about them.

Despite Moritz's insistence on his innocence with regard to same-se desire, hints of homoeroticism surface in Anton's exaggerated friendships, ¿ Robert Minder notes: "After particularly discouraging rejections, the yout joins 'the dirty street kids' and their 'wild behavior'; the best student b comes the friend of 'two dissolute boys,' two teenagers, with whom he 'sta lying in bed for whole days'" (cited by Lothar Müller 464). One of Reisel earliest wishes, revealed shortly after Reiser has mentioned sickness and re gion as important elements in his life, is the desire to know other youths: "I felt most strongly the need of friendship with his own kind: and often, wh he saw a youth of his age, his whole soul hung on him, and he would ha given anything to become his friend" (14–15). He announces his friendsh with the character Philipp Reiser with extravagant, effusive declarations love (238–39) and suffers severe melancholy in the absence of the loved o (271–72). Reiser subsequently becomes utterly infatuated with a young C thusian monk, "with pale cheeks of exceptionally beautiful structure" (39 especially when he discovers that the young monk entered the order beca lightning struck his (the boy's) best friend (398). Finally, Anton develops real love and fondness" for a character named Neries (410). On the nov last page, Anton murmurs his new best friend's name as he walks in tears a theatrical mission that will turn out to be as ill-fated as the rest of his l "While walking he frequently spoke aloud the name Neries, whom he re¿ loved, and cried violently as he did so" (436).

The fictional character Reiser's friendship with the historical figure V helm August Iffland, while not as passionate, may have meant even more those readers looking for signs of "Greek love" in that era, because the mous playwright was notorious for his homosexual leanings. The Vienn police reported on March 26, 1809: "They say namely: Iffland is a me ber of secret societies and harbors an immoral tendency toward his own

cault points out in a late interview, however, the decline, beginning in the sixteenth century, of friendship as a non-sexual male bonding resulted in the eighteenth-century emergence of male homosexuality "as a social/political/ medical problem" (Gallagher 58). Especially in the light of "medical problems," Reiser's friendships deserve closer scrutiny here. These friendships differ from nonsexual male bonding in their undisguised exclusion of women. Reiser identifies enthusiastically with every aspect of Goethe's Sturm und Drang classic *Werther* (1774) except for the matter of love: "In short, Reiser believed he found himself in *Werther*, with all his thoughts and feelings, up to the point of love" (253). Given that *Werther* is primarily a love story, this is a queer reception of the novel, indeed!

Anton claims on several occasions that he cannot imagine himself in a love relationship with a woman: "Participation in the sufferings of love took some effort on his part . . . , because it was impossible for him to think of himself as the object of the love of a woman" (256; see also 244, 287). The novel contains a few striking images of women—the pale maid in black at Paulmann's church (72), the beautiful young woman grieving for Philipp Reiser's drowned friend (251)—and a fair number of passages concerning Anton's mother and other women of her generation who deny or provide him care. Other than these visions of somber femininity and the confrontation with the maternal, however, Anton's main thought about women is that he could never be loved by one, a thought that distinguishes the novel from the usual rhetoric of friendship, which generally protects itself from the suspicions of even suppressed homosexuality by giving the friends a few girlfriends.

Not only does Anton Reiser exclude women from his horizon, he actually attempts to replace them. The novel further distinguishes itself from the friendship tale of the Sturm und Drang when its hero plays female roles on the stage. In one play, Anton is Clelie, the beloved of Medon (400, see also 408). Of course, at all-male educational institutions men had to play women's roles in student productions, but he plays the role of Clelie so well and is so satisfied with it that he "forgets himself" (403). Given his professed love of his fellow students, and his inability to identify with romantic stories involving men loving women, his ability to identify so well with female characters loving men signifies a desire to replace the woman as the object of the man's desire.

Moritz's response to this homosexual desire is to locate it at the heart of a disconsolate novel of anomie. The motif of self-loss and self-destruction is perhaps the strongest single unifier of this novel. It begins with the references to the pietist Madame de Guyon's philosophy of returning to one's "nothingness" (*Nichts*), and destroying all passion and all selfhood (9). It resurfaces with his love of another classic of the Sturm und Drang, Friedrich Maximillian Klinger's *The Twins* (*Die Zwillinge*, 1776) and Guelfo's "self-contempt and the drive for self-destruction" (343). Klinger, incidentally, will be of interest to us when we look at the Faust myth, for his version of the story emphasizes the kind of male-male connections in which Moritz was also interested. The self's desire to destroy its passions and return to nothingness is especially understandable when it harbors desires that it considers pathological and immoral. Here Reiser anticipates another queer trademark, the self-hating and self-destructive side of gay and lesbian creativity that Thomas Vollhaber has documented in his study *Void. Fear. Experience. Studies of Contemporary Gay Literature* (*Das Nichts. Die Angst. Die Erfahrung. Untersuchung zur zeitgenössischen schwulen Literatur*, 1987). Once again the signifiers of homosexuality are settling into place even before the signified is fully extant. This particular signifier — self-loathing — can trace its origins to the pathologizing discourse of medical psychology.

Both authors present societal claims that nonnormative gender roles and expressions of sexuality as phases to be outgrown, illnesses awaiting cures. Wieland's *Agathon* shows how society condemns homosexuality and active female sexuality as pathological. Moritz's psychologically informed *Anton Reiser* links homosexuality and the need for self-destruction. At the same time, good arguments suggest that Wieland laughingly proposes that one kill the doctor and ignore reasons, that he satirizes the pathologization of forms of sexuality and gender when he refers to *Don Quixote*. By the same token, it can be argued that Moritz demonstrates the cheerlessness of a world in which nonheterosexual desires are proscribed. But despite the possibilities of a positive reading, it remains important to hang on to the presence of a medical discourse that describes paternalistic families as "healthy" and pathologizes alternatives to such families. Ignoring such discourses would be a grievous underestimation of the power of institutional discourses and the role in nineteenth- and twentieth-century Euro-American culture of literary genres such as the Bildungsroman in propagating this power. In order to be true to the ironies of eighteenth-century literature, it is important not to blur the dialectics of the Enlightenment, dialectics exemplified both by the ability of medical discourses to produce both liberating improvements in human well-being and oppressive patriarchal structures and by the ability of literary texts to critique and reinforce such discourses simultaneously.

If the eighteenth century saw the first pathologization of same-sex desire, the late twentieth century has witnessed a repathologization. The advent of Acquired Immune Deficiency Syndrome (AIDS) has made the discursivity of medicine all the more clear. In the case of AIDS, the imbrication of medicine and rhetoric starts at the most elementary level of linguistics, where language can be a *pharmakon* and medicine uses the linguistic structure of signifier and signified; it continues to the most complicated levels of storytelling and mythic thinking. Regarding AIDS, Avital Ronell remarks on "the co-constitutive status of rumor and disease. Here it appears that rumor spreads the plague and, inversely, the plague carries rumor" ("The Worst Neighborhoods" 128). Paula Treichler writes, "the very nature of AIDS is constructed through language and in particular through the discourse of medicine and science" (31); she concludes that AIDS brings with it "an epidemic of meanings or signification" (32). Although seemingly far from the subject of German literature of the age of Goethe, the signification of AIDS demonstrates basic issues of medical semiotics that go back at least to the eighteenth century. A brief review of the semiotics of AIDS puts into a larger perspective the benefits of studying sexuality and textuality together from the perspective of medical history.

To begin with, the naming of AIDS provides an excellent case study in the construction of signifiers and signifieds and their relationship to each other and to other signs. The very name Acquired Immune Deficiency Syndrome indicates the arbitrariness of signifiers and the nosological difficulties of signification. Originally, when the disease first appeared among gay male populations in urban areas of the United States, it was called GRID, Gay-Related Immune Deficiency. HIV (Human Immunodeficiency Virus), the virus that causes AIDS, is similarly a name that was invented as a compromise between two competing names — HTLV III (Human T-cell Lymphotic Virus, type 3) and LAV (Lymphadenopathy-Associated Virus).

While the nosological activity of naming new diseases is obviously linguistic, it does not reveal the heart of semiotic problems as clearly as the activity of deciding what is to be named: AIDS also demonstrates the arbitrariness of the signified. Unable at first to find a specific cause of the disease, researchers simply defined it as the sum of the opportunistic diseases that afflicted a person with an impaired immune system. Someone "had AIDS" if they contracted a certain number of the opportunistic infections recognized by the Centers for Disease Control as indicators of the illness. These signifiers of AIDS, primarily observed among gay men, tended to exclude other people afflicted by opportunistic infections less common among gay men. (For instance, the omission of certain vaginal infections had the obvious effect of excluding women from the ranks of those who "had AIDS.")

Furthermore, AIDS has spawned whole new vocabularies and altered old ones: "safe sex" was not a concept before the advent of AIDS and the meanings of "protection" and "responsible behavior" have taken on a new coloring. Susan Sontag shrewdly suggests that those debilitating computer problems called "viruses" would have another name if AIDS had not surfaced (69–70). The ambiguity of language is evident in some of these labels, which began with an implicitly derogatory subtext, but allowed the "gay community" and even the "IV-drug using community" to become solid entities with some political clout. In this case, language made a poison function pharmaceutically as a cure; the signifier AIDS had the power to help alter social reality.

The case of AIDS also makes clear the process of mythmaking, which is to say the linkage, often ideological, of several signifiers. AIDS demonstrates this process not only because it is linked with countless other incendiary signifiers, but also because its very structure mimics the process of signification in mythology. Curiously, long before AIDS became known, Barthes speculated that the syndrome, that collection of signs that always refer together to a certain diagnosis, corresponded to "the group of stereotyped words" that refer to a culturally accepted norm (*Semiotic* 209). AIDS fits this pattern in that its own configuration is analogous to a myth and, perhaps in part for that reason, has generated countless myths.

Barthes sees mythology as a kind of metasignification, a sign in which the signifier points to a signified that consists of another sign, in which the signifier points yet further away (*Mythologies* 115). Semiotically, AIDS functions in a similarly mythological way. The symptoms of opportunistic infections mean various sicknesses in the body, like Kaposi's sarcoma (KS), cytomegalovirus (CMV), and pneumocystosis carinii pneumonia (PCP). The presence of these sicknesses means AIDS. Then the sign AIDS, consisting of both its signifiers and its signifieds, goes on mythologically to signify a series of additional signifieds: homosexuality, drug abuse, Africa, blackness, immorality, decadence, depravity, and so on.

AIDS has proven an inordinately fertile spawning ground for ideological constructions via the more general connotations of AIDS — its myths. It has revived old iconographies linking disease with divine punishment, especially for sexual acts perceived as passive, receptive, or feminine (Gilman, "AIDS and Syphilis"). It has also been linked with the Holocaust, with all that such a comparison means in terms of state-sponsored genocide and a popular conspiracy of indifference. It also strengthens mythologies surrounding the black and the homosexual, being associated with both and thus also connecting each category to the other, in a way not unrelated to the issues of orientalism discussed in the previous chapter.

"Whatever else it may be, AIDS is a story," writes Treichler (42). She means "story" not only in the sense of a journalistic sensation, but also in the sense of a narrative. Speculation about the origins of the disease are a crucial part of its narration. The orientalist discourses of colonialism and exoticism informing the American mythologies of AIDS make certain that the beginning of this story always already takes place somewhere else, often Africa (Treichler 56).[3] In myth, where there is a beginning there is usually an end. Pessimists see closure in the story happening when AIDS brings about the end of the gay world, the sexual revolution, the healthcare system, and/or Africa (although not everyone views all of these endings as unfortunate). Optimists might see the development within the gay community of a more serious moral tone through its encounter with mortality, or the discovery of a "magic bullet" that will cure the disease as possible happy ends to the story of AIDS.

Finally, the dramatis personae of AIDS tell about characterization. Like any good story, AIDS has its good and bad characters. At the microscopic level, the Human Immunodeficiency Virus itself is a degenerate invader, fought off by the valiant but overwhelmed T cells. An example of such dramatization appeared in an article in the *New York Times* from 1994: "The signaling molecules called cytokines that normally control the body's battle plan, telling the T cells, B cells, macrophages and antibodies when and where to strike, start to babble or stammer or grow tongue-tied, sending all the wrong signals at the wrong times" (Angier). This particular quotation is additionally fascinating for its reliance on war metaphors and the trope of the tower of Babel—did humanity in its pride sin against the Lord before this fiasco of communication took place? This anthropomorphic view of the

3. Conversely, it is widely believed outside of the United States that the CIA (or sometimes the KGB) developed HIV (Bornemann 233–34). Germany, seemingly relishing the role as a kind of intermediary between the U.S. and the Third World, tends to believe a combination of both American and African stories: while it assumes that the disease began in Africa, the German press has consistently tended to demonize the rich American gay tourist as the spreader of the disease (Jones).

virus and the division of the microscopic world into good and bad characters makes this story an excellent narrative.

On the mythological level, there are even more characters: a demonized figure, like the rich American homosexual tourist or Randy Shilts's "patient zero."[4] Blame can likewise be attached to greedy scientists, lazy and corrupt governmental officials, sexually promiscuous gays, or mendacious bisexuals. Conversely, adulation and glory surround the hardworking scientist, the muckraking journalist, or the gay activist willing to stand up against the above-mentioned villains. These heroes share their position on the good side of the ledger with children, patients of careless dentists, and spouses of bisexuals.

Some of these tropes are culled from quite familiar files in the cultural archives. "Patient zero" as the oversexed, vindictive homosexual is one such figure taken from popular images of gay people. Jeff Nunokawa sees in him the doomed-to-death Dorian Gray (313–16), while Ellis Hanson finds Bram Stoker's undead, bloodthirsty, sexually ambiguous, nocturnal, flying Count Dracula in the man who was a gay flight attendant. Daniel Selden sees the whole narrative structure of AIDS, its emergence among outsiders, and governmental denial followed by successful medical action anticipated in the movie *Jaws*. Literature, understood in its broadest sense, has clearly affected the mythologies of AIDS.

While literature constructs myths, it also deconstructs them, identifying their discursive origins and logic. Paul Monette's moving memoir *Borrowed Time*, for example, challenges clichés about the person living with AIDS (Yingling 298). If Monette's book was typical of first-generation responses to AIDS that emphasized the tragic, David Feinberg's *Eighty-Sixed* was one of the first in a series of novels using humor to strip away sentimental ideologies that tended to victimize people living with AIDS. Tony Kushner's ambitious seven-hour drama *Angels in America* attempts to give meaning to the plague by placing it within American political and religious discourses. African-American poet and filmmaker Marlon Riggs uses AIDS to deconstruct mythologies of race and sexuality in his poetry and films. While literature helped engender the modern image of AIDS, AIDS has given birth to a whole range of new literature.

The German-speaking literary world has formulated responses to AIDS as well. The biting satire of Rosa von Praunheim's films is familiar in the

---

4. Gaetan Dugas is the allegedly sex-crazed flight attendant—French Canadian, not a U.S. citizen, not a native speaker of English—who supposedly spread the disease in bathhouses across the American continent, allegedly maliciously.

United States; less familiar is the fiction that has appeared in the German language. A recent article by Joachim Pfeiffer shows how Stefan Reichert, coeditor of an edition of Paul Celan's poetry, modifies Baudelairian poetics in his interpretation of the disease. Traditions of solitude shape both Reichert's poetry and Christoph Klimke's poetic narrative. Walter Vogt's *Die Betroffenen* (*The Affected*) makes a Brechtian attempt to provoke its audience to action rather than move them to tears. Like the second generation of Americans to write about AIDS, a number of German authors, such as Detlev Meyer and Napoleon Seyfarth, use comic and revolutionary traditions to depict AIDS. All of these authors would probably agree with Wolfgang Max Faust, who in his memoirs writes that a new language is needed: "We no longer write and read in the traditional way" (cited by Pfeiffer, "Jegliches Mitleid," 15). From yet another linguistic tradition, Hervé Guibert writes that AIDS has made it possible for him "to radicalize several narrative systems, as well as my relationship to truth, the inclusion of my person to a degree that I myself would not have thought possible earlier" (cited by Pfeiffer, "Jegliches Mitleid," 15). In critiquing the discourses of AIDS, writers have changed those discourses.

A discussion of the signification of AIDS demonstrates the interrelationships between medicine and literature. AIDS thus reflects the process of signification in language, showing how signifier and signified are constructed and evolve and how mythmaking takes place around signs; at the same time, its dramatization in the media exhibits the role of character and narrative in discourses about medicine. Similar interrelationships also obtain in eighteenth-century German texts, which at first glance seem far removed from the present day and AIDS. Indeed, an analysis of earlier manifestations of the relationship between medicine and literature could be very useful in responding to catastrophes like AIDS as well as understanding the interactions between textuality and the medical aspects of a phenomenon like sexuality.

5

PEDERASTY AND PHARMAKA

IN GOETHE'S WORKS

Read some "Meister," but was ridiculously horny (certainly not because of the reading).

Klaus Mann, diary entry, March 12, 1932

Any discussion of the Bildungsroman must of course eventually turn to Johann Wolfgang von Goethe, whose *Wilhelm Meister's Apprenticeship* (*Wilhelm Meisters Lehrjahre*; 1796), is generally credited as being the first truly successful example of the genre. Any discussion of medicine and its ambivalences will probably turn at some point to drugs, *pharmaka*, those inherently ambivalent means of healing that can also lead to addiction and death. Goethe and his texts provide insight into both categories. *Wilhelm Meister's Apprenticeship*, for instance, is written in a medical discourse; same-sex desire turns out to be the dangerous prescription that helps a young man develop into a family father. In fact, throughout his works pederasty in general is for Goethe a pharmakon that reflects all the ambivalences of literature itself.

Goethe's works are interesting not only because they thematize queer sexuality or because they helped contribute to the discursive construction of modern sexual identities. They are also compelling because they point to the inevitable instability of linguistic identity. Studying Goethe's writings reinforces the notion that modern sexuality is a fabric constructed out of a number of discursive strands, like classicism, orientalism, and medicine, but also underscores the ramifications of that discursive nature. If sexuality has a discursive element, that element must lend itself to deconstructive analyses that point to sexuality's rhetoricity, its infinite interpretability. As the reader queers Goethe, Goethe queers sexual identity.

Like Wieland and Moritz, Goethe cultivated extensive connections in the medical community. According to his autobiography, he frequently socialized with medical students both in Leipzig and in Strasbourg (*HA* 9:259, 361).[1] In addition to knowing the medically well-informed Wieland and Moritz, he also knew personally many of the prominent physicians of his day, including Zimmermann and his own physician, Hufeland. A diary entry on July 1, 1795, lists a number of progressive physicians in whose work he was interested, such as Hufeland, John Brown, Melchior Adam Weickard, and Johann Christian Reil (*WA* 3.2: 34). Goethe even participated in a number of psychiatric cures (Diener).

Goethe's interest in medicine carries over to many of his literary works. The question of whether a bad mood is a sin or a sickness preoccupies Werther and Charlotte. Mephisto makes fun of the medical profession as he encourages a witless student to become a doctor. In the lesser-known play *Lila*, Goethe depicts a psychiatric cure (Diener). In *Wilhelm Meister* issues of illness and health, particularly psychosomatic sickness and psychological well-being, appear in details as trivial as Aurelie's headaches and Barbara's toothaches and in plot elements as significant as the Harper's madness and Mignon's literal heartsickness. Indeed, the possession of medicine distinguishes between the novel's haves and have-nots: Natalie and her *Oheim* keep a surgeon in their retinue, while the entire Tower Society frequently consults the physician to recommend treatment for such varied complaints as Lothario's gun wound, the Beautiful Soul's melancholia, the Harper's mania, and Mignon's heart condition. In contrast, the characters outside the orbit of the Tower Society are not only without medicine, but in fact sick and in many instances, by the end of the novel, dead. In many ways Wilhelm Meister's story is in part the story of his medical empowerment, as he moves from a kind of sickness at the beginning of the novel to a sort of health and in *Wilhelm Meister's Journeyman Years* (*Wilhelm Meisters Wanderjahre*; final edition 1832), eventually to a modest position as a surgeon within the healing profession itself.

1. The *Hamburger Ausgabe* (= *HA*) is used for most Goethe citations, as it is the most widely distributed edition. Passages from Goethe's oeuvre not included in the *HA* are cited from the *Weimarer Ausgabe* (= *WA*).

Goethe was also certainly aware of a wide variety of expressions of sexuality and possible familial constructions. As we have already seen, Goethe's essay on Winckelmann (*HA* 12:96–129) is shot through with positive allusions to the art historian's well-known love of men (Derks 203–11). His constant support of the historian Johannes Müller, who was embroiled in a scandal that revealed his homosexual inclination, also demonstrates Goethe's sophistication on issues of sexuality.

Some believe that they can find more than tolerance in Goethe's life. A few biographers have made very bold claims indeed. Rainer J. Kaus even asserts that "for the psychologist . . . there can be scarcely any doubt that Goethe also acted upon the homosexual aspects of his psyche" (77). The doyen of German-American psychoanalysis, Kurt Robert Eissler, also puts together, based on evidence from the *Apprenticeship* and its predecessor, the fragmentary *Wilhelm Meister's Theatrical Mission* (*Wilhelm Meisters theatralische Sendung*), a sketchy case for a possible homosexual activity in Goethe's youth (2:1456–57).

Kaus cites in particular the letter that Goethe's man-servant Philipp Seidel wrote to a friend on October 15, 1777: "We have a relationship with each other like man and woman. As I love him, so he loves me, as I serve him, so he expresses authority over me. — But why do I confide in paper what my dear holy secret is!" (quoted in Kaus 77). Seidel is not the only man who felt like Goethe's wife: the Sturm-und-Drang poet Lenz also wrote veritable love letters to Goethe and assumed the position of the adoring woman in those letters.

As early as 1963 the biographer Richard Friedenthal found Goethe's relationship with Duke Karl August somewhat queer: "It is the most curious ministerial conference that one can image, from bed to bed or next to each other on a broad sofa" (231). The letter written from Rome to the Duke on December 29, 1787, documents Goethe's Italian discovery of male-male love. After complaining that the female prostitutes had venereal diseases and the unmarried maidens insisted upon marriage, Goethe explains that the men in Italy love each other: "After this contribution to the statistical knowledge of the land you will ascertain how tight our situation is and will understand a remarkable phenomenon that I have seen nowhere as strong as here, it is the love of men amongst themselves [*die Liebe der Männer untereinander*]" (*WA*: 4.8:314–15). Goethe's assumption that this love "is *rarely* driven to the highest degree of sensuality but rather dwells in the more moderate regions of inclination and passion" (*WA* 4.8: 315; my emphasis) implies that it sometimes does go beyond the bounds of propriety.

Like many Europeans who lived in the eighteenth century, Goethe ran across work that associated Italy with homosexuality. He translated the Italian artist Cellini's autobiography, which refers to sodomy. He also translated one of Richard Payne Knight's travel journals to Sicily for inclusion in his study of Phillip Hackett, the Prussian artist who spent much time in Italy. While this journal does not mention sexuality in any particular way, Knight, who was infamous in the eighteenth century because of his *Discourse on the Worship of Priapus and Its Connection with the Mystic Theology of the Ancients* (1786–87), was part of a homocentric and phallus-obsessed world of Northern European connoisseurs that vibrated with homosocial and homosexual tensions (G. S. Rousseau 68–137).

Goethe's trip to Italy seems to have been generally important for the development of his personal sexuality. In his study of the journey, Eissler concentrates more on Goethe's relationship with women and his father, reaching the famous conclusion that Goethe first overcame his father and had an orgasm with a woman in Italy (for instance, 2:1130, 1146, 1158). Goethe's artwork from Italy, both his images of male nudes with prominent genitalia (Gilman, *Sexuality*, 229) and — with a little imagination — his ejaculatory images of erupting volcanoes, suggest that male as well as female sexuality preoccupied him in this period of time. Given the importance of Italy as the site of homosexual desire in the minds of many eighteenth-century Europeans, it is not a coincidence to find the following couplet specifically among the *Venetian* epigrams:

Boys I have also loved,
But I prefer girls;
If I'm tired of her as a girl,
She can serve me as a boy as well!

[Knaben liebte ich wohl auch
Doch lieber sind mir die Mädchen;
Hab' ich als Mädchen sie satt,
Dient sie als Knabe mir noch.] (*WA* 1.5.2:381)

Whether this is an autobiographical confession or a play on the ancient tropes of erotic epigrams, it points to Goethe's knowledge of homosexual practices.

Kaus, Eissler, and Nicholas Boyle, the author of an extensive recent biography of Goethe, all seem to agree that Goethe had some sort of sexual, even pederastic, feelings for Frau von Stein's young son, Fritz (cited and discussed by Kaus 83, 147). The pederastic feelings for young boys show up in Goethe's loving portrayals of male youth in, for instance, *Faust II*. Both Boyle and Eissler consider the poem "Erlkönig" clearly pederastic, pointing to the moment when the spirit ruler threatens to take the young endangered boy by force: "I love you, your beautiful figure charms me; / And if you're not willing, I'll use violence" [*Ich liebe dich, mich reizt deine schöne Gestalt; / Und bist du nicht willig, so brauch' ich Gewalt*] (*HA* 1:155). Boyle writes about this "most terrifyingly erotic poem": "It is the true voice of desire, speaking to the boy with a directness scarcely paralleled elsewhere in Goethe's verse, it will brook no refusal, and its object is unequivocally unnatural" (340). That Boyle would be using the word "unnatural" in 1994 to describe same-sex desire demonstrates how nonqueer readings are sometimes less historically accurate than the queer ones, for, as we shall see, Goethe himself views that male-male desire as in some ways natural.

THE PHAMARKON

On April 7, 1830, Goethe commented in a discussion about Johannes Müller that "Greek love" was as old as humanity, adding that "one could therefore say that it was at once rooted in nature and at the same time against nature" (Friedrich Müller 71). The trope also appears in Voltaire's essay on Socratic love, in which Voltaire wrote: "How can it be that a vice, one which would destroy the human race if it became general, an infamous assault upon nature, can nevertheless be so natural?" He answers his question by suggesting that boys are like girls and thus able to confuse male desire, a line of argument that relies upon the one-sex theory of gender (Bullough 490). In 1796, Ramdohr sums up Enlightenment thinking on the subject of pederasty by declaring that it is "in nature and not in nature and against nature" (cited in Hössli 1: 255).

In describing pederasty as something both natural and unnatural, Voltaire, Goethe, and Hössli grant male-male sexual desire the power to disrupt the binarisms that construct our society in a way that Eve Kosofsky Sedgwick, using English and American authors, outlines in *Epistemology of the Closet* (11). Goethe's reference to pederasty's position in nature suggests that same-sex desire is paradigmatic for literature itself. Pederasty, with its power to unsettle the duality of natural versus unnatural, fulfills a function similar to that of writing in Jacques Derrida's essay on "Plato's Pharmacy"—the function of a pharmakon that can both poison and heal. Pederasty and writing, which both refer constantly to diametrically opposed concepts, are "heterotextual" in that they mean both themselves and the other. Pharmaka that are at one and the same time natural and unnatural, poisonous and curative, pederasty and writing show the link in Goethe's works between sexuality and textuality.

Like Goethe, Derrida goes back to the Greeks, specifically Plato, to talk about the pharmakon, which is both a poison causing forgetfulness and ignorance and a remedy to those conditions.[2] His pharmakon is of course writing, not pederasty, yet there is a link between sex and his drug. Rhetorically Derrida's examples make clear that Plato's pharmaceutical writing has an erotic component. The pharmakon operates "through seduction" (70). Socrates allegedly uses his pharmaceutical powers to bewitch Agathon (117–18). The example of Helen shows that the pharmakon has "the power to break in, to carry off, to seduce internally, to ravish invisibly" (116–17). The pharmakon is not always used nefariously, to seduce the unwilling; rather, in its "good" and "beautiful" manifestations, its rhetoric relates to reproductive sexuality: some writing can "engender," "regenerate," "bear fruit" (152). Language is a "pharmakon which can equally well serve the seed of life and the seed of death, childbirth and abortion" (153). Regardless of the outcome then, writes Derrida, "the entrance of the pharmakon on the scene" necessarily leads to "games and festivals, which can never go without some sort of urgency or outpouring of sperm" (149–50). Clearly if writing is the pharmakon, then it is, in Derrida's view of Plato, linked to a sexuality of dissemination.

Derrida emphasizes queer sexuality when looking for metaphors of the pharmakon. He starts with the *Phaedrus*, a text famously associated with male-male love. He remarks explicitly on homosexuality in "Plato's Pharmacy," linking it with writing, Derrida's primary concern: "One could cite here both the writing *and* the pederasty of a young man named Plato" (153; see also 164, n. 80). In this passage Derrida associates not just sexuality, but specifically homosexuality, with the pharmakon of writing: pederasty, like writing, is "a lost trace, a nonviable seed, everything in sperm that overflows wastefully," whereas reproductive sex, like "living speech," bears fruit (152). Throughout the essay Derrida describes the pharmakon of writing in ways that could easily also refer to nonreproductive sexuality. Writing as a phar-

2. Unless otherwise indicated, all references to Derrida are to "Plato's Pharmacy," in *Disseminations*.

makon substitutes "the prosthesis for the organ, . . . a limb by a thing, . . . the passive, mechanical . . . for the active" (108), just as the queer sexuality of, say, a Marquis de Sade emphasizes the mechanical nature of what was once allegedly a wholesome, organic act.

Derrida emphasizes the nonreproductive aspect of writing instead of the fruitful aspect of living speech because he doesn't want to push potentially dangerous drugs. For Avital Ronell, the addict needs a drug to fill the lack that ultimately derives from the signifier's inaccessibility to the signified. Addiction stems from that condition that renders literature necessarily ambiguous: we can never know if the work is supposed to mean one thing or another. Derrida uses metaphors of nonreproductive sexuality to describe writing because literature is queer to the extent that it does not transmit the meaning—the genes, so to speak—of its author to future generations. The pederast and other practitioners of queer sex stand for a sober understanding of the limits of literature's ability to mean. Their sobriety will help them withstand the temptations of addiction, confirming Ronell's psychoanalytic observation that "the pervert does not do drugs" (*Crack Wars* 17). The metaphor for the spoken language that the addict wants is reproductive—not perverse—sexuality that transmits presence and meaning from author to reader. If homosexuality appears in literature as a pharmakon or drug, it is because it characterizes, with its queerness, literature itself, which is the drug that can either cure (if this condition of "nonreproductive" textuality is accepted) or kill (if it is not) the addict. The pervert, the homosexual, understands the queer nature of literature and avoids addiction, while the addict yearns for straight writing.

In a footnote Derrida declares the pharmakon "analogous . . . to that of *supplément* in the reading of Rousseau" (96, n. 43),[3] a reading that on the one hand emphasizes the diametrically opposed tendencies (both adding to and replacing nature and speech) of writing as a *supplément* and, on the other hand, stresses Rousseau's use in the *Confessions* of the phrase "dangerous supplément" to mean masturbation (*Grammatology* 144–45, 149–50). Once again the deep ambiguity of writing is linked this time via *supplément*, in the earlier example via pharmakon, to queer sexuality. Derrida's comparison of Plato's ancient Greek pharmakon to Rousseau's eighteenth-century European *supplément* pivots the discussion back to Goethe and his age. When Foucault moves from the erotics of the ancient world to the love of the modern world, he sees Goethe's *Faust* as emblematic for the shift from the love of

3. See also the translator's note 46 on page 110.

boys to that of women (*History* 2:229–30). Goethe's comments about pederasty—about its ancient, original ambiguity, its naturalness and unnaturalness—suggest that for him, male-male love had not yet completely lost its value as a pharmakon or supplément.

Although Goethe drank many a bottle of red wine on the way to the twelve-step programs of his late writings, he takes the recommended dosage of this drug, pederasty, under the doctor's supervision. As Ronell suggests, Goethe, the master of renunciation, is almost the opposite of the "addict," who is "a non-renouncer par excellence" (*Crack Wars* 9). Goethe uses the twin pharmaka of writing and homosexuality to renounce the kind of textuality that claims presence, that corresponds to procreative sexuality, in favor of a queer textuality more comparable to nonaddictive pederasty.

ROMAN ELEGIES AND *THE WEST-EASTERN DIVAN*

In fact, homosexuality appears frequently in Goethe's oeuvre. Goethe's "To the Moon" ("An den Mond"), with its stanza about resting on the breast of one's good male friend, has attracted the attention of queer readers for centuries. Two other works in particular raised eyebrows when they first appeared because of their alleged endorsement of pederasty. Although he generally liked the *Roman Elegies*, August Wilhelm Schlegel objected to a passage in the tenth elegy that included in a list of great warriors Frederick the Great, along with Alexander, Caesar, and Henry IV. He apparently found the passage problematic because of anxieties caused by rumors surrounding the sexuality of Frederick the Great as well as the monarchs to whom he was compared.[4] More clearly provocative in the *Roman Elegies*, however, is the reference in the nineteenth elegy to Amor, who attempts to steal heroes away from Fama by offering them first women, then men:

Girls he offers; whoever foolishly scorns them
Must bear truly grim arrows from his bow;
He excites man for man, drives desire to the animal.

[Mädchen bietet er an; wer sie ihm töricht verschmäht,
Muß erst grimmige Pfeile von seinem Bogen erdulden;
Mann erhitzt er auf Mann, treibt die Begierden aufs Tier.] (*HA* 1:172)

---

4. Schlegel, *Sämtliche Werke* 10: 70. Cited by Derks 268. For further reactions to the *Elegies*, see Femmel and Meckel 11–14.

This passage incensed Schlegel and other contemporaries because of its casual treatment of "unnatural" passions (Derks 268).

The four elegies that were not published might have outraged audiences even more. One calls upon the phallic god Priapus to sodomize all those hypocrites who read the *Elegies* voyeuristically:

Now watch the hypocrites . . .
If one should near . . .
. . . then punish him from behind
With the pole that springs red from your hips!

[Nun bemerke die Heuchler . . .
Naht sich einer . . .
. . . so straf ihn von hinten
Mit dem Pfahle, der dir roth von den Hüften entspringt!] (*WA* 1.53:6)

Ammer, the editor of an edition of Goethe's *Erotische Gedichte*, positions this poem as a "guard" at the beginning of his reconstruction of the "original" *Roman Elegies*. Goethe, incidentally, possessed a drawing of a thief being sodomized by a priapic monument (Femmel and Meckler 175). On the one hand, this passage emphasizes the violent, nonerotic use of sodomy; on the other hand, the use of sodomy to punish voyeuristic readers points to Goethe's constant interest in linking queer behavior metaphorically to writing.

Much later in life Goethe continues to use homoerotic motifs in his poetry, specifically in *Das Schenkenbuch*, the section in *The West-Eastern Divan* (*West-östlicher Divan*) that most emphasizes the pederastic slant of the Persian literature that inspired Goethe to write the *Divan*. The German title of *Das Schenkenbuch* bears some discussion. It stands out in the table of contents of the *Divan* because, whereas all the other titles of the *Divan* are structured as genitive phrases along the lines of "The Book of the Singer" ("Das Buch des Sängers"), "The Book of Hafis" ("Das Buch Hafis"), or "The Book of Love" ("Das Buch der Liebe"), only *Das Schenkenbuch* is constructed as a compound noun. The unique structure within the *Divan* of this book title allows Goethe to leave pointedly unclear whether this is "The Book of the Cupbearer" ("Der Schenk") or "The Book of the Inn" ("Die Schenke"). In fact, in the inn the poet dallies amorously with the cupbearer, so it is a book about both. Goethe's linguistic subterfuge does not work in English, so translators must choose between inn and cupbearer; those who, like the recent translator Whaley, opt for "The Book of the Inn" eliminate what Goethe's contemporaries felt to be the subject of the book. In their dictionary, the brothers Grimm credit much of the modern nuancing of the word *Schenk* (cupbearer) to precisely this book, adducing "Goethe's procedure in *The West-Eastern Divan* (Book of the Cupbearer)" (*Deutsches Wörterbuch* 8:2539). The "Announcement" for *The West-Eastern Divan* that appeared in the *Morgenblatt* of February 24, 1816, also refers to "The Book of the Cupbearer" (*Das Buch des Schenken*; WA 1.6:430).

While the Grimms did not object morally to the *Divan*, other contemporaries did. Adelbert von Chamisso, for instance, accuses "father Goethe" (*Vater Goethe*) of setting a precedent for "coquetting with the love of boys" (Derks 271). This is something like the pot calling the kettle black, as Chamisso's narrative *Peter Schlemihl* (1814), about a young man who cannot have children and is not considered a "real man" all because he lacks a shadow, has sent out queer vibrations since it appeared.

But, returning to Goethe, when recent translators ignore what Goethe's contemporaries considered to be the book's centerpiece, they merely pass on the opinion of revered twentieth-century Goethe editors like Erich Trunz, who, anxious to allay fears about homosexual tendencies, have hastened to reassure readers by giving Goethe's word that the book depicts "a truly pedagogical relationship" (*HA* 2:202, 649).

Goethe must have had a different view of pedagogy than such modern readers, though, for this student-teacher relationship is replete with love of a decidedly physical kind. The cupbearer, a wily student indeed, exclaims:

But I love you more
When you kiss to remember;
For the words pass,
And the kiss—it stays inside.

[Doch ich liebe dich noch lieber
Wenn du küssest zum Erinnern;
Denn die Worte gehn vorüber
Und der Kuß, der bleibt im Innern.] (*HA* 2:95)

To find this relationship innocent of all erotics is to disagree with both Goethe, who emphasized the erotics of the passage, and his contemporaries, who found it morally objectionable. In his commentary to the *Divan*, Goethe writes: "Neither the immoderate taste for half-forbidden wine, nor the tender feeling for the beauty of a growing boy, could be absent from the 'Divan'; the latter was to be treated however — in accordance with our traditions — in all purity" (*HA* 2:202). Like Wieland in *Agathon*, Goethe apparently chooses to treat this subject "in all purity" only because that is "in accordance with our traditions." In another passage, Goethe reflects moodily on the increasingly restrictive nature of the customs of his times: "What the ancient Greeks were allowed to say is no longer appropriate for us to say and what appealed to Shakespeare's stronger contemporaries, the English of 1820 can no longer bear, so that in recent times there is a felt need for a family Shakespeare" (cited in Vaget 11). Goethe seems to censure his own era's inability to handle sexuality more than the deviations of earlier times.

The *Roman Elegies* and *The West-Eastern Divan* both show Goethe's willingness to use the motif of homosexuality in his writing; they also show the unwillingness of critics from both Goethe's and our own era to accept this homosexuality. More important, however, they also point to Goethe's linking of the motif of homosexuality with the theme of language and writing. The connection between sexuality and poetry is one of the famous points of the *Elegies*, particularly in the fifth elegy, in which the poet uses his hands in the daytime to leaf through the works of the ancients and in the nighttime to feel his lover's body. The dream of a union of lived sexuality and poetry reaches its apogee when the poet taps out hexameters on his lover's back (*HA* 1:160).

In his commentary on the *Divan*, Goethe follows his references to the "tender feeling for the beauty of a growing boy" by recounting in some detail one of the stories by the Persian poet Saadi about teacher-student relationships, a story that resembles Plato's *Phaedrus* in its blending of erotics and grammar, of high-minded education and carnal manipulation. The poet Saadi likes the boy partly because of his looks, but also because the boy, grammar in hand, is learning pure language thoroughly (*HA* 1:203). In fact, the "pedagogy" in "The Book of the Cupbearer" has to do with teaching language. The book begins with a poem that asks, "Where was the parchment, the pen where, / That captured everything?" [*Wo war das Pergament, der Griffel wo, / Die alles faßten?*] (*HA* 2:89). It continues to circulate around the theme of inspired, intoxicating, beautiful writing, speculating that one poet wrote beautiful letters despite drunkenness and discussing the inspired nature of the Muslim scriptures. With the cupbearer himself, the poet discusses the nature of poetry and song, teaching the cupbearer otherwise when the youth says he prefers kisses to words.

Homosexuality and language are both present in the *Roman Elegies* and the *Divan* because they are both pharmaka. In another poem, written while in Italy, Goethe makes clear the relationship between eros and those characteristics that identify the pharmakon. In 1788, Goethe wrote a poem to Cupid, who fills a role analogous to the Amor of the *Roman Elegies*:

Cupid, loose, stubborn boy!
You asked me for quarter for a few hours.
How many days and nights you have stayed!
And now have become imperious
    and master of the house.

[Cupido, loser eigensinniger Knabe!
Du batst mich um Quartier auf einige Stunden.
Wie viele Tag' und Nächte bist du geblieben!
Und bist nun herrisch und Meister im Hause
    geworden] (*WA* 1.4:104)

While the more usual, heterosexual interpretation of this poem might assume that Cupid is the spirit that has caused the singer to fall in love with a woman, Sander Gilman intriguingly suggests that this "paean" could in fact address "the young and beautiful boy" (*Sexuality* 228), a suggestion made more plausible by the poet's conclusion that Cupid has "warped and misplaced" his "tool" (*HA* 1:237). The warped and (perhaps because) misplaced tool reflects the idea that pederasty might actually have an effect on or be an effect of the physical construction of the genitalia. Klaus Müller reports that around 1800 physicians were beginning to suspect that pederasts could be identified by their thin and not very long members (95).

Goethe, who reused parts of this poem in *Claudine of Villa Bella* (*WA* 1.11:230), comments on the self-contradictory nature of eros in its broadest implications when he reprints the poem yet again in the *Italian Journey* (*Italienische Reise*):

If one does not take the following little poem in a literal sense, doesn't imagine that spirit that one usually calls Amor, but rather imagines a collection of active spirits that speak to the innermost part of humanity, challenge it, pull it back and forth, confuse it with divided interest, then one will participate in a symbolic way in the circumstance in which I found myself. (*HA* 11:478)[5]

Regardless of whether this Cupid is homosexual or not, he is definitely a pharmakon, a pleasure and a pain. Here Goethe explicitly asks the reader

---

5. See also Goethe's *Gespräche mit Eckermann*, 5 and 6 April 1829, in Goethe, *Gedenkausgabe*, vol. 24.

to dismiss the idea of sexuality, Cupid or Amor, as a single demon, and see it as a complex of self-contradictory impulses that affect humanity in the deepest way. He points here to the pharmaceutical nature of sexuality, its inborn ambiguity, which relates it so closely to textuality. Goethe's own understanding of the figure known as "Amor" supports Müller-Sievers's case that Goethe's sexually liberating experiences—in Italy or anywhere else—are not interesting only in and of themselves (442). Rather they are interesting because Goethe sees them as apt symbols for poetry. In a number of Goethe's poetic works the ambiguity of sexuality—its pharmaceutical nature, which emerges out of its linguistic constitution—becomes clear.

WERTHER

Two of the protagonists in Goethe's novels show the way in which this sexual-linguistic pharmakon can poison and cure growing young men. In 1796 Goethe published in *Die Horen* two collections of *Letters from Switzerland* (*Briefe aus der Schweiz*), the first of which purportedly consisted of letters from Werther's youth. Werther, a product of the Sturm und Drang, with its emotional cult of friendship, is no stranger to effusive declarations of love to other men. Kaus is one of the few critics who points out the male-male erotics of the final scene of *The Sorrows of Young Werther* (*Die Leiden des jungen Werthers*), in which a male youth kisses the dead Werther and must be torn away from him by force: "the oldest, whom he had loved most, hung from his lips until he passed away; the youth was torn away by force" (HA 6:124). This will not be the only time that such necrophiliac fantasies with beautiful dead male youths appear in the writings of Goethe and other German classicists: we recall Jean Paul's dying warriors, embracing and embraced, and we shall return to the subject when we look at the dead fisherman's son in the *Wilhelm Meister's Journeyman Years* and the dead Marquis de Posa in Schiller's *Don Carlos*.

Despite the deathbed scene, it is nonetheless clear in *The Sorrows of Young Werther* that Werther is obsessively in love with a woman, Lotte. Werther's love of Lotte is so all consuming that it seems queer that Anton Reiser, in Moritz's novel, would identify with every aspect of Werther, except for his love of Lotte. But perhaps Anton Reiser has an insight into Werther's love that has generally been lost in straight interpretations of the novel. It turns out in the *Letters*, however, that in his youth his desire developed less straightforwardly. Although Werther and his friend Ferdinand mention

female beloveds and flirt with the women they encounter, Werther nonetheless develops an appreciation of the male body before encountering the
female body:

I arranged for Ferdinand to bathe in the lake; how splendidly my young friend is
built! how proportionate are all of his parts! what a fullness of form, what a splendor of youth, what a profit for me to have enriched my imagination with this perfect example of human nature. . . . I see him as Adonis felling the boar, as Narcissus
mirroring himself in the spring. (*WA* 1.19:213)

This incident may have origins in the adventures of the two Counts Stolberg, with whom in 1775 Goethe first visited Switzerland and who enjoyed
bathing in the nude so much that they were eventually asked to leave the
country (Eissler 1:373). Eissler, incidentally, sees a general pattern in Goethe's
life linking homosexuality and Switzerland (1:370). In any case, Adonis and
Narcissus are doomed to an early death in Greek mythology. Werther's passionate deathbed kiss fits in with this vision of male-male desire.

Werther therefore begins to look for Venus. The gender restrictions of
the time make it more difficult for him to find a naked woman, so he must
hire a prostitute, who is less willing to pose nude for his observation than
to have intercourse with him. Once the prostitute poses for him, however,
Werther shifts his desire from his fellow man to his fellow woman. Even
though his discovery of this beauty occurs in the most unnatural situation
possible — a brothel, where sex is sold, being used as an artist's studio, where
reality is portrayed — Werther declares that her unclothed body is nature revealed: "What a strange sensation, as one piece of clothing after the other fell
off, and nature, stripped of its foreign shell, appeared strange to me and —
I'd like to say — made almost a frightening impression on me" (*WA* 1.19:217-
18). As queer as it is, this is nature. Heterosexual desire is perverted. At the
same time, homosexuality becomes a natural phase through which Werther
grows. Its naturalness in his development becomes clear in its setting — the
beautiful lakes of Switzerland. In fact, Eissler argues that most of Goethe's
homosexual bonding takes place in nature (1:374). Goethe thus holds fast to
the belief he expressed in the conversation with Müller that homosexuality
was in, although against, nature.

The passage in the *Letters from Switzerland* also shows the relationship
between homosexuality and language that recurs in Goethe's writing, for a
diatribe against high society, in which Werther particularly objects to speaking French — a language in which he believes he sounds "silly" (*albern*) —
immediately follows Werther's discovery of the beauty of the male body.

Werther observes that the "dunce" expresses himself "just as in a foreign tongue," "with already coined, traditional phrases," whereas the "witty person" "quickly, vivaciously, and characteristically grasps and easily expresses that which is delicate and proper in the present" (*WA* 1.19:215–16). Werther's early encounter with sexuality coincides with his discovery of the power of language or textuality.

WILHELM MEISTER'S APPRENTICESHIP

The same year that Goethe published the flashback to Werther's youth saw the arrival of the first of the Wilhelm Meister novels, *Wilhelm Meister's Apprenticeship*, in which a similar pharmaceutical use of homosexuality also appears, although Klaus Mann certainly doesn't seem to have registered it! The reconception of Wilhelm's family from a sprawling unit with an actively involved grandmother in *Wilhelm Meister's Theatrical Mission* (the first, uncompleted, attempt at a Wilhelm Meister novel, begun in the 1770s and titled in German *Wilhelm Meisters theatralische Sendung*) to a tightly knit, self-contained bourgeois nuclear family in the *Apprenticeship* reveals Goethe's uncanny sensitivity to the sociological changes in family structures taking place in his era (Kittler, "Wilhelm Meister," 15–29).

While there is a subtle hint of possible lesbianism or tribadism in Philine's affair with the "girl" (who turns out to be Friedrich), these allusions to homosexuality otherwise hover around the men in the novel, particularly Wilhelm. At least one male character besides Wilhelm can be construed as tainted by a whiff of homosexuality—Philo, the beloved of the Beautiful Soul. The Beautiful Soul had fallen in love with him, but when he confessed certain things that he had withheld from her, she could "assume the worst" (*HA* 7:392): "With infinite sadness of heart I saw in Philo some sort of counterpart to the hero of Wieland's novel *Agathon*, who had to repay the cost of his education in the sacred grove of Delphi with heavy overdue interest" (*HA* 7:392). Subsequently in describing this catastrophe, the Beautiful Soul alludes to David and Bathsheba (*HA* 7:393). In his commentary, Trunz implies that these confessions are sexual, and assumes that they are heterosexual (*HA* 7:776–77). David, however, is linked not only to Bathsheba, but also to Jonathan. And Agathon is quite definitely linked not only to Danae, as Trunz emphasizes, but also to homosexual love, specifically in the Delphic groves that the Beautiful Soul mentions. As mentioned earlier, in *Agathon* as in his other works, Wieland treats the subject of homosexuality. In one specific case the protagonist Agathon, who as a youth dreams of being loved by the gods like Ganymede, is homosexually abused by a priest disguised as Apollo in a coppice near Delphi (1:555–60). Homosexual abuse, rather than heterosexual activity, could therefore easily explain why Philo's confession prompts "experiences which were quite new" to the Beautiful Soul (HA 7:392). Importantly, this touch of homosexuality causes the Beautiful Soul to realize that she is no better than he is and to recognize the evil within her. This process of self-recognition then contributes to her development. The poison of homosexuality is therefore part of her cure.

Turning to Wilhelm, however, one can begin with the observation that Wilhelm's first love, for Mariane, has an interesting parallel to Werther's admiration for the female body. Just as Werther had discovered "nature" in the artificially lit brothel, Wilhelm discovers "much natural" in Mariane's boudoir, filled with makeup, cosmetics, and all the decidedly unnatural accoutrements of an actress (HA 7:19). The sexologist Havelock Ellis reports that Wordsworth flung away the novel at this point, because it was too smutty! Perhaps what really irritated Wordworth is that Goethe sees male-female desire as a product of culture, just as he repeatedly shows same-sex desire to have some roots in nature. Indeed, the earliest heterosexual urges that Wilhelm relates in his childhood take place on the stage and are therefore performed speech acts. This sexuality, by virtue of its rhetoricity, can be queered and thus open to constantly changing, self-contradictory interpretations.

While it might seem eccentric to emphasize the homosexual in Wilhelm, who notoriously goes through a chain of women and even begets a child along the way, there is something queer about his relationships with women. Mariane herself hints at Wilhelm's sexual ambiguity when she identifies him with the figure of Jonathan from his puppet theater: "[Mariane] stayed with her Jonathan. She knew how to treat him so charmingly and then to transfer her endearments from the puppet to our friend so that once again a trifling play became the introduction to happy hours" (HA 7:16). Jonathan, because of his love for David, was in the eighteenth century, like Ganymede, a signifier for homosexuality (Faderman 107, 121).

The most obvious example of the queerness present in Wilhelm's youth is Mignon, the dark waif he adopts while traveling. Both Wilhelm (HA 7:91) and the narrator, who refers to her with a feminine pronoun only five times in the novel (Keppel-Kriems 87), have difficulty determining her gender. Even her name, with its masculine ending, puts her gender into question, underscoring her lack of conformity to the heterosexual norms present at the novel's end. In addition, although editors of Goethe editions anxiously insist that "Mignon," like "Liebling," could apply innocently to both men and women, the name was, like Ganymede, a byword for a male homosexual prostitute in the late eighteenth century.[6]

Mignon is of course almost synonymous with pathology as well as androgyny. She cannot take part in the happy end of the novel because of her fatal heart attack brought on by the bourgeois primal scene—the appearance, at least, of a nuclear family, with Therese kissing Wilhelm while "Felix tugged at her skirt and cried, 'Mother Therese, I'm here too!'" (*HA* 7:544). If Mignon's lack of gender definition gives her medical leave from taking part in the bourgeois nuclear family, Philine, the most entirely and aggressively feminine among the female characters of the novel, represents the eighteenth-century medical "problem" of excessive female sexuality. From the moment she is introduced, she exhibits strong desires, aggressively asking Wilhelm for flowers (*HA* 7:91). This behavior—for instance, when she kisses him on the street (*HA* 7:133)—discomforts the queer Wilhelm.

He has other quarry on his mind anyway: While he is fascinated with the fight over her between Friedrich and the supermanly stablemaster, he doesn't honor her with a glance. His mirror image comes not from Philine, but from Wilhelm's rivals, as the scene in which Friedrich and the stablemaster fight for Philine shows: "What he saw was an exaggerated display of his own self, for he too had been consumed by fierce jealousy, and if his sense of propriety had not prevented him, he too would have indulged his wildest fancies, gleefully and maliciously harmed his beloved, and challenged his rival. He would gladly have obliterated everybody who seemed to be there just to exasperate him" (*HA* 7:140).

Wilhelm finds, in the masculine stablemaster and the passionate Friedrich, images of male desire that appeal to him far more than the object of that desire, which he too would like to wound (Roberts 78). He therefore diligently avoids looking at Philine and concentrates exclusively on the two men fighting for her: "The duel was for Wilhelm an additional externalization of his own feelings. He couldn't deny that he himself would have liked to direct a rapier, or still better, a sword, at the stable master, although he soon observed that the man was a far better fencer than he was. But he did not deign to cast on Philine a single glance" (*HA* 7:141). Wilhelm is still narcissistically infatuated with images—not of Philine, who eludes his memory as quickly

6. For the anxious denials see Trunz, *HA* 7:726, and Schings's commentary in the *Münchener Ausgabe* of Goethe's works, 5:736. For more adventuresome speculations, see Wolff 110.

as she leaves his bed—but of his male competitors for her (*HA* 7:140–41). He's not sure exactly what, but he'd like to point something hard and sharp at the stablemaster even though, or perhaps because, the stablemaster wields his tool quite professionally.

Eventually Philine gets her way, however; everything points to her as the possessor of the delicate arms and breast that he didn't have the strength to resist on the night of the successful performance of *Hamlet* (*HA* 7:327; 523–24). Wilhelm, however, cannot even remember who is in bed with him when he sleeps with her (*HA* 7:327, 523): so immaterial is the identity of the person with whom he sleeps on that night that he even thinks it might be Mignon, who by all accounts has a considerably different body type than Philine. Indeed, the famous point about Mignon is her youthful androgyny, bringing Wilhelm even closer to the reproach of pederasty.

Predictably, given eighteenth-century anthropology, Philine's behavior leads to no good. Wilhelm cannot marry her, as she pales in his mind in comparison with the passionless Natalie (*HA* 7:228), who admits to lacking an understanding of love (*HA* 7:538). Mignon's death and Philine's fading charms turn out to be typical for nonnormatively heterosexual behavior in *Wilhelm Meister*. Androgyny and "excessive" female sexuality are at the beginning of Wilhelm's life. Because Wilhelm's beginnings are saturated with illness such as that eighteenth-century illness, "theater mania" (Flaherty, "Stage-Struck"), this queer behavior with which he is initially surrounded becomes textually linked to illness. The sexual deviance associated with Wilhelm's wounds and illnesses must presumably be cured just as much as they.

An organization called the Tower Society, similar to the Masons and bearing the standard of Enlightened thinking (including medicine), attempts to socialize Wilhelm Meister to a heterosexual "healthiness." Just as Moritz had done in his *Journal*, they cure him of his mania for the theater by letting him act on stage until he loses interest in drama (Flaherty, "Stage-Struck"). The treatment for *Theatermanie* involves the typically homeopathic eighteenth-century tactic of using an illness to cure itself. Similarly, the Tower Society uses Wilhelm's initially strong homosexual drives to turn him into a heterosexual.

After attracting Wilhelm with her male cross-dressing, Therese, an associate of the Tower Society, teaches Wilhelm (a) a series of ideological gender distinctions based upon, to use Laqueur's terminology, a "two-sex system" and (b) the imperative of loving someone from the other gender. In a long passage, she relates to Wilhelm how Lothario had convinced her that while disharmony epitomizes the masculine world of politics and business, the housewife has a true internal autonomy: "man . . . for the sake of some goal he never attains, . . . must every moment abandon that highest of all goals: harmony within himself. But the sensible housewife really governs, rules over all that is in the home" (*HA* 7:452). Interestingly, this wisdom about the world really goes from man to man, from Lothario, via Therese, to Wilhelm, thus confirming some of Luce Irigaray's suspicions about the "hom(m)osexual" or homosocial nature of bourgeois society.

Finally, Natalie, sister of Lothario, who is the leader of the Tower Society, inducts Wilhelm into a mature heterosexual relationship. She, whose eyes contain — homeopathically — "poison and antidote" (*Gift und Gegengift*; *HA* 7:606), first attracts Wilhelm by playing to his homosexual impulses when she appears in a man's coat as the Beautiful Amazon (*HA* 7:226). Only later does she reveal herself to be a woman in every sense of Therese's definition of the word, at which point Wilhelm can love her.

Natalie first appears on the scene not only as an Amazon, but also as a bringer of medical care for the wounded Wilhelm. She warms him with her masculine cloak, has her surgeon attend to his immediate needs, and leaves twenty gold pieces behind to pay for his subsequent medical care (*HA* 7:227, 234). Thus her androgyny, which Wilhelm finds so fetching, is intimately connected with her cure of Wilhelm. Friedrich puts his finger on her pharmaceutical nature when he compares her to the princess whose love both poisons and cures the prince, with whom he in turn compares the sick Wilhelm: "What's the name of the Beautiful Woman who enters and carries in her demure rogue's eyes poison and antidote at the same time?" (*HA* 7:606). "Poison and antidote" is a typical representation of the pharmakon. Derrida devotes the second half of an extensive footnote in "Plato's Pharmacy" to the word *Gift* (131–32, n. 56). The positive sense of the German word *Gift* is contained in the German *Mitgift* (dowry) as well as the English word "gift." The homeopathic phrase applies well to Natalie's erotic appeal, which is initially androgynous and thus homoerotically tinged — a poison — but leads to the cure of the prototypical nuclear family consisting of Wilhelm, Natalie, and Felix.

The princess to whom Friedrich compares Natalie is Stratonice, the bride of Seleucus, who was the father of Antiochus and who — to complete the circle — was in love with Stratonice. Wilhelm had been fascinated with this quasi-Oedipal story of the son in love with his stepmother ever since his childhood, when a painting of the lovesick prince from his grandfather's collection caught his eye. This painting is important because it suggest that Wilhelm's innermost feelings, his love, have been prefigured by myth, art, culture, and civilization—that is to say, by the pharmakon. Here again the signifiers turn out to precode that which they signify: in Wilhelm's case, real love follows artistic representation of love, not vice versa. But the story in the painting is particularly interesting in our context because it has a queer side as well. Hössli records something that few Germanists have noted: According to Demetrius, when Antiochus showed signs of lovesickness, his doctor Erasistratus observed the youth "when a boy or a girl stepped in to the room, watching all parts of the body that tend to be changed with a change of the soul" (2:99). Thus the foundational myth of Wilhelm's erotic life begins with the question of whether the male protagonist loves a girl or a boy.

WILHELM MEISTER'S JOURNEYMAN YEARS

In 1796, Goethe clarified the homosexuality inherent in Werther's youth and alluded to homosexuality in Wilhelm Meister's personality. Apparently the allusions in *Wilhelm Meister* were not suggestive enough, however, for several decades later Goethe provided his readers with a subsequent flashback to the homosexuality of Wilhelm's youth, just as he had in Werther's case. The importance of the homosexuality for Wilhelm's subsequent "healthy" development into a heterosexual is stressed in *Wilhelm Meister's Journeyman Years*, in which the reader learns of only one new incident in Wilhelm's life before the *Apprenticeship*: the story of the fisherman's son, with whom Wilhelm falls in love.

As Eissler notes, the story is told haltingly, divided into several sections by dashes or asterisks in the text, suggesting its emotional import (2: 1449). Wilhelm was supposed to visit some friends, but in such a way that he would be at home by nightfall: "for sleeping out of his long-accustomed bed seemed an impossibility" (*HA* 8:270). The parental concern about sleeping arrangements proves justified, for Wilhelm spends the afternoon with "a youth, who had especially attracted me with his first appearance" (*HA* 8:271), in a sultry, sensual environment, learning to fish—which in this case turns out to be a metaphorical activity. He is surrounded by dragonflies, for which his friend uses the unusual name "sun virgins [*Sonnenjungfern*]" (*HA* 8:272), suggesting that virginity is at stake. Eventually he and the friend are both naked together in the water, overwhelmed by each other's beauty, and, after dressing again, exchanging "fiery" kisses: "so beautiful was the human figure, of which I had never had a concept. He seemed to observe me with the same attentiveness. Quickly clothed, we stood, still undisguised in front of each other, our spirits were attracted to each other, and we swore an eternal friendship amidst the most fiery kisses" (*HA* 8:272). The last scene has the same erotic implications as the scene in the *Letters from Switzerland* in which Werther watches Ferdinand bathe. Even Trunz has to remark on the "soft erotic tones" of "the first friendship" (*HA* 8:636). Within the narrative the pastor's wife also suspects that something is wrong when she refuses to let Wilhelm take his new friend home "with a quiet remark on the impropriety" (*HA* 8:272). While Eissler believes the situation is inappropriate because of the class differences between the two boys, it seems just as probable that the mother was concerned about sexuality. Wilhelm never sees his friend, who dies trying to rescue some wayward swimmers, alive again.

Just as Werther had associated Ferdinand with doomed figures from Greek mythology, so Wilhelm links his friend with Hyacinth, one of Apollo's male lovers who is killed by Zephyr, who is also in love with the youth. As his friend is—unbeknownst to Wilhelm—dying, Wilhelm falls in love with a girl, with whom he walks in a garden where the beautiful hyacinths are past their prime. Goethe provides the readers of the *Journeyman Years* with one flashback of Wilhelm Meister's youth to emphasize the importance of Wilhelm's male-male attraction at the beginning of his development. Like the hyacinth, this development is natural, but it blooms in the early spring of the young man's life and passes away before the peak of the human cycle.

Although the flowers in the garden point to the fleeting nature of Wilhelm's homosexual desire, Wilhelm himself is still overwhelmed by the death of his friend when he sees "nude, stretched out, brilliant white bodies, glowing even in the dim lamplight" (*HA* 8:275). Seeing his friend's body among the dead, he floods the youth's "broad chest with unending tears" (*HA* 8:276). That these unending tears flooding the beautiful body of his nude friend might be a euphemism for another, less easily mentioned bodily fluid becomes possible when Wilhelm admits: "I had heard something about rubbing [*Reiben*] that was supposed to help in such a case, I rubbed my tears into him and deceived myself with the warmth that I aroused" (*HA* 8:276). Recalling Johann Valentin Müller's remark that lesbians were called "fricatrixes" or "rubbers," it seems possible that this "rubbing" has a sexual side to it (214). The masturbatory nature of this "rubbing" is further intimated by its pointlessness: this necrophiliac pleasure has no living object, does not further a relationship with a living other. Like Rousseau's supplément, this rubbing arouses only deceptive warmth.

The final indication of the erotics of this mortuary encounter comes when Wilhelm tries to resuscitate the dead boy artificially, an effort that glides smoothly into memories of their kiss in the lake: "In the confusion I thought I would blow air into him, but the pearly rows of his teeth were clenched tightly, the lips, upon which the farewell kiss seemed yet to rest, denied the lightest sign of response" (8:276). The deathbed scene, reminiscent of Werther's death, further emphasizes the erotic nature of the friendship between the boys. This homoerotically charged episode is also intimately linked with medicine as it determines, supposedly, Wilhelm's desire to become a surgeon. Thus homosexuality (both a disease and a drug) and medicine (both the supplier of metaphors for Wilhelm's development and the product of that development) are reinforced as basic structures in Wilhelm's growth.

Such is the "happy end" of *Wilhelm Meister*. The Tower Society, with the help of medicine, can utilize Wilhelm's "illnesses" or "vices" to cure themselves; his love of the theater brings him away from the theater and into the bourgeois world, while his homosexuality brings him away from homosexuality and into a heterosexual relationship. Proponents of the bourgeois cause find the ending felicitous because it implies that such "problems" will heal themselves in the bourgeois order. Detractors, however, rely on the novel's irony to argue that Goethe was describing, rather than advocating, the changes taking place in his society. His novel portrays too clearly the dangers of the equation of health and the bourgeois family: Many characters (the Harper, the Beautiful Soul, Laertes) will not be able to follow Wilhelm's journey to the position of father in the bourgeois family and are therefore doomed, in the novel's world, to sickness (Hirsch). Thus, while the study of the medical discourse in *Wilhelm Meister's Apprenticeship* makes clear that Wilhelm develops from a state that the Tower Society calls sick (including theater and homosexuality) to one it calls healthy (including a practical career and a heterosexual relationship), this does not mean that the reader must greet such development as exemplary.

The reader should use the occasion to observe the mechanisms of this "cure," particularly the drugs, the pharmaka, that bring it about. The most efficacious pharmakon is pederasty in its natural unnaturalness. On many levels Goethe relates pederasty to writing itself, in all of its polyvalence. Sexuality, the product of discourse, allows for the analysis of discourse. In the final analysis, pederasty is for Goethe always part of the cure: a pharmakon, with all the medical connotations of that word, the drug that endangers many of the characters of Goethe's world, but also cures them. For the reader, homosexuality functions similarly: as a metaphor for the text. Like pederasty, the text should be a pharmakon, both natural and unnatural, meaning both itself and the Other — in a word, heterotextual. This equation of pederasty, pharmakon, and writing suggests that sexuality in Goethe's works refers finally to the textuality of these works. Indeed, perhaps it goes beyond the works themselves to point to the textual nature of sexuality in general. And, in pointing to the textual, or discursive nature of sexuality, it opens that sexuality up to a multitude of queer interpretations.

6

PERFORMING GENDER
IN *WILHELM MEISTER*
Goethe on Italian Transvestites

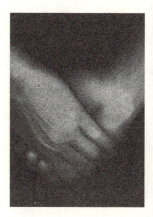

The efficacy of pederasty as a pharmakon to ensure the development of the complete male has a specific grounding in gender. In keeping with the eighteenth-century attitude toward the pharmakon as a kind of homeopathic medication—just enough toxin to bring about a positive effect—Goethe seems to argue that a touch of femininity could help produce a man. Like homosexuality, effeminacy could help "man" construct his masculinity, according to Goethe. In the November 1788 issue of a German journal, *The German Mercury* (*Der teutsche Merkur*, edited, incidentally, by Wieland), Goethe anonymously published a short piece entitled "Women's Roles on the Roman Stage, Played by Men" (*Frauenrollen auf dem römischen Theater, durch Männer gespielt*; WA 1.47:267–74). He had seen an all-male performance of Carlo Goldoni's *Mine Hostess* on January 3, 1787. This was in Rome, where the strictest prohibitions against women appearing on the stage had been in place for two centuries. Ten years after the performance Goethe saw, Napoleon's conquest of Rome swept away these restrictions on women's performances, which makes Goethe's essay, according to its translator into English, "an eyewitness report by a modern man of letters of one of the last all-male performances" in a tradition going back at least to Shakespeare's day (Ragusa 47).

On the one hand, Goethe's defense of cross-dressing is open to the charge that he promotes the exclusion and mockery of women. On the other hand, his essay suggests that gender is a constructed, performed, and performative discourse rather than an innate essence, which allows for a critique of patriarchy. It therefore suggests that the contradictory reactions to cross-dressing in current discussions emerge from structures of sexuality and gender already present in eighteenth-century discourses. In addition, it underscores the constant ambivalence and irony of signification that helps queer Goethe's writings.

Goethe admits that he visited the Roman theater "not without prejudice" (*nicht ohne Vorurteil*; WA 1.47:272). He assumes that his readership will also be opposed to the practice, casually writing, "So much has been said against this Roman tradition" (WA 1.47:269). In 1777, he himself had produced Goldoni's play using women for the women's roles, for which reason he writes: "I am convinced, and have seen myself, that a clever and intelligent actress can earn much praise in this role" (WA 1.47:273). If Goethe and his readers are any indication, the time for the elimination of the Roman practice of using male actors for female roles was ripe when Napoleon took over.

Goethe, however, chooses to say something in favor of the Roman practice, for, despite his negative predisposition, he enjoyed his evening at the theater: "I felt a hitherto unknown pleasure, and noticed that many others shared it with me" (WA 1.47:272). The fact that Goethe shares his pleasure with the other members of the audience suggests that some kind of male bonding over the representation of femininity is in fact going on. He initially explains his pleasure as the product of an encounter with a bit of antiquity, much like seeing a ruin, a lost trace of the past: "It must be allowed to say something in its praise, or at least (in order not to seem too paradoxical) to draw attention to it as to an antique remnant" (WA 1.47:269–70). Goethe reminds his readers that the ancients, like the modern Romans, did not allow women on the stage: "The ancients did not allow women to set foot on the stage, at least in the best era of their art and morals. Their plays were either so structured that women were more or less disposable; or the women's roles were performed by an actor who had been especially trained for them" (WA 1.47:269). As a devotee of the classics, Goethe would be loath to dismiss the ancient tradition.

The connection to antiquity turns out to be the last word of the essay as well. In closing, he argues such performances are a chance to relive the past and prove what many had doubted: "Male actors were often success-ful to the highest degree in delighting in female clothes a tasteful nation" (*WA* 1.47:274). Apparently there had been some doubt about whether an-cient drama could have been that good without actresses—and with cross-dressed men. Thus, Goethe's first and last justification for the Roman prac-tice of using men to play women's roles is its legitimization of the power of ancient drama, which had replaced women with cross-dressed men.

To make matters worse, according to Lesley Ferris, Goldoni's *Mine Hostess* is explicitly misogynist. The play centers on a woman, Mirandolina, who is courted by two noblemen. A third nobleman, the Knight, cannot understand why anyone would waste his time on a woman: "What! Let a woman worry you? Let a woman upset you? A woman? I'll never come to that! A woman! But I'm in no danger, for to be upset by a woman is to be upset by nothing" (act 1, scene 4; p. 7). Eventually Mirandolina seduces even the woman-hating Knight into becoming infatuated with her, where-upon she promptly rejects all three aristocratic suitors and marries her ser-vant, Fabrizio. Ferris argues that Goethe, like many of his contemporaries, viewed Mirandolina's decision to marry a social inferior as pure contrariness ("Goethe" 59).

In her polemic against Goethe, Ferris emphasizes the passage where Goethe sees the all-male cast in the Papal States as an opportunity for men to avenge themselves on such contrary women. It was entertaining, he writes, that the youth "knew the dangerous characteristics of the beloved sex so well and . . . avenged us on the fair sex for everything similar that we have suf-fered at their hands" (*WA* 1.47:247). In this passage Goethe, with his "we" and his "us," assumes that both the spectators at the performance and his readers were all men, which furthers the exclusionary tendencies of his re-marks about classical theater. Add to this exclusionary talk the notion that all these men need to wreak vengeance on the fair sex, and one can under-stand why Ferris entitled her chapter on this subject "Goethe, Goldoni, and Woman-Hating" (see also Ferris, "Legacy").

A large body of feminist criticism would support Ferris's interpretation of Goethe's appreciation of the Roman cross-dressing. Mary Daly declares that, "like whites playing 'black face,' the [drag queen] incorporates the op-pressed role without being incorporated by it" (67). Jill Dolan writes that the old, all-male tradition of the theater allowed men to play the Other in order "to appropriate and reject women." She then moves from premod-ern drama to modern drag performances, in which, in her words, "women are nonexistent . . . but woman-as-myth is constructed in an agreed upon exchange between the male performer and the usually male spectator" (6). Frye similarly argues that cross-dressing "is a casual and cynical mockery of women" (137).

Oddly, on this issue orthodox feminism overlaps with orthodox psychoanalysis, which sees cross-dressing as being, despite appearances, all about the phallus. According to this line of reasoning, the male impersonating a female does not want to emphasize his femininity but actually to emphasize that which distinguishes him from real women, which is to say his genitals, which represent the phallus. In a classic essay called "The Psychology of Transvestism," Otto Fenichel writes that "the patient himself represents a woman with a penis" (169; see also Tyler 41–42). Thus when Goethe dons his mother's jacket in 1772 to make a fool out of himself skating, Kurt Robert Eissler, in his psychoanalytic biography of Goethe, interprets the act as transvestitism that is intended to mock the mother and caricature the female sex (1:141). Ferris is of course presumably not relying on orthodox psychoanalysis in her interpretation of Goethe, but she might well agree with Eissler that Goethe's reference to man's desire to avenge himself on women through cross-dressing suggests that there is a deep-seated personal motivation for Goethe's interest in cross-dressing.

All of these arguments on the antifeminist and misogynist implications of Goethe's essay assume that Goethe wants to use the cross-dressed actors to make a statement about women. Marjorie Garber critiques Freud's analysis of another famous cross-dresser, Schreber, for precisely the same assumptions. She argues that he looks *through* the transvestite, rather than *at* the transvestite (*Vested* 208). On this account, the viewer should not see in the cross-dressed man some kind of statement about women or mothers, but rather the action of cross-dressing. The viewer should concentrate on the representation rather than the represented. Garber's interpretation has a poststructuralist inflection that harks back to Jean Baudrillard, who writes about transvestitism: "Here the signs are separated from biology, and consequently the sexes no longer exist properly speaking. What transvestites love is this game of signs" (12–13). Feminists like Luce Irigaray also see a value in "mimicry" that allows a woman to "assume the feminine role deliberately . . . so as to make 'visible,' by an effect of playful repetition, what was supposed to remain invisible" (76). Most recently, Judith Butler argues forcefully for the possibility of both male and female mimicry of gender through cross-dressing:

As much as drag creates a unified picture of "woman" (what its critics often oppose), it also reveals the distinctness of those aspects of gendered experience which are falsely naturalized as a unity through the regulatory fiction of heterosexual coherence. *In imitating gender, drag implicitly reveals the imitative structure of gender itself—as well as its contingency.* (*Gender* 137)

At the same time, Butler makes clear that not all drag is subversive (*Bodies* 125). Does the cross-dressing in Rome pass the test? Does it underscore the iterative and imitative, rather than the original and natural, elements of gender?

Goethe gives ample indication that he would support an analysis that concentrated on the general representation of gender in drag rather than on any particular statement that drag might make about a particular gender. Goethe in fact does not say that he enjoyed the all-male performance of the play because it demonstrated the nature of woman, but rather because the actors represent artifice rather than crude reality: "In such a performance the concept of imitation, the thought of art, always remained lively and, through the clever play, only a sort of self-conscious illusion was produced" (*WA* 1.47:272). This notion appears at least four times in the essay, including near the end, where Goethe sums up his argument again in terms of mimesis and art: "one felt here the pleasure of seeing, not the thing itself, but its imitation, of being entertained, not by nature, but by art, of observing, not an individual, but a result" (*WA* 1.47:274). The line of thinking that emphasizes mimesis, art, and reiteration is Goethe's most frequently repeated argument in favor of cross-dressing on the stage. In the center of his analysis stands the belief that the transvestite performance of the piece allows us to see an artistic representation of woman rather than a woman herself: "In the same way a double charm arises in that these people are not women, but represent women" (*WA* 1.47:272). Insistently, Goethe stresses that cross-dressing invites the audience to consider the signifiers of gender.

The pleasure of seeing artifice, rather than nature, emerges partly because the consciousness associated with artifice can tell the audience more specifically about the nature of that which is depicted. For this reason, one learns more about femininity from the cross-dressed male actor than from a real woman, according to Goethe:

The youth has studied the characteristics of the female sex in its essence and behavior; he knows them and produces them as an artist; he does not play himself, but a third and actually foreign nature. We get to know this nature all the better because someone has observed and thought about it, and not the thing, but rather the result of the thing, is performed for us. (*WA* 1.47:272)

Alienation from the object of one's attention allows for more insight into that object, according to this line of thinking. Goethe's use of the phrase "third nature" anticipates Hirschfeld's notion of the "third sex"; it also looks ahead to Garber who sees the drag queen as providing a critique of dichotomies such as "male" and "female" by offering a "third term" (*Vested* 11). Intentionally or accidentally, then, the cross-dressing actors of Rome become a third term that demonstrates the performativity of gender.

Now this argument may be no better than the earlier defenses for cross-dressing that Goethe gave. Ferris emphasizes that the "thing" that Goethe rejects in favor of its "imitation" is "woman." However, in his essay, Goethe in fact discusses the entire gender system, not just men cross-dressing as women. For him, the cross-dressing of the Roman theater takes place in the context of the city's general joy in transvestitism: "The more modern Romans have in general a special inclination to exchange the clothes of both sexes at masquerades" (*WA* 1.47:270). In contrast to the men who dress up as women, one finds "women of the middle classes as Pulcinelle, higher class women in officer's clothes, quite beautiful and happy" (*WA* 1.47:270). The men do the same: "Coach drivers and servants often make quite respectable women" (*WA* 1.47:270). By placing the transvestitism of the Roman stage in the context of carnival, he hints at an even broader disruption of gender, because carnival is a time when traditional dichotomies are disrupted. When he compares the Romans who cross-dress to Tiresias, the ancient Greek seer who had been both male and female, he suggests that they are on their way to transcending traditional binary constructions of gender: "it is quite remarkable how both sexes take pleasure in this show of inversion, and attempt to usurp the privilege of Tiresias as much as possible" (*WA* 1.47:271). Significantly, he asserts that "both sexes" can participate in the attempt to usurp Tiresias's position as member of a third sex.

Heterosexuality gets undermined when the boundaries between the two sexes begin to blur. Thus the homosexual connotations of both Italy and cross-dressing in the eighteenth century also suggest that in his essay, Goethe addresses a larger issue of gender rather than femininity alone. Terry Castle writes "the implication . . . that sodomy follows from transvestitism became a standard notion in the eighteenth century" (46). Similarly, as we have seen, Italy was becoming a gathering place for European homosexuals in the eighteenth century. Goethe's letter of December 29, 1787, in which he tells the Duke that although he doesn't dare commit much to paper about the subject, he has never seen so much love between men as in Italy (*WA* 4.8:314–15), suggests that he also connects the Italians with homosexuality. The connections between cross-dressing, carnival, Italy, and homosexuality make one wonder then if the *sich* in the following sentence is reciprocal or reflexive: "In carnival many young guys wander around in the clothing of women of the lowest classes, and seem to please themselves/each other quite a bit therein [*scheinen sich gar sehr darin zu gefallen*]" (*WA* 1.47:270). Do the young men dressed as women please themselves, or each other? The links from trans-vestitism and Italy to homosexuality suggest that Goethe's essay on cross-dressing on the Roman stage point in the direction of a rewriting of gender that will be so dramatic that it will escape the binary thinking of hetero-sexuality.

Goethe's essay seems to emphasize that gender is a performed and per-formative discourse. In this light, the revelation that the second-string actors sometimes reveal their biological sex loses much of its sting: "it is undeni-able that Columbine sometimes cannot completely hide her blue beard" (*WA* 1.47:271). Admittedly, Goethe refers to this situation as a problem, but is it not possible that the obvious artificiality of their performance of women actually strengthens Goethe's point about the presence of mimesis on the stage rather than nature?

If the second-rate actors accidentally reveal the arbitrariness of the signifiers of gender, even the good cross-dressing actors seem to support Butler's analysis that drag shows that gender structures are always already parodic and imitative. Consciously, the actors avidly want to appropriate femininity and rid themselves of their masculinity: "They observe the de-meanor, the movement, the behavior of women most exactly; they attempt to imitate them . . . ; in short, they attempt to rid themselves of their own sex as much as possible" (*WA* 1.47:271). The second-rate actors show gender up by failing to hide their beards, but even the best actors always remain "art," showing up gender by reiterating it.

It is possible, therefore, to see Goethe's essay on cross-dressing in a feminist, as well as a misogynist, light. The essay points to an eighteenth-century awareness of the arbitrariness of the signification of gender, which allows for the possibility of change. It is true that while Goethe argues that men, through their distance from women, can study the essence of femininity better than women, who merely are women, he does not make an explicit counterclaim: that women, from a distance, could perform masculinity more accurately than men.

However, one of his favorite actresses in Weimar, Christiane Becker, née Neumann (also known as "Euphrosyne") frequently played men's roles in the 1790s. Goethe listed "disguised pants roles" (*verkleidete Mannsrollen*) as one of her specialties (*WA* 1.36:245). In 1791, for instance, she played a certain "Arthur" quite to Goethe's satisfaction (*WA* 1.35:19). In 1794, she not only played the role of Jakob in Iffland's *Old and New Time* (*Alte und neue Zeit*), but she actually delivered a prologue to the play, written by Goethe, in which she drew attention to her cross-dressing: "I'm supposed to be Jacob? a boy?" (*WA* 1.13.1:164). Thus, biographically at least, Goethe saw a role for women to expose the artifice of masculinity by playing men's roles.

If Goethe fails to make the claim that men can learn about their gender through cross-dressed women in his essay on Italian transvestites, he makes precisely this claim in *Wilhelm Meister*, completed not too long after the essay on cross-dressing. In *Wilhelm Meister*, Goethe carries on the experiment of determining whether cross-dressed female characters can show Wilhelm Meister how masculinity functions, allowing him to learn to perform his gender. Wilhelm Meister learns to become a husband and father from a series of cross-dressed women: Mariane, Mignon, Natalie, and Therese. The Tower Society's treatment of Wilhelm makes clear that it believes that Wilhelm's lovesickness stems from his insufficient manliness. An important part of its program of socializing is its effort to develop his gender identity.

The most obvious symptom of Wilhelm's inadequate masculinity, in the mind of the Tower Society, is his fascination with transvestites of androgynous appeal. In the novel, androgynous, cross-dressed women exert a powerful attraction on the hero. Mariane's mannish attire lends her boyish good looks. Wilhelm tells Mariane that one of his first literary loves, Chlorinde in Torquato Tasso's *Jerusalem Liberated*, charmed him because of her androgynous nature (*HA* 7:26). Wilhelm's acquaintance, the Baroness, loves to disguise herself as a pageboy or a hunter (*HA* 7:188). One of the women to whom Wilhelm proposes, Therese, dresses frequently as a man, partly in order to impress the man whom she loves (*HA* 7:454–55). And the woman whom Wilhelm finally does marry, Natalie, has haunted him as "the lovely Amazon" (*HA* 7:235, 513) long before he knows her personally. Goethe's own era found even more of the female characters androgynous: Aurelie, according to Schiller, is destroyed by her own androgyny (letter to Goethe, July 2, 1796; Mandelkow 2:233), and even Philine, of all characters, is, according to Daniel Jenisch, author of the first book-length study of *Wilhelm Meister* (published in 1797), a "moral hermaphrodite" (79–80).

Fitting into this pattern as well, of course, is Wilhelm's attraction to Mignon, one of the most famous and influential androgynous and transvestite characters in German literature. Derks offers a whole list of cross-dressed characters who appeared in Mignon's wake in the early nineteenth century (413). Further demonstrating the character's iconicity, MacLeod has reprinted a charming gallery of wonderful nineteenth-century portraits of Mignon in her book *Embodying Ambiguity* (112–18). Although characters like Aurelie urge her to wear feminine clothing suitable for her sex, she insists on wearing boyish clothing. Neither Wilhelm (*HA* 7:91) nor the surgeon (*HA* 7:236–37) can determine her gender at first, while the narrator refers to her with pronouns of three different genders (MacLeod, *Embodying*; Aurnhammer 166). Her Italian heritage fits well with her cross-dressing, given Goethe's assertions about Italian habits at carnival.

In order to grasp the importance in the novel of transvestites, it is important that clothing too is a semiotic system, one that, according to Barthes, works along the lines of classical representation:

The woman of fashion is a collection of tiny, separate essences rather analogous to the character parts played by actors in classical theater; the analogy is not arbitrary, since Fashion presents the woman as a representation, in such a way that a simple attribute of the person, spoken in the form of an adjective, actually absorbs the person's entire being. (*The Fashion System* 254–55)

Fashion, according to this view, predates the emergence of that whole, coherent, organic entity "humanity" that was to have some special extra-linguistic residue of personality. Fashion belongs instead to classicism, that mentality that believed in transparent clothing codes that could easily tell the observer the class, gender, ethnicity, and nature of the wearer. In such a system, the transvestite confounds the established binarisms by refusing to refer smoothly either to "male" or "female." It is thus no surprise that, as we saw in the analysis of Friedel's *Letters on the Gallantries of Berlin* (1782) — in which the "warm" would signal their sexual proclivities with certain codes that were then appropriated by others — fashion, playing with clothing codes, would become part of the gay tradition. This tradition emerges at the end of the eighteenth century as "man" walks into view out of the rubble of classicism.

The many sumptuary laws proclaimed from the Middle Ages through the Enlightenment show that the classical era was not naive about representation. It knew that signs of clothing could be manipulated to disguise class or — increasingly more important — gender, but this possibility resulted in watchful vigilance rather than complete skepticism with regard to the system of representation. Jarno mirrors this mentality in *Wilhelm Meister* when he distinguishes between "dainty hermaphrodites [*artige Hermaphroditen*]" like the Baroness, who merely appear to be men but do not possess manly virtues, and "real amazons [*wahre Amazonen*]" (*HA* 7:439) like Therese, who both appear and act masculine. While he warns of the possibility of subverting and misusing the semantic system of clothing as signifier for character, he does not fundamentally attack the validity of the union between clothes, body, and characters (Neumann, "Ich bin gebildet," 51–52).

Jarno's assertion that he can distinguish not just between a cross-dressed woman and a biological man, but between artificial hermaphrodites and real amazons, is comparable to the Tower Society's belief that it can ensure that its pharmakon, its "Bildung," will cure and not poison. Just as the pharmakon disrupts the polarity between toxin and anti-toxin, the transvestite pharmaceutically confuses male and female. In her analysis of the frequent occurrence of drag shows in socially conservative institutions, Garber suggests these institutions are using transvestitism as "a version of the poison as its own remedy" (*Vested* 66). Like the pharmakon, the transvestite is, therefore, as the Cuban writer Severo Sarduy claims, a "metaphor for what writing really is" (cited in Garber, *Vested*, 150). Sarduy refers to the imperfect simulation of the transvestite here. By showing the distance between the signifier (a woman in drag, say) and the signified (who is "really" a man), the transvestite foregrounds representation in a way that challenges the notion of a perfectly transparent language. The Tower Society is playing with poison when it plays with cross-dressers: transvestitism is a symbol for the breakdown of an entire semiotic system, yet the Tower Society hopes to manage it successfully in order to cure the system.

The Tower Society's use of medicine in its work with transvestites is additional evidence pointing to the pharmaceutical nature of the cross-dresser in *Wilhelm Meister*. Garber points out that frequently in transvestitism the doctor is "the ultimate agent of discovery" (*Vested* 203). In *Wilhelm Meister*, Mignon is afraid to see the surgeon about her arm because "he had thought she was a boy" (*HA* 7:236–37). Actually, everyone knows about Mignon's gender status at this point except for the Tower Society: Jarno scornfully calls her a hermaphrodite and the surgeon thinks she is a boy. But once the Tower Society fixes her gender as a girl passing for a boy, it uses her for its own gender constructions. Indeed, although it pathologizes her condition, regarding her as a upas or kind of poison, it also medicalizes her in the sense that it turns her into a kind of medicine, a pharmakon. Despite her noxious androgyny she becomes, like all the mannish women in the *Apprenticeship*, part of Wilhelm's cure.

Most of the transvestites in *Wilhelm Meister* are like Mignon in that they go from female to male. Goethe almost certainly knew of some of the many examples of such behavior in the eighteenth century, which was fairly common and becoming threatening to society. As MacLeod notes, such eighteenth-century fashion journals as the *Journal des Dames* and the *Journal des Luxus und der Moden* report on the increasing popularity of men's clothes for women (*Embodying* 92). These fashions provoked reactions. Whereas medieval and renaissance sumptuary laws had been directed primarily at members of the bourgeoisie who attempted to dress in a way that was above their station, eighteenth-century laws tended to target women who dressed as men. While there was some admiration for women who were forced to take on a man's role in order to survive (Vicinus 436–37), female-to-male cross-dressers were increasingly seen as dangerous or at least unsettling to the gender constructions developing in the era (Straub). In England there were fifteen cases of women prosecuted for impersonating men between 1761 and 1815 (Faderman 58). In Paris, an ordinance of 1800 strictly forbade female-to-male cross-dressing (Garber, *Vested*, 153). And in Germany, Catharina Margarethe Linck had been executed in 1721 for impersonating a man and marrying a woman (Faderman 51; Vicinus 439). Goethe's interest in the "gynocracy" of the "Bohemian Amazons" and the attendant male revolution against that assertion of power by women (*WA* 1.42:93–94) suggests his awareness of the anxieties that female insubordination could cause.

When the women in the novel cross-dress, they generally seem to take on male characteristics that go beyond clothing. Thus, at the beginning of the *Apprenticeship*, when Mariane enters her room dressed as an officer and confronts her servantwoman about the choice of her lover, she is her most obstreperous and least ladylike. As Mariane puts aside her phallic "sword and plumed hat" (*HA* 7:9)—the same accessories that Mephisto will wear, incidentally—Barbara, the servantwoman, seizes the initiative and attempts to change her charge into a woman by changing her wardrobe: "I have to see to it that you are soon in a long dress again . . . I hope that you will apologize, as a girl, for the harm you did me as a flighty officer: off with that coat and with everything underneath it. It's an uncomfortable costume, and dangerous for you, I see" (*HA* 7:10).

Barbara clearly believes that Mariane is developing manly qualities by wearing men's clothes. When Mariane subsequently contemplates her own heroic behavior in the face of rejection by a world that does not understand her illegitimate child, she agrees with Barbara that male character traits deserve masculine attire: "Don't I deserve to appear in men's clothing today? Haven't I been bold?" (*HA* 7:480). Mariane's question implies that men's clothes are a reward for particularly courageous behavior. Similarly, the Beautiful Soul is pleased that her father considers her almost a son (*HA* 7:360) and she is proud of her "manly defiance" (*HA* 7:379). Later in the novel, Therese apologizes to Wilhelm that her men's clothing is "unfortunately . . . only a costume" (*HA* 7:446). The novel presents the aspirations of these women to manliness as something to be proud of. This positive assessment of masculinity in women is generally what explains the affirmative treatment that some women who cross-dressed as men received in the eighteenth century. Many eighteenth-century thinkers such as, for instance, Kant, found it understandable that a woman would try to live as a man, because they assumed that everyone agreed that men were naturally better (Schiebinger 230).

The novel puts clear limits on these aspirations, however. Natalie, a wealthy and powerful "Amazon," could seriously destabilize the gender structures that, as shall be seen, the Tower Society is constructing. Therese's more overt cross-dressing, which first appeals to Wilhelm but which he then rejects, stands as an implicit warning, perhaps to Natalie and certainly to readers that women must not take their desires to become men too seriously, lest they be relegated to also-rans in the marriage contest.

The relationship between Natalie and Therese stands in a hallowed tradition going back at least to Shakespeare, an author who was of course immensely important for Goethe and whose works play important roles in *Wilhelm Meister*. Writing about similar structures in *Twelfth Night*, in which Olivia is, like Natalie, a strong, independent woman, and Viola, like Therese, is a parody of a woman trying to be a man, Jean Howard notes that "the figure of the male-attired woman [is] used to enforce a gender system that is challenged in other contexts by that figure" (432). Therese's presence suggests that mobility is possible on the gender continuum, but that too much of a good thing is not desirable. Her own manliness points to the Tower Society's belief that it can manage its poisons, using such potentially dangerous behavior salubriously.

Under the management of the Tower Society, cross-dressing loses much of its potentially transgressive power. MacLeod notes that those androgyne women, like Mariane and Mignon, whom Wilhelm knows prior to his encounter with the Tower Society, fade away, "leaving the male hero with his experience of enlightenment" (*Embodying* 138). The amazonian women—like Therese, Natalie, and the Beautiful Soul, who are within the orbit of the Tower Society—are androgynous only in an abstract way, allowing them "to lead the lives expected of them in the patriarchal *Turmgesellschaft* without any apparent contradiction" (*Embodying* 138). Their cross-dressing underscores the centrality of masculinity rather than putting gender categories into doubt. It limns the borders of masculinity and serves primarily to raise Wilhelm as a proper young man.

Male-to-female cross-dressing was also an important phenomenon in the eighteenth century, and not just on the Roman stage. Edward Hyde, Lord Cornbury and the colonial governor of New York and New Jersey from 1702 to 1708, dressed as a woman, apparently in order to represent his relative and sovereign, Queen Anne (Garber, *Vested*, 53). His behavior attributes great power to the ability of clothes to represent concepts like the monarchy even across the barrier of gender. More sensational still was the Chevalier d'Eon, born in 1728, who was, according to Garber, "the most famous transvestite in Western history." Born a man and trained as a spy, d'Eon cross-dressed until the English judicial courts and French royal court required that his gender identity be fixed. It was decided he was a woman. At the time, the world was astonished that a woman had passed as a man so long; when, however, d'Eon died in 1810 and the surgeon determined that he had anatomically normal male genitals, the world—including the surgeon and d'Eon's female companion, Mrs. Cole—was just as surprised to discover that a man had passed as a woman for so long (Kates; Garber 265; Bullough, *Sexual Variance*, 488–90). So spectacular was d'Eon's story that Havelock Ellis wanted to name the phenomenon of cross-dressing "eonism."

Goethe mentioned the Chevalier in a letter to his wife (September 23, 1814; *WA* 4.25:41), but there were other cross-dressers even closer to home. The author of *Kyllenion: A Year in Arcadia*, August, the Duke of Sachsen-Gotha and Altenburg, with whom, as mentioned in Chapter 2, Goethe had some contact and with whose older relatives Goethe had been quite close in the 1790s, dressed in women's clothes at his court (Derks 413). As mentioned earlier, in a coded way Goethe refers somewhat negatively to the Duke's proclivities when he complains about him as "problematic," "effeminate," and "pleasant yet disgusting" (*WA* 1.36:34).

Goethe's veiled contempt for the young Duke August suggests that he may have associated cross-dressing with emasculation. In any case, male-to-female cross-dressing in his fictional works (as opposed to his essay on the Italian stage) is often portrayed negatively. While many of the female characters in *Wilhelm Meister* aspire to male virtues by wearing masculine clothes, the male characters do not explicitly reciprocate so often. This would make sense if the role of female-to-male cross-dressers is to state allegorically the qualities of masculinity so than a young man like Wilhelm, uncertain of his gender, can learn the difference between men and women. Transvestism becomes an act done in the service of teaching gender. The closest thing to overt male transvestitism takes place in Wilhelm's mind when he sees Philine with a young person in an officer's uniform, who he somewhat irrationally assumes is his long-lost mistress Mariane. Although he saw a man, he cries out: "let us see the disguised girl!" (*HA* 7:337). In fact, the "girl" is Friedrich, dressed up as a girl dressed up as an officer. The Shakespearean quality of the multiple disguises points, incidentally, to the archaism in Friedrich's character that manifests itself in his Baroque "foolishness" as well. It is also, as MacLeod notes, a wonderful example of advanced cross-dressing—dressing up as a cross-dresser. This motif will return when we look at Lichtenberg's fragments.

Otherwise, to find male characters in Goethe's oeuvre who explicitly don female attributes one must leave the *Apprenticeship* and turn to, for instance, *Faust*, where the move is associated with shame. When Mephistopheles adopts the appearance of the Phorkyas he worries that he will be called "hermaphroditic!" (*Faust* 8029; *HA* 3:343). Similarly, in the Classical Walpurgisnacht, Thales expresses concern about the ambivalent gender of Homunculus: "Unless I err, there is another problem: / He seems to be hermaphroditic" [*Auch scheint es mir von andrer Seite kritisch: / Er ist, mich dünkt, hermaphroditisch*] (*Faust* 8255–56; *HA* 3:250). This negative portrayal of male-to-female sex changes shows that Goethe's gender continuum—like that of many writers—often seems slanted against women. While it may be advantageous for women to don male clothing, it is shameful for men to lose their gender identity.

Wilhelm, however, benefits from the cross-dressing of the female characters because he can specularly identify with their androgyny and learn masculinity from them. Thus he loves Mariane, dressed as an officer, because she mirrors, or to use Goethe's word, "echoes," him (*HA* 7:57). Similarly his mirror relationship with Mignon allows him to explore a whole range of emotions, variously identifiable as female, childish, or poetic. Further indication that Wilhelm mirrors these cross-dressed women is his attempt, identical to their own, to achieve masculinity by dressing up as a "real" man, the Count. The Baroness, who enjoys dressing up as "a page boy, or a huntsman" (*HA* 7:188), encourages Wilhelm to follow her example and dress up as the Count. At this point in his development, he is therefore in a situation similar to the women, who are aspiring to manly power by wearing male clothing. The difference of course is that Wilhelm will be able to become a man.

The use of the semiotics and didactics of drag to allow Wilhelm to become a man is clearest in his relationship with Natalie, whom he first sees dressed in her (obviously male) uncle's coat, for which reason he calls her the lovely Amazon through most of the novel. When he first sees her he is lying wounded, tended by his similarly wounded mirror-image, Mignon, and Philine, who serves as a caring nurturing maternal figure (*HA* 7:224–25). He is thus in a childlike state of undifferentiated gender, mirroring androgynous characters, and happy to view the woman with a man's coat as an androgynous Amazon, or to speak psychoanalytically, a mother with a phallus.[1] Natalie, however, attempts to show him the importance of shedding his androgynous nature and becoming a man by handing him her phallus or avuncular coat (*HA* 7:228). With this move she reveals herself as woman and dresses him up as a man.

The Tower Society uses Wilhelm's interest in androgynous characters to attract him to women like Natalie and allow him to develop the masculinity they desire for him, which demonstrates the basic homeopathic structure of the Tower Society's cures. For the Tower Society's male "patients," whose telos is manhood, this strategy offers great possibilities: they can move, via the symbolism of drag, from self-identification with androgynous women to self-identification as men. Cross-dressing becomes the mechanism through which Wilhelm can use a series of women for his own individuation and development. This makes his story of becoming a man a rich one, full of psychological complexity, while at the same time it clearly relegates the position of the female to that of a stage that one goes through.

The Tower Society thus uses the transvestite "as a figure for development, progress, or a 'stage of life,'" a strategy that Garber considers "to a large extent a refusal to confront the extraordinary power of transvestitism to disrupt, expose, and challenge" (*Vested* 16). Garber repeatedly calls this looking through rather than at the transvestite (*Vested* 150); the attitude corresponds to the notion of a transparent signifying system. Goethe, in his essay on women's roles in the Roman theater, shows his awareness of looking at the transvestite as an artistic phenomenon; the Tower Society is not so astute, however. Just as the Tower Society believes it can manage the pharmaka of art and language to get the cures it wants, so it attempts to use androgyny and cross-dressing to develop a strong man. Goethe's essay and his novel *Wilhelm Meister* know more than the Tower Society. These works know that the Tower Society's use of cross-dressing as a pharmakon points out the constructed status of gender.

1. Eissler 2:205; Kittler, "Wilhelm Meister," 51; Neumann, "'Ich bin gebildet,'" 51.

7

MALE MEMBERS

Ganymede, Prometheus, Faust

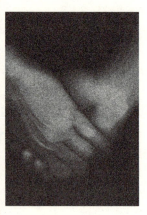

Two of the bits of Faustian flotsam and jetsam that wash
up occasionally on literate shores for use in the general
press, "the Faustian bargain" and "the eternal feminine,"
reflect the story's masculine origins and Goethe's addition
of the feminine to that legacy. A queer reading of Goethe's
Faust further uncovers the gender biases in Goethe's writing. It shows that despite the desire of his male characters
to attain a kind of femininity, they can never escape their
man-to-man world. The interaction between the men in
this masculine world, however, destabilizes traditional
gender categories to the point that Goethe's gender biases
deconstruct themselves.

The entire Faust tradition, beginning long before
Goethe, has always contained a bargain or deal, usually a
male-male affair. The resonance of Goethe's addition of the
feminine to the masculine Faustian world is audible in the
common currency of the phrase "eternal feminine," along
with the popularity of Margarete, whose tragedy within
the drama has captured the sympathy of countless readers
since its first publication. In adding the feminine to the
Faustian tradition, Goethe does not, however, displace the
male-male dynamics of the pact. Instead, he establishes
a triangle of desire that confounds and upsets traditional
gender dichotomies: Faust's masculine desire for the eternal feminine must be routed through the male Mephistopheles, in the process putting into question the nature of
male and female. A queer reading of *Faust* thereby points

to the discursive nature of gender and emphasizes Goethe's interest in the masculine.

Goethe's lifelong interest in questions of gender make clear why he would turn to the masculine Faust tradition and add to it the feminine. Although many examples from his oeuvre might serve as well, "Prometheus" and "Ganymede" provide a useful example of how Goethe consistently directs male desire for the feminine through other men. Throughout his life, Goethe linked "Prometheus" to other literary works he composed entirely or in part between 1773 and 1775, writings such as "Ganymede" and *Faust* (*HA* 1:483–85; *HA* 3:477–78). Concerning "Prometheus," Goethe wrote to his friend Carl Friedrich Zelter on May 11, 1820: "I refrain from any comparison; but note that an important part of *Faust* also comes from this time" (*WA* 4.33:28). While he intended these linkages to block radical political receptions of "Prometheus," they also underscore a series of fundamental dichotomies in Goethe's thinking. Ever since Goethe published "Ganymede" and "Prometheus" together in 1789, the two poems have embodied for critics opposing yet complementary postures toward the world, with "Ganymede" seen as dissolution of the self and "Prometheus" as an assertion of the self. As Drux writes, "Prometheus" traditionally manifests the Goethean concepts of "systole," "concentration," and "self-assertion," while "Ganymede" is said to promote "diastole," "expansion," and "selflessness" (24). Often critics see "Ganymede" and "Prometheus" as exemplifying, respectively, the feminine and masculine as well.[1] Goethe, however, flatly disrupts these elegant bifurcations, because both Ganymede and Prometheus are male. A gendered analysis, in fact, conflates the binary oppositions of the two poems into a single masculinity, striving, but unable to represent the feminine and construct a larger dichotomy.

On the pronominal level, "Prometheus" (*HA* 1:44–46) strongly asserts identity, from its elision of the "you" in the opening lines to its resounding, self-confident line, "As I" [*Wie ich*] (line 58). The Promethean strength found in grammar carries over to other areas as well. In the first stanza, Prometheus alludes to the hut he has built and the fire he has created, pointing to his own technological prowess. In the fourth stanza, he refers to his victory over the Titans and his escape from death and slavery, claiming for himself freedom and autonomy. Not surprisingly for an eighteenth-century bourgeois fantasy, this assertive, technologically gifted, free self is also male. The speaker's masculinity emerges in references to his unfulfilled "Boyish-morning / Flower-

1. Heller 100; Lugowski 115; Rolf Christian Zimmermann 2:158–61.

dreams" [*Knabenmorgen / Blütenträume*] (lines 50–51). While these boyhood dreams were in the past, the speaker makes clear that now it is Zeus who is boyish: "And practice, like a boy" (line 3) while time and fate have initiated him into manhood: "Has not all-powerful time / Forged me to a man, / And eternal Fate" [*Hat nicht mich zum Manne geschmiedet / Die allmächtige Zeit / Und das ewige Schicksal*] (lines 43–45). This linkage of a powerfully asserted self and autonomous, technological strength with outspoken masculinity suggests why critics have frequently connected the Promethean with the masculine.

This masculinity, however, goes beyond Zeus' castratory ability to chop off the tops of oak trees and mountains, an ability that Prometheus belittles by comparing it to playing with thistles. The last stanza also shows that the poem's strongly asserted "I" is fertile enough to produce his own descendants when it refers to Prometheus creating human beings after his own image. This passage reflects eighteenth-century thinking that came to German via Herder from Shaftesbury about the metaphorical meaning of Prometheus as a poet who is a kind of god, a "second maker." Goethe's familiarity with this tradition is indicated by his essay on Shakespeare, written in the same years as "Prometheus," in which he compared Shakespeare to Prometheus as a maker of humans: "He competed with Prometheus, forming humans in his image trait by trait" (*HA* 12:227).[2] The allusion to Prometheus is graphic enough to retain the strength of its literal image: a man creating other human beings without procreating. Besides male parthenogenesis, the Promethean plenitude includes the ability to still pains and quiet tears—maternal rather than paternal characteristics. Indeed, even Prometheus' technical inventions, home and hearth, belong to the feminine sphere. The Promethean masculinity thus attempts to transcend the traditionally male to incorporate or appropriate the generative, nurturing, healing characteristics of the feminine.

In stark grammatical contrast to "Prometheus," "Ganymede" (*HA* 1:46–47) positions the "You" prominently, from the emphatic *Du* of the poem's second line to its final lines, ending in the second person with an elided "I." Whereas "Prometheus" had defiantly asserted the identity of its speaker, "Ganymede" is a poem of self-dissolution. Correspondingly, while "Prometheus" celebrates the autonomous individual, "Ganymede" speaks of a porous, vulnerable individual into whose body the spring's warmth, the flowers, and the grass all force their way (*sich drängen* is the verb). Recurrently,

2. See Drux 11–12 and also Pizer.

outside forces, such as the nightingale's music that calls toward him and the clouds, have an effect on Ganymede. Whereas Prometheus acts, Ganymede is a passive object of actions, penetrated by the spring and nature. Ganymede's selflessness and porousness contribute to the "feminization" that some critics have noted in the hymn.[3] Specifically, this passivity has led to a critical understanding of Ganymede as the feminine object of masculine, divine love. The rape or rapture of Ganymede could then be seen Neoplatonically as the story of the soul rising to God, or a fable with a moral having to do with a passive openness to penetrating divine powers.[4] Goethe could have learned of such interpretations via his mystical studies of Pietism and alchemy, traditions that relied heavily on Neoplatonic thinking (Rolf Christian Zimmermann 1:205). In this interpretation, the "Ganymedic" can express the selflessness, vulnerability, and openness that humans need to experience divine and spiritual forces.

Just as interpretations that claim Prometheus' ability to create his own descendants point to the poet's ability to create new worlds ignore the literal idea of male pregnancy, the refashioning of the rape of Ganymede into the story of a feminized soul rising to God dismisses any discussion of male homosexuality from the scholarly discourse. Since Ganymede is a boy, however, the relationship between Ganymede and Zeus is of course a male-male one. The subject matter gives the critics pause: "But remarkable," exclaims one, "the spring is the male beloved, not the female beloved [*der Geliebte, nicht die Geliebte*]" (Conrady 229). In the first sentence of his essay, another critic suggests avoiding the issue entirely: "One should first attempt to visualize this hymn without putting its name all-too-powerfully in the front field" (Lugowski 103). The limited amount of new scholarship on the subject is just as reticent: as recently as 1985, Pietzcker writes: "But Ganymede is not much more than a name here" (*Trauma* 21).

While Goethe was certainly familiar with Neoplatonic thinking, he did not feel the need to interpret the sexual out of his symbolic purview. Alongside the edifying, Neoplatonic, interpretation another tradition, almost as old as the myth itself, has flourished, a tradition that adduced the Ganymede story as a defense of a noncritically understood homosexuality (Barkan 29). Plato asserts that the Cretans were already using the "chartering power" of this myth: "And you know it is our universal accusation against the Cretans that they were the inventors of the tale of Ganymede; they were con-

3. Lugowski 115; Rolf Christian Zimmermann 2:158–61.
4. Panofsky 212–18; Baird-Lange 238–40; Saslow 59–62, 187–190.

vinced, we say, that their legislation came from Zeus, so they went on to tell this story against him that they might, if you please, plead his example for their indulgence in this pleasure too" (*The Collected Dialogues* 636d). In the Renaissance and in the eighteenth century, Ganymede had become a symbol for male-male desire, in whatever form it manifested itself in those eras, without allusions to transcendent meaning. In the Renaissance, Ganymede is a "part of homoerotic lexicography" and a phrase in the "vernacular of homoeroticism," according to Gregory Bredbeck (264, 267).

As for eighteenth-century Germany, we have already seen repeated examples of the use of Ganymede to carry homosexual meanings: Frederick the Great scandalously referred to the apostle John as a "Ganymede," the *Gallantries* described male prostitutes as "Ganymedes," and Wieland flirts with the subject matter in his poem "Juno and Ganymede," while the captain of the ship in *Agathon* attempts to seduce Psyche, calling her his "Ganymede." There is more evidence to support the sexual implications of the term: In 1773, in the foreword to his translation of Petronius' *Satyricon*, called in German *Begebenheiten des Encolp*, the novelist Wilhelm Heinse uses "Ganymede" to refer to the beloveds of the ancient Greeks: "Who would prove to the Greeks that the pleasures they take with beautiful Ganymedes should not have delighted them more than the pleasures with their women? Every person carries the measure of his own pleasure in his own breast."[5] The open-mindedness implicit in this statement is quite astonishing.

Goethe's allusions to the Ganymede story throughout his life indicate his awareness of this non-Neoplatonic tradition. In *Gods, Heroes, and Wieland* (*Götter, Helden und Wieland*, also composed in the early 1770s, incidentally), Merkurius expresses his desire to see Wieland with the following command: "And if he were Ganymede's tutor, he would still have to come to me" (*HA* 4:205). Given the slipperiness of the distinction between pedagogy and pederasty in the Greek tradition, calling Wieland Ganymede's teacher fit neatly into a text designed to tweak the older author's dignity. A charming Venetian Epigram of 1790 alludes to the sexual nature of Zeus' relationship with Ganymede:

Don't turn, dear child,
your little legs toward the sky;
Jupiter sees you, the rogue,
and Ganymede is worried.

5. Cited by Ulrichs, *Forschungen über das Räthsel der mannmännlichen Liebe. Inclusa*, 53.

[Kehre nicht, liebliches Kind,
die Beinchen hinauf zu dem Himmel;
Jupiter sieht dich, der Schalk,
und Ganymed ist besorgt.] (*WA* 1.1:317)

Goethe's subsequent translation of the passage in Benvenuto Cellini's autobiography in which the Italian artist defends sodomy with an allusion to Ganymede shows the translator's knowledge, at least by 1797, of the tradition equating Ganymede, quite non-Neoplatonically, with sodomy. Called a sodomite, Cellini retorts, in Goethe's translation: "Oh, you fool, I said, you've gone beyond the limit! But would God that I understood such a noble art; for we read that Jupiter practiced it with Ganymede, and on earth the greatest emperors and kings did the same; I however, as a lowly humble little person, wouldn't know how to behave in such a peculiar custom" (*WA* 1.44:196). Goethe was clearly quite familiar with the use of Ganymede as in apologies for male-male sexual desire.

Time spent demonstrating the awareness of Goethe and his era that Ganymede was a signifier of male-male sex is not idle provocation, but an important step in interpretation, because this knowledge makes clear that the poem "Ganymede" is not about a feminine loss of individuality, but rather a male imitation of femininity in the form of passive male sexuality toward other men. While Prometheus attempts to attain femininity through a phallic plenitude which allows for male mothering, Ganymede attempts to attain femininity through passive receptivity to male power. Thus, the apparent dichotomy between the Promethean and the Ganymedic pales in comparison to the unspoken dichotomy between masculine and feminine.

As suggested earlier, "Promethean" and "Ganymedic" are simply labels for attempts in Goethe's works at achieving the feminine through male-male relationships. Similar structures appear in Tasso's struggles with Antonio, which are a part of his love for Leonore von Este; in Werther's competition with Albert, which is a part of his love for Lotte; and perhaps even in Wilhelm's bonding with Lothario and other members of the Männerbund of the Tower Society as he graduates to the love of Natalie. Precisely this structure also appears in *Faust*, where an analysis emphasizing gender shows the collapse of the distinction between Mephistopheles and Faust into an eternal masculinity incapable, but desirous, of reaching the feminine.

The homoerotic has deep roots in the Faust tradition. The shadowy historical Faust was allegedly kicked out of several communities, not only because of his sorcery, but also because of shameful sodomitical acts. Rumors of Faust's perversity may have sparked Christopher Marlowe's interest in the subject, because Marlowe was interested in male-male sex and wrote *Edward II*, which Derek Jarman has convincingly rendered as a queer film. Thomas Mann's twentieth-century novel *Doktor Faustus* also has homosexual innuendoes, particularly in the relationship between Adrian Leverkühn and Rudi Schwerdtfeger. The homosexual touches to Goethe's *Faust* are thus par for the course.

In the eighteenth-century German world, Goethe was not the only author of a *Faust*. In addition to Lessing's *Faust*-fragment, Friedrich Maximilian Klinger wrote a *Faust*, which appeared in 1771. Sodomy shows up in this *Faust* often enough for the work to merit a mention in the "Bibliography of Homosexuality" published in the first *Yearbook for Sexual Intermediary Types* (1899). Admittedly, sodomy is not represented positively, but rather as part of a scathing anticlerical attack. The Pope offers indulgences for sodomy because he hopes that the money for the indulgences will pay for the cavalry, which, being particularly prone to the vice, will end up paying for itself (2:172). The Pope's son, Cesare Borgia, takes a youth for his own pleasure and writes, "never has a victor received a more charming Ganymede as booty, and, if lustful Jupiter still ruled, I would fear a dangerous and powerful rival" (2:177). Klinger's use of the Ganymede myth in his version of the Faust story hints that something brings the two traditions together. Eventually the Pope himself makes "certain proposals" to Satan, whereupon the Devil strikes him dead, making clear the nature of those proposals: "Sodomy [*Sodomie*] and the adoration of the Devil! By Satan, the ruler of the dark realm, a pope cannot go to Hell at a nicer time in his life" (2:183). Later the Devil tells Faust that his own son is being used in a similar way: "Your second son serves a prelate who uses youths for the same purposes that the Pope wanted to use me" (2:193).

Dichotomies between the Promethean and the Ganymedic as well as between the masculine and the feminine obviously play a role in the philosophy outlined in *Faust* and lead to the queer aspects of the play. Faust's famous speech to Wagner about the "two souls" in his breast (*HA* 3:41; lines 1112–18) shows, within one person, a pattern of polar opposites. While a simple structure of dual desires is the main point here, a very tentative linkage could be made between the Promethean self-assertion of the one soul that "hangs . . . on to the world" and the Ganymedic desire for rapture or ascension to another world expressed by the other soul that "violently rises . . . to the fields of high ancestors." Critics have tended to emphasize one or the other sides of Faust: Boyle sees him as Ganymede-like (1:222–24), Heller and Brown as Promethean (100, 185). The queer point is the conflation of these gendered dichotomies.

This admixture of the Ganymedic and the Promethean can be seen in many of the early scenes of *Faust*. In the scene "Night," for instance, Faust yearns in a Ganymedic way for a divine force that will penetrate him and fill his heart (*HA* 3:22–23; lines 434–81). Confronted by the spirits, however, he asserts his identity in a Promethean fashion (*HA* 3:24; lines 499–500). Faust's striving upward, although generally perceived as aggressive and thus fitting into the Promethean mode, overlaps in many ways with the Ganymedic desire for transcendence, as indicated in the use of *streben* ("to strive") in the ode as well as in the play. This demonstrates how closely entwined the concepts of Ganymedic and Promethean are.

Faust claims in his speech about the two souls in his unhappy breast that they want a divorce: "The one wants to separate from the other" (*HA* 3:41; line 1112). A close analysis of the play will show that while Faust can never sort out these categories, he develops the Promethean at the cost of the Ganymedic. When first making the pact with the devil, Faust's initially receptive posture — thrice asking Mephisto to enter (lines 1530–32) — exemplifies his early Ganymedic tendencies. Later, in "Dismal Day," Mephistopheles cleverly twists the question of who seduces and who is seduced, who penetrates and who is penetrated, when he asks: "Are we imposing [*aufdrängen*] on you, or you on us?" (*HA* 3:138). Faust passively receives Mephisto's penetrating visits, implying that Mephisto is the aggressor, but Faust also calls for those visits, implying that he arranges his own seduction. The spirit world's program of teaching Faust a more Promethean approach toward the world begins with the "spirit choir," which calls Faust "a titan" and "powerful among the sons of earth" (*HA* 3:54–55; lines 1612, 1617–18), titles appropriate for Prometheus. As ironic as these lines are, they point to Mephisto's plan to instruct Faust in a more phallically penetrating attitude toward women and men. He teaches Faust to drive "right into the heart of things" [*recht ins Innere*] (*HA* 3:97; line 3047) by seducing Margarete. Near the beginning of this process of seduction, he introduces Faust to the art of entering rooms by bringing the newly rejuvenated scholar into Margarete's chamber. In the room, Faust's masculine daydreams of a paternal throne (*Väterthron*; *HA* 3:87; line 2697) reveal his incipient phallic desires. After Mephisto has taught Faust to seduce Margarete, he teaches him how to use phallic instruments for the less romantic penetration of men. He has Faust pull out his "sword" (*Flederwisch*, literally "duster"; *HA* 3:118; line 3706) in order to fight Valentin.

Valentin, who is concerned with Margarete's lost virginity, most painfully when he calls her a whore (*HA* 3:118; line 3730), is certainly aware of the phallic nature of Faust's intrusions.

Throughout the play's second part, Faust gains more and more control over the phallic idiom. Act 1, at the beginning of part 2, reveals that considerable anxiety about the breakdown of distinctions between the masculine and the feminine still exists. This anxiety manifests itself in the Chancellor's rejection of "Doubt" as an hermaphrodite (*Zwitterkind*; *HA* 3:154; line 4902). It also shows up in the discussion of gender in the masquerade called *Mummenschanz*, exemplified for instance by the flower girls' essentialist statement on the nature of women: "For women's nature / Is so closely related to art" [*Denn das Naturell der Frauen / Ist so nah mit Kunst verwandt*] (*HA* 3:159; lines 5105–6). The Herald, too, is concerned about gender when he tells Boy Charioteer that "One could shame you by calling you a girl" (*HA* 3:173; line 5548). Such concern turns out to be justified when Mephistopheles, disguised as Greed, changes from female to male (*HA* 3:176; line 5665). This concern about gender reflects the transitional nature of gender at this point in the play, as Faust develops toward the Promethean and Mephisto develops toward the Ganymedic, both of which tendencies become increasingly evident in *Faust II*.

Faust's increasingly Promethean, phallic stance becomes clear when one follows the phallic symbols. In act 1, for instance, Faust receives "the little thing" [*das kleine Ding*] (*HA* 3:193; line 6261), the all-important key to the mothers, which, as Bennett notes, shares with the male member the property of growing when it is handled (83). Shortly after the Herald strikes Mephistopheles, he lends his staff to Faust, who is dressed as Plutus:

How it flashes and explodes,
      sprays forth sparks!
The staff, it's already glowing.

[Wie's blitzt und platzt, in Funken sprüht!
Der Stab, schon ist er angeglüht.] (*HA* 3:178; lines 5743–44)

In act 4, the kaiser refuses to give Mephistopheles the general's staff, preferring to lend it to Faust: "The staff I cannot grant you / You do not seem to me to be the right man" [*Den Stab kann ich dir nicht verleihen, / Du scheinst mir nicht der rechte Mann*] (*HA* 3:322; lines 10703–4). Mephistopheles responds to this slight to his manhood with sour grapes: "May the stumpy staff protect him!" [*Mag ihn der stumpfe Stab beschützen!*] (*HA* 3:322; line

10707). Notwithstanding the aspersions Mephistopheles casts on the size of Faust's masculinity, by this point the trend is clear that Faust is becoming more phallic and thus more Promethean. By act 5, Faust's Bildung to a phallic Promethean outlook on life has reached the point that, like Prometheus, he is creating new worlds, although sometimes with criminal means.

In contrast to Faust, Mephistopheles begins the play as a phallic presence. In the "Prologue in Heaven" he assertively introduces himself, attacking God just as Prometheus did to Zeus. When he intrudes into the receptive Faustian study, he comes bedecked in phallic symbols, "The cock's plume in his hat / With a long, sharp rapier" (HA 3:52; lines 1538–39). In this garb, incidentally, he is somewhat reminiscent of Mariane in Wilhelm Meister, who also wears "a feather hat and a rapier" (HA 7:9). Before Faust has sat on his paternal throne in Margarete's room, Mephistopheles sits on the throne in the witch's kitchen holding a phallic scepter:

Here I sit
　　　like the King on the throne,
I hold the scepter here,
　　　only the crown is lacking.

[Hier sitz' ich
　　　wie der König auf dem Throne,
Den Zepter halt' ich hier,
　　　es fehlt nur noch die Krone.] (HA 3:79; lines 2448–49)

In this feminine space Faust becomes entranced with the image of femininity, "the most beautiful image of a woman!" [Das schönste Bild von einem Weib!] (HA 3:78; line 2436). Mephistopheles insists, however, on respect for the trappings of his masculinity: "Don't you have more respect for the red leggings? / Can't you recognize the cock's feather anymore?" [Hast du vorm roten Wams nicht mehr Respekt? / Kannst du die Hahnenfeder nicht erkennen?] (HA 3:80; lines 2485–86). Mephistopheles tries to convince Faust to ride phallic broomsticks to the Walpurgisnacht party (line 3835), where the coarse old witch vulgarly praises the size of his endowment (lines 4140–43). In "Dismal Day," Mephistopheles echoes the Promethean scorn of the supposedly divine ability to throw lightning bolts and provoke storms: "Are you grasping for thunder? Good that it wasn't given to you miserable mortals! To dash the innocent passers-by, that is such a tyrannical nature to let off steam in one's weakness" (HA 3:138).

While Mephistopheles is primarily mocking Faust's undirected and helpless rage, his argument contains a secondary critique—reminiscent of Prometheus—of the gods in general who use their strength to punish the innocent tyrannically. Finally, appearing in the *Mummenschanz* as "Greed," Mephistopheles seems to emphasize his masculinity by undergoing a sex change from female avarice to male greed and declaring: "Am of the male sex, Greed!" (*HA* 3:178; line 5665). In this scene, he parades his masculinity even more outrageously by molding gold into offensive figurines, presumably penises (*HA* 3:179; lines 5781–94).

But perhaps Mephistopheles protests too much: despite his dirty statues and assertions of masculinity, he no longer controls the phallic symbols in act 1. Indeed, as early as "Night," in Margarete's room, where Faust learns of the "throne of the fathers," Mephistopheles, not his pupil, cries out, twice, "Enter" (*Herein*; *HA* 3:86; line 2684). When he appears in the *Mummenschanz* as Zoilo-Thersites, Mephistopheles receives a blow from the Herald's phallic rod: "So upon you, you raggedy dog, let fall / a master stroke of the pious staff" [*So treffe dich, du Lumpenhund, / Des frommen Stabes Meisterstreich!*] (*HA* 3:171; lines 5471–72). Similarly, after his escapade with the gold figurines, the Herald drives him away with his "Staff" (*HA* 3:179; line 5796). Obscenely well endowed in the first Walpurgisnacht, in the Classical Walpurgisnacht he, as Phorkyas, worries about the accusation of hermaphroditism: "They call me, oh shame!, hermaphroditical" [*Man schilt mich nun, o Schmach, Hermaphroditen*] (line 8029). (Incidentally, the same verb, *schelten*, is used for this statement and for the reproach that Boy Charioteer could be called a girl, linking the fates of the two characters.) Throughout *Faust II*, Mephistopheles becomes increasingly emasculated and feminized. He continues his female impersonation in the play's final act, when Faust wants the property of Philemon and Baucis and Mephisto acquires it for his master with illicit means. Mephistopheles refers to the Biblical story of Naboth's vineyard to explain his role: According to the metaphor, Baucis and Philemon are Naboth, who loses his vineyard, Faust is King Ahab, and Mephistopheles takes on the role of Isabel, the King's beloved, who arranges the immoral take-over (*HA* 3:340; lines 11286–87).

Increasing evidence of Mephisto's sexual interest in men accompanies his loss of masculinity. Subtle traces of this queer sexuality manifest themselves in Mephisto's overly warm descriptions to Helen of the beauty of Faust. Asked about his appearance, Mephisto, as Phorkyas, replies:

. . . I do like him.
He is a cheerful, bright, well-built,

and unusual for the Greeks,
    an understanding man.

[. . . mir gefällt er schon.
Es ist ein munterer, kecker, wohlgebildeter,
Wie unter Griechen wenig',
    ein verständiger Mann.] (*HA* 3:272; lines 9010–12)

To Helen's attendants, Mephisto-Phorkyas describes Faust's entourage as a "fresh, golden-locked bevy of boys. / Youth itself!" [*goldgelockte, frische Bubenschar. / Die duften Jugend!*] (*HA* 3:273; lines 9044–45). These fairly innocent indications of Mephisto's susceptibility to male beauty become much more obvious in the final scene, after the angels shower him with rose petals. He wants to kiss the angels: "You're so pretty, verily I want to kiss you!" [*Ihr seid so hübsch, fürwahr ich möcht' euch küssen*] (*HA* 3:354; line 11771). He tries to turn the reproach of queer sexuality around by claiming that the heavenly forces are worse than the hellish ones because the angels seduce both men and women (*HA* 3:354; lines 11780–83). He thereby implies that the devils seduce only women, but his come-hither calls to one angel in particular belie his words: "You, tall boy, you I like most of all" [*Dich, langer Bursche, dich mag ich am liebsten leiden*] (*HA* 3:355; line 11794). Mephisto's interest in the "members" (*Glieder*) of the angels points additional to his appreciation of male beauty:

. . . so come down,
Move the blessed members a bit more secularly.

[. . . so senkt euch nieder,
Ein bißchen weltlicher bewegt
    die holden Glieder] (*HA* 3:354; lines 11787–88)

By this point, the formerly phallic Mephistopheles has become as receptive and Ganymedic as the formerly receptive Faust has become phallic and Promethean.

The see-saw relationship between Faust and Mephistopheles reflects the Goethean structure—already seen in the poems "Ganymede" and "Prometheus"—of two forms of masculinity, each approaching the feminine from a different perspective and playing against the other in order to achieve a more complete femininity. While a discovery of the Ganymedic within the Promethean and vice versa unsettles the dichotomy between Mephisto and Faust, it might seem to strengthen the one between the masculine and feminine. As Avital Ronell has Margarete say to Ernst Jünger in a discussion that also includes Marguerite Duras: "I was the excluded negativity that made it possible for you to displace virility" (*Crack Wars* 157). The truly feminine figures — Margarete and Helen — are excluded by their effacement as the generalized "eternal feminine," so that the passive Ganymedic and the virile Promethean, like Faust and Mephistopheles, can intertwine. Jürgen Flimm, in his 1983 production of *Faust* in Cologne, seems to have captured the exclusion of the feminine from the male-male relationship between Mephistopheles and Faust. The theater critic C. Bernd Sucher wrote: "Gretchen interests this Faust from Cologne much less than Mephisto" (14).

Yet, this phallocentric view of the world ends up deconstructing itself. The angelic exclamation, "Saved is the noble member" (*Gerettet ist das edle Glied*; *HA* 3:359; line 11934), reveals how Faust's discourse, while remaining trapped in the masculine, undermines the distinctions between the Promethean and the Ganymedic. By the play's conclusion, Faust's drive to become more Promethean has been so successful that his "immortal part" (*Unsterbliches*) is nothing but a "member" (*Glied*). *Glied* can mean "limb," of course, and chaste ears may choose to hear that meaning in Mephisto's infatuation with the "members" (*Glieder*) of the angels. But Goethe is bawdy enough that the word could mean "male sexual organ" in both passages, especially when one recalls Mephisto's parodic line "Saved are the noble devil's parts [*Gerettet sind die edlen Teufelsteile*]" (*HA* 3:355; line 11812), uttered just after Mephisto has withstood the homoerotic temptation of the angels. *Glied* is at the same time "Faust's immortal part," so the word is also linked via the concept of soul to the Promethean goal of identity. In becoming a "member," Faust's Promethean, phallic striving reaches a climax.

Here a little philology is helpful. Somewhat disapprovingly, because he sees the original meaning of the word as "joint," Adelung lists the male member as one of the meanings of *Glied*: "In a somewhat less appropriate way, the male member [*das männliche Glied*] also bears this name, after which some people, in a completely indecent way, have constructed the female member [*das weibliche Glied*], which has just as little right to be called a member as the nose or other parts of the body do" (2:721). The Grimms have fewer problems with the meaning of the word as penis, finding a long and complicated historical linguistic tradition: "Euphemistically the sexual parts are called *glied*. . . . The use comes from the designation for the penis, corresponding to Latin, *membrum virile*, and has spread to the entire male sexual part." In one of his footnotes, Hans Rudolf Vaget points to the linguistic difficulties that Goethe and his contemporaries had in the poetic designation of the male member, which Goethe thematizes in an epigram from 1790:

Give me instead of *der Schwanz* another word, O Priapus,
For I, as a German, am plagued wickedly

. . .

The *Schwanz* is something from behind
And from behind I never had a happy pleasure.

[Gib mir statt "der Schwanz" ein anderes Wort, O Priapus,
Denn ich Deutscher ich bin übel als Dichter geplagt

. . . .

Der Schwanz ist etwas von hinten,
Und von hinten war mir niemals ein froher Genuß.][6]

This priapean poem, of which only the second line is published in full in the *Weimarer Ausgabe*, indicates not only that Goethe thought and wrote about the male anatomy, but alludes also to an awareness of sodomy, which is important for a discussion of the homosexual overtones of the relationship between Faust and Margarethe.

Since for Goethe, however, the Promethean is only one of two necessary approaches to life, he chooses the word *Glied* to represent these Promethean qualities, for *Glied* in the sense of *Mitglied* or "member" points in a Ganymedic direction toward losing one's sense of phallic identity as a member of a larger group. The angelic refrain, "Saved is the noble member of the spirit world," can also be seen as calling Faust a "link" in the great chain of being that is the spirit world. Thus Stuart Atkins's straightforward rendering catches almost all of the possible meanings of this difficult line: "This worthy member of the spirit world" (Goethe, *Faust I & II*). Faust becomes a member both phallic and selfless, both Promethean and Ganymedic.

As Faust loses his sense of identity by becoming nothing but a *Glied*—both a "(male) member," that is, autonomous, assertive phallic symbol, and a "member, for instance, of society," that is, nonautonomous and submissive—he achieves the status that Mephistopheles had when Faust asks him: "You call yourself a part, and stand entire before me? [*Du nennst dich einen Teil, und stehst doch ganz vor mir?*]" (*HA* 3:47; line 1345). At the culmination of Faust's journey, concepts like part and whole, rebellious autonomy and selfless submission—indeed, even characters like Mephistopheles and

6. Vaget 42; see also Borchmeyer 138–39; Boyle 1:648.

Faust—conflate as seen by Goethe's use of the word "*Glied.*" Two seemingly diametrically opposed approaches to the feminine, the Ganymedic and the Promethean, the passive and the active, the Mephistophelean and the Faustian, collapse, unable to be differentiated, and unable to escape membership in masculine society. Once again, the categories of sexuality and gender in Goethe's works have proven themselves to be discursively constructed and hence inherently ambiguous, self-deconstructing, and queer.

8

THOMAS MANN'S
QUEER SCHILLER

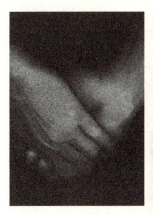

Wherever we find Goethe, we are sure to find Friedrich
Schiller (1759–1805), the other half of the pair who con-
stitute German classicism. Schiller, whose star waned
somewhat in the twentieth century, was, if anything the
more popular of the two German writers in the nineteenth
century. His plays *The Robbers, Wilhelm Tell, Wallenstein,
The Maid of Orleans, Maria Stuart, Intrigue and Love,* as
well as his many ballads and poetic and philosophic essays,
ensured for him a prominent place in the constellation
of German literary stars. And like so many figures in that
constellation, there is a homoerotic strand to his writing,
even though he rejected Ramdohr's aesthetics as spending
too much time "down there" (Derks 379).

Tonio Kröger, in Thomas Mann's 1903 short story
of the same name, offers his beloved Hans Hansen the
gift of Friedrich Schiller's *Don Carlos,* a play so beautiful
"that it gives one a jolt, that there is, so to speak, a bang"
(210).[1] According to Kröger, it is a play about a lonely king
betrayed by a marquis out of love for a prince. Hansen,
perhaps intrigued by violent images, wants to know how a
play could have a "bang" (*knallen*), but otherwise doesn't
pay much attention, preferring the more virile art of horse
riding. Unlike Hansen, however, Mann's readers have paid
attention to Tonio's analysis of *Don Carlos*—and usually

1. Thomas Mann's short stories are cited from *Die Erzählungen.
Erster Band.* All translations are my own.

found it wanting. While Anthony Heilbut, in his 1996 biography of Mann, describes Kröger's interpretation as "the homosexualizing of *Don Carlos*—to show the private uses of art" (161), most academics, more cautious by nature than freelance biographers perhaps, have simply viewed the boy's analysis as a misreading. Is this queer Schiller in Mann's text "homosexualizing" for a purpose or "misreading"? A closer reading of Schiller's texts themselves shows that *Don Carlos* lends itself willingly and elegantly to appropriation by Mann and indeed other queer and querying readers.

Thomas Mann's interest in Schiller's possibly deviant sexuality was openly discussed in his household. In a diary entry of August 16, 1931, Klaus Mann recounts the topic of conversation at one dinner party at his father's: "Was Schiller homosexual [*homosexuell*]?" (19). Nor is *Don Carlos* the only bit of Schilleriana that Mann uses homosexually in his writings. In *Difficult Hour* (*Schwere Stunde*), published in 1905, a couple of years after *Tonio Kröger*, Schiller appears as a bookish man who must mentally tell his wife that he will never belong completely to her because of the strong Hansen-like Goethe hovering in the background (Heilbut).

In one of the last texts Mann wrote, his *Essay on Schiller* (*Versuch über Schiller*), composed in 1956, he states more explicitly that the love of Schiller's life was none other than Goethe: "The great adventure of his life, his experience of passion, of passionate attraction and repulsion, of deep friendship, deep desire and admiration, of give and take, of jealousy, of melancholy, envy and proud self-assertion, of lasting affective tension—was an event between man and man . . .—it was his relationship with *Goethe*" (*Leiden* 433). Mann asserts that Schiller was "the completely masculine" writer who wanted to attribute to Goethe "a feminine manner," although "others, like Schlegel, emphasized precisely the masculine in him" (*Leiden* 433). If Mann is right, Schiller's heterodox effort to regard Goethe as feminine is on the one hand an endorsement of a queer strategy of appropriating texts—reading in a writerly way, as Barthes would say. On the other hand, it shows Schiller's discomfort with the implications of a male-male relationship and his hope to remold his relationship with Goethe on a heterosexual model. In any case, it is clear that for Mann, Goethe and Schiller bring issues of gender and same-sex relationships to the fore.

Other readers of Mann's era agreed that there was something homosexual in Schiller. The author was prominently cited in early homosexual emancipation circles, which included, incidentally, a great-grandson of Schiller, Alexander von Gleichen-Rußwurm. As early as 1891, a certain G. Portig published a monograph entitled *Schiller in His Relationship to*

Friendship and Love, as Well as in His Relationship to Goethe (*Schiller in seinem Verhältnis zur Freundschaft und Liebe, sowie in seinem inneren Verhältnis zu Goethe*). In his attempts to use the classics of literature to defend same-sex love, Elisar von Kupffer referred to Schiller in his work *Ardor for Favorites and Love of Friends in World Literature* (*Lieblingsminne und Freundesliebe in der Weltliteratur*). In an essay from 1930 entitled "The Love of Friends as a Cultural Factor: A Word to Germany's Male Youth," Adolf Brand, the editor of *The Exceptional: A Magazine for Male Culture* (*Der Eigene: Ein Blatt für männliche Kultur*),[2] a journal devoted to promoting erotic male bonding, mentioned both Goethe and Schiller in a list that also included Anacreon, Pindar, Virgil, Horace, Hafis, Michelangelo, and Shakespeare, all as proponents of male-male love (Oosterhuis 151).

Another member of the circle, a physician named Otto Kiefer who wrote for *The Exceptional* under the pseudonym "Reifegg," specifically discussed *Don Carlos* in an essay entitled "On the Importance of the Love of Youths for Our Time" (*Über die Bedeutung der Jünglingsliebe für unsere Zeit*). He lamented that "already now in our materialistic, egotistical time, boys and youths who let themselves be beaten bloody for their beloved friend, as Schiller reports of Don Carlos, are becoming rare" (Oosterhuis 171). *The Exceptional* reprinted Schiller's ode "Friendship" (*Die Freundschaft*), an act that was deemed immoral in one of the many court cases against the journal. In 1914, the prominent homosexual sexologist Magnus Hirschfeld discussed Schiller's work, particularly the *Maltese*-fragment, in his treatise *Homosexuality in the Male and the Female* (*Die Homosexualität des Mannes und des Weibes*), as Paul Derks reports. In October 1927, a certain Herr Wegener published an article called "The Homophiles in Schiller's Prose Writings" (*Die Homoeroten in Schillers Prosaschriften*) in the homosexual journal *Papers for Human Rights* (*Blätter für die Menschenrechte*).

A prominent appropriation of Schiller's *Don Carlos*, one that had implications far beyond the boundaries of Weimar's queer subcultures, takes place in Leontine Sagan's film *Mädchen in Uniform*, which was released in 1931. This astonishing film, directed by a woman, based on a play by a woman

2. The translation of *Der Eigene* is rather difficult. "Eigen" is an adjective most commonly meaning "own," as in "my own" [mein eigener]. By extension, it can also mean "peculiar," as in "die Grobheit, die ihm eigen ist" ("the rudeness that is peculiar to him"). By further extension it can actually mean "strange" or "queer," according to *Cassell's German-English Dictionary*, as in "es ist mir eigen zu Mute" ("I feel queer"). Thus, *Der Eigene* could be translated with something like *One's Own* or even as *The Queer*. For reasons of historical continuity, I have chosen to follow the precedent set by Harry Oosterhuis and his translator Hubert Kennedy, who refer to *Der Eigene* as *The Exceptional* in their collection of excerpts from the journal.

(Christa Winsloe's *Gestern und Heute* [*Yesterday and Today*]), and featuring an all-woman cast, is a feminist landmark. It also has an iconic status in lesbian filmmaking as the first film to feature lesbian subject matter. Young Manuela, who is from an impoverished aristocratic family, enters an authoritarian girl's school. There she falls in love with the progressive teacher Fräulein von Bernburg. When the school's principal reproaches Fräulein von Bernburg about the affair, the young educator responds with the ringing declaration, "What you call sin, I call love." Because of this passage in particular, the film was censored heavily in the United States and in other countries. But while the film shocked some audiences, it titillated others and was sold out for weeks in Paris (Kessler 727).

Don Carlos occupies a central role in the film, as the girls perform it under the direction of Fräulein von Bernburg. Most of the authoritarian faculty want to appropriate the play for their own conservative purposes, hoping to use the German classics to repress fantasy and enforce discipline. Some note that the classics can also be transgressive, finding that Schiller is at times a bit too free.

Mädchen in Uniform leaves little doubt that the transgressive Schiller is the author who has significance in the twentieth century. Just as students are practicing Posa'a famous lines about freedom of thought [*Gedankenfreiheit*], one of the teachers demands absolute obedience, barking out the order "obey!" [*Gehorchen!*]. In the movie, as in Schiller's drama, smuggled letters are of vital importance. Just as King Philip II restricts the free passage of letters, so too does the school.

Sagan's film puts Manuela in the role of the Prince, just as Mann's *Tonio Kröger* does for its title character. The role of the prince, for both these early twentieth-century interpreters, is Hamlet-like. Weak and indecisive, he does not feel adequate for the task at hand. Similarly, Manuela is "strangely sensitive" [*sonderbar empfindlich*], even though she is the daughter of a soldier [*Soldatentochter*]. Thus, *Mädchen in Uniform* not only explicitly thematizes Schiller's *Don Carlos*, but also incorporates many aspects of it into its own narrative and characterizations.

In 1940, Gad Beck and his gay friends were reading and finding points of identification in Don Carlos and the Marquis de Posa: "I consider both these figures gay [*schwul*], always this exalted Schiller — 'O!,' it doesn't get any gayer than that! When Carlos and Posa appear on the stage, they play a love pair, without any doubt, and whoever has not noticed just does not want to see it" (70). Beck notes this in his memoirs published in 1995, demonstrating that the tradition of appropriating Schiller has survived until this day.

So loud was the noise made in homosexual circles about Schiller that the satirical magazine *Jugend*—not necessarily aimed at homosexual audiences—took note with the cartoon of Goethe and Schiller unclasping hands discussed in the preface of this book. An earlier image in the same journal, from October 16, 1897, showed two naked male youths resting together on an outcropping overlooking a bridge and a tower, accompanied by a quote from Schiller's ode "The Artists" (*Die Künstler*). Thus, Tonio Kröger is not alone. The queering of Schiller is at home in a large body of early twentieth-century German thought.

The accusation that these early twentieth-century homosexuals were projecting their own historical biases into these texts by discovering "homosexuals"—products, after all, of mid- to late nineteenth-century discourses—in an eighteenth-century text loses some of its force in discussions of *Don Carlos*. Schiller, who had a chair in history at the University of Jena, knew his history well enough to write a lengthy book on the Spanish involvement in the Netherlands, in which he discusses historical figures like King Philip II of Spain extensively. He knew perfectly well that he had changed historical dates to suit his fiction. (For instance, as Batley notes, Don Carlos, Elizabeth, and Egmont were all dead twenty years before the defeat of the Armada, an event that is nonetheless mentioned in his play.) Schiller also knew that King Philip was actually forty-one at the time that the events with his son and his second wife were transpiring, not nearly sixty, as the play would have one believe (Kittler, "Carlos"). He was also aware, as were many of his own contemporaries, of the anachronism of putting late eighteenth-century ideas about the rights of humanity into the mouth of the Marquis de Posa, a sixteenth-century Maltese knight (Klaus-Detlev Müller). Schiller himself concedes, in his "Letters on Don Carlos" (*Briefe über Don Carlos*) that Posa's belief in the freedom of the individual is the "favorite subject of our decade," not of earlier eras (2:251).[3] Historical accuracy of this sort was in no way the prime motivator of his writing. This anachronism is not a problem for Schiller; in fact, to modern readers Schiller's own example suggests some possibilities for the uses of history in literature.

Despite Schiller's own appropriation of history, and the queer tradition of appropriating Schiller, most responses to his plays have been decidedly straight. Since the nineteenth century, criticism has tended to see Schiller in terms of stirring defenses of liberty, humanity, and freedom or analyses of

3. Unless otherwise indicated, Schiller references are to Friedrich Schiller, *Sämtliche Werke*, 5 vols., ed. Gerhard Fricke and Herbert G. Göpfert, 5th ed. Translations are my own. Italics in the English always indicate Schiller's emphasis.

Da stieg der schöne Flüchtling aus dem Osten.
Der junge Tag, im Westen neu empor,
Und auf Hesperiens Gefilden sprossten
Verjüngte Blüthen Joniens hervor.

Sascha Schneider (Dresden).

(Schiller, Die Künstler.)

Sascha Schneider, untitled (?) (from *Jugend* 42.16 [Oct. 16, 1897]: 982). *Queer Schiller?*
A fragment of a Schiller poem illustrated by an image of two male figures.

the concept of history and the characteristics of genre. The subtitle of Wolfgang Wittkowski's collection of essays on Schiller is typical: "Art, Humanity, and Politics of the Late Enlightenment." As far as the play *Don Carlos* goes, the most famous lines in the criticism have been the Marquis de Posa's strident denunciations of monarchical abuse of power and ringing pleas for freedom of thought: "I cannot be a servant of lords" [*Ich kann nicht Fürstendiener sein*] (line 3020) and "Give me / Freedom of thought" [*Geben Sie / Gedankenfreiheit*] (lines 3213–14).[4] Reviews of productions of *Don Carlos* in *Theater Heute* in the late 1990s suggest that the theatrical world has also seen nothing particularly revolutionary in Schiller's constructions of gender and sexuality. K. D. Schmidt's production in Berlin's Maxim Gorki Theater in 1997 could deal with the male-male bonding in the play only in an embarrassed and embarrassing adolescent way. Similarly, a review of an English production of *Don Carlos* in the *Times Literary Supplement* also suggests that it was quite conservative sexually (Ashton).

Olga and Thomas Nesseler have recently published one lengthy monograph that does address homosexuality in Schiller's works, asserting that, "as his correspondence makes clear, the relationship of the poet Schiller to Andreas Streicher, to Reinwald, Körner, Huber, and even to Goethe and to others, has unconscious, latently homosexual connotations" (207). About *Don Carlos*, they argue that "Schiller unconsciously fantasizes between Carlos and Posa, not a 'platonic' friendship, along the lines of the friendship cult of the eighteenth century, as traditional Germanists have argued, but latent homosexuality" (110). While the Nesselers are open to discussions of homosexuality, they operate only in the most reactionary and pathologizing of psychoanalytic modes. What is striking about both their account is their constant assumption that heterosexuality is the natural telos of human development. This requires among other things a blind adherence to preset categories of male and female, which Judith Butler has begun to shake up.

Let us leave the realm of psychoanalysis and return to Schiller. As Jane Bennett points out, confining Schiller to the purely abstract, to concepts like liberty and humanity, vitiates some of his most heartfelt beliefs. Schiller was quite capable of writing abstract theses, and chose instead to write dramatic plays. In the abstract theses that he did write, he went to bat for aesthetics—for that realm of experience that attempted to bridge the gap between body and mind, that attempted to connect sensual pleasure with thought. Schiller's

4. All references from *Don Carlos* are to line numbers as they appear in volume 2 of the Hanser edition.

hope, in the *Letters on the Aesthetic Education of Humanity* (*Briefe über die ästhetische Erziehung der Menschheit*) was that people could *will* to do what they *ought* to do. This "willing" is ultimately a sensual, physical, bodily act. The drama attempts, as literally as possible, to flesh out the moral problems that Schiller confronts by giving these problems to people with actual bodies. By ignoring the sensual, the physical, the bodily in Schiller's dramas, readers have tended to turn him into an intellectual, conceptual artist, which is at odds with his philosophy of art.

Schiller had begun his career with writings on the mind-body problem, inspired by medical models that denied the separation of mind and body. In *Don Carlos* the connections between mind and body are made evident in the way the characters frequently turn scarlet or pale: the priest Domingo loses his color, making a particularly nefarious suggestion (line 2102), Posa turns pale upon hearing of Carlos's love (line 2282), Posa refers to the blushes of embarrassed lady lovers (line 2379), Carlos turns red when he hears that the queen will see him (line 2448), the king complains that the queen made him turn red before his entire court (line 2623). This far-from-exhaustive list emphasizes the involvement of the body in Schiller's play. The moment in the play when the king cries moves Tonio Kröger precisely because it is about the ability of bodily fluids to break through strict intellectual and moral self-control. *Don Carlos* itself therefore avoids excluding the body and reducing humanity to abstract ideas like freedom and humanity.

Certainly, Schiller's passionate devotion to friendship seems at times to move into the bodily realm. In addition to the ode "Friendship" (published in 1782), which was originally going to appear in a novel with the mellifluous title, *From the Letters of Julius to Raphael* (*Aus den Briefen Julius' an Raphael*), the 1789 short story *Play of Fate* (*Spiel des Schicksals*) demonstrates Schiller's powerful interest in friendship and its sexual implications. In *Play of Fate*, a prince is quite taken with a young man named G*, "the perfect image of blooming health and Herculean strength" (5:36). Although the prince admires G*'s mind, it is his exterior, his body, that really turns him on: "If the prince was fascinated by the mind of his young companion, this seductive exterior carried away his sensuality irresistibly" (5:36). This relationship clearly goes beyond friendship: "Equality of age, harmony of inclinations and character established quickly a relationship between both of them that possessed all the strength of friendship and all the fire and all the violence of love" (5:36–37). In the course of time, a count, Josef Martinego (the only character with a name, and an Italian-sounding one at that, which, as we know, makes it exotically and sexually suspicious in eighteenth-century northern

Europe), manages to insinuate himself into the good graces of the prince. In order to have the prince all for himself, the Italian count urges the prince to indulge in unnamed "vices." Knowing that "nothing is more entitled to a bolder intimacy than the co-knowledge of secretly held weaknesses, the count awakens passions in the prince that had until now still slumbered": "He carried him away to the kind of indulgences [*Ausschweifungen*] that tolerate the fewest witnesses and accessories" (5:39). Derks argues convincingly that these unnamed, secret vices are very probably sexual; the fact that the prince subsequently has a string of other male "favorites" allows one to presume that the vices are homosexual in nature.

The relationships related in *Play of Fate* are typical for many of Schiller's works, which tend, as one critic writes about *Don Carlos*, to "wallow in men's greatness" (cited in Orton 250). In her outstanding piece on Schiller, Hammer argues that among the symptoms of the "diseased mythos" of masculinity in Schiller's plays are the "intermale relationships so passionate that they interrupt and violate the standard circuit of male homosocial bonding" (155). In this world of "murky male desires" (155), she maintains that Schiller implies "that men's relationships with each other are, at least under patriarchy, both murderous and covertly homosexual" (167). These intense male friendships in many of Schiller's writings have resulted in the inclusion of his works in various compilations of "gay literature," like Bullough's *Annotated Bibliography of Homosexuality*.

Hammer writes specifically about *Wallenstein*, "the dramatic creation most overtly concerned with manhood, homosocial bonds" (161). Although they rarely mention the sinister sides of this male bonding, it is certainly true that modern queer readers have frequently looked to *Wallenstein* as a source for gay male history. To begin with, the play is predominately masculine: its characters are mostly men primarily interested in the male world of war. Hammer is right to quote Sedgwick, who points out that, "for a man to be a man's man is separated only by an invisible, carefully blurred, always-already crossed line from 'being interested in men'" (Hammer 167). Indeed, Wallenstein does seem to wander across that line. In *Wallenstein's Death* (*Wallensteins Tod*), Wallenstein approaches Max, reminding him of past help, and cries out: "I myself was your nursing woman, I wasn't ashamed / Of small services, I tended you / With womanly caring activity" [*Ich selbst war deine Wärterin, nicht schämt ich / Der kleinen Dienste mich, ich pflegte deiner / Mit weiblich sorgender Geschäftigkeit*] (lines 2149–51). In this passage, Wallenstein's femininity is emphasized repeatedly. Gender-bending is a frequent phenomenon in Schiller's other plays as well. Johanna, in *The Maid of Orl-*

eans (*Die Jungfrau von Orleans*), possesses "a masculine heart" (*ein männlich Herz*; line 196). Maria Stuart, in the play that bears her name, trumps Queen Elizabeth with declaration, "*I* am your king" (line 2451). For an author who wrote such notoriously gendered poems as "Castratos and Men" (*Kastraten und Männer*, published 1782) and "Dignity of Women" (*Würde der Frauen*, published 1796), Schiller is surprisingly flexible.

Schiller's notes for his planned play *The Maltese* (*Die Malteser*) contain some of the most remarkably open discussions of male-male sensuality of any literary text from the eighteenth century, even if one hesitates to call them, as Hirschfeld did, proof of an intimate understanding of homosexuality. *The Maltese* was going to be about the Knights of Malta, an organization that Schiller perceived as an exemplary all-male secret society. In a letter to Wilhelm von Humboldt of October 5, 1795, Schiller wrote enthusiastically that the play consisted exclusively of male characters: "The plot is simple and heroic, as are the characters, who are at the same time exclusively masculine, and it is therefore the representation of a sublime idea, the kind that I love" (Seidel 1:174). While in his "Letters on Don Carlos" Schiller denies that passionate friendship is at the center of *Don Carlos*, he states that that subject is reserved for a later project, which turned out to be *The Maltese*.

While many of Schiller's plays have large numbers of male characters, the *Maltese*-fragment goes beyond Schiller's usual generalized interest in the homosocial and masculine realm to address male-male love quite specifically. Two of the main characters, Crequi and St. Priest, were to be lover and beloved. In one projected table of contents, Schiller refers to a "Scene of the lover with the beloved" [*des Liebhabers mit dem Geliebten*]" (3:177). He clarifies the distinction between the two in a footnote to his plans for the project: "But only one is the lover, the active one; the younger and beloved behaves passively [*Doch ist nur einer, der Liebhaber, der Handelnde; der jüngere und geliebte verhält sich leidend*]. But the lover acts with a blind passion, forgetting the whole world, and verges on the criminal" (3:173). Although Schiller denigrates Ramdohr's approach when he writes to Goethe about the aesthetician, he actually seems to have a similar view of the polarities necessary in human relationship, regardless of whether these relationships are same-sex or not (Ramdohr 1:171–72). This understanding of male-male love as something inherently directional and not necessarily reciprocal or egalitarian is typical for the ancient Greeks, as both modern historians of sexuality and eighteenth-century classicists know. Therefore, Schiller alludes in a footnote directly to the ancient Greeks in his notes on the two men: "Love of the Greek youths for each other" (3:173).

As we have seen, male-male love in ancient Greece was well known in the eighteenth century. In fact, it was one of the few arenas in which same-sex behavior could be discussed with any degree of openness. At times, the Greek love was regarded as asexual, friendship. More often, though, it was understood as having a sexual component. Schiller did not steer away from this component. He refers to "the most dignified and accurate use of the motif of the love of the two young knights in its entire range" (3:170). This range includes the sensual: "Their love is of the purest beauty, but it is however necessary not to remove from it the sensual character [*den sinnlichen Charakter*] with which it is attached to nature. It may and must be felt that it is a transfer, a surrogate [*Surrogat*], of sexual love [*Geschlechtsliebe*], and an effect of a natural drive [*eine Wirkung des Naturtriebes*]" (3:172). Although Schiller begins with the obligatory assurance that this love is "pure," his insistence on its sensual nature, its similarity to sexual love, and its naturalness is quite astonishing for this era. As remarkable as his beliefs are though, his determination in arguing that this love has to be *felt* rather than merely thought fits in with his writings on aesthetics.

The "surrogate" nature of this male-male love appears elsewhere in Schiller's notes: "The love of men in the play is the completely valid surrogate for the love of women [*Die Männerliebe ist in dem Stück das vollgültige Surrogat der Weiberliebe*] and replaces that love for poetic purposes in all parts, indeed, it [the love of men] even exceeds the effects [of the love of women]" (3:173). In another passage, Schiller equates Crequi's love with heterosexual love, or at least indicates that it is indistinguishable from such love: "His passion is true sexual love [*wahre Geschlechtsliebe*] and manifests itself through a detailed tender care, through raging jealousy, through sensual glorification of the figure, through other sensual symptoms" (3:173). "Care" (*Sorge*) is the activity that characterizes Wallenstein's feminized love for Max. In addition, the medical vocabulary of the symptom also recurs frequently: "The love of the two knights to each other must have all the symptoms of sexual love" [*Die Liebe der zwei Ritter zu einander muß alle Symptome der Geschlechtsliebe haben*]" (3:172). What these "other sensual symptoms" of love might be are not spelled out, but—especially since they are medical, and thus have to do with the body—it seems highly likely that they are the physical aspects of love. In any case, Schiller is willing and almost anxious to exhibit this love, even though it might arouse suspicions: "The lover [*Der Liebhaber*] may show his tenderness blatantly, even though that might appear suspicious" (3:171–72).

Schiller's use of the words "surrogate" (*Surrogat*), "suspicious" (*ver-*

dächtig), "to appear" (*scheinen*), and "symptom" (*Symptom*) suggests that ultimately Schiller differentiates between male-male love, a sickly surrogate with a suspicious appearance, and male-female love, which is presumably the real thing (it doesn't "appear" to be anything other than it is) and healthy to boot. At the same time, however, this male-male love, despite its sickliness, in other ways exceeds in merit the male-female love. Moreover, to compound the paradoxes that surround same-sex love in Schiller, the two categories of love are virtually indistinguishable — despite the difference between surrogate and original. The imitative, appearance-oriented, sickly-symptomatic side of this male-male love makes it difficult for modern readers (like Derks, for example) to accept Hirschfeld's view, which understands Schiller's depiction of the love of the Maltese as a positive one. The quality of the homosexual counterfeit of heterosexual desire, though, is so good that same-sex desire becomes, in Schiller as in Goethe (see Chapter 5), an apt symbol for the power of language to operate as a pharmakon, in the Derridean sense. In Schiller's world, same-sex desire, like language, is a surrogate for the "real thing," heterosexual desire, but it is not always possible to distinguish the original from the copy.

The classic pharmakon is the poison that cures, the curative that kills, the drug that can do both good and bad. The doubled nature of *Gift* (in German, "poison," but etymologically related to *Mitgift*, "dowry," as well as to the positively charged English "gift") is thematized throughout *Don Carlos*. Don Carlos refers to what he thinks is the page's knowledge of his affair with the queen as "poison" (line 1310); Domingo, who speaks eloquently of the two-sidedness of words (lines 1974–78), believes that the "poison of the innovators [*Gift der Neuerer*]" (line 2039) is already lurking in the hearts of the queen and the marquis. When Domingo suggests that the queen and Carlos are having an affair, the king demands a "drop of poison" [*Tropfen Gift*] (line 2734) from him. The marquis hopes that Eboli's poison hasn't crossed her lips, equating "poison" specifically with words (line 4123). The king's knowledge that this "poison" can also be a curative makes it a pharmakon: "poison itself, / I find, can, in benevolent natures, / Nobly become something better" (lines 3265–67). Conversely, the marquis knows that some healing interventions are almost poisonous: "The remedy / Is almost as bad as the danger" (lines 3458–59). As these characters learn about the positive sides of poison and the negative sides of cures, they are also learning the trickiness of language, the impossibility of determining its sincerity and authenticity, and the multiple, sometimes self-contradictory interpretations that it provokes as well as the vagaries of sexuality.

The Grand Inquisitor, with his rhetorical questions, links the pharma-kon specifically with issues of gender in a speech that begins when he grills the king: "Was . . . poison no longer poison?" (lines 5199–5201). Connect-ing pharmaceutical poisons with fundamental truths, he demands to know, "Had between good and evil / And true and false the partition fallen?" (lines 5201–2). Then linking these fundamental truths with gender, he compares masculine fidelity with feminine moodiness:

What is constancy,
What is male loyalty, when in a half-hearted
Moment a sixty-year-old rule
Melts like a woman's mood?

[Was Beständigkeit,
Was Männertreue, wenn in einer lauen
Minute eine sechzigjährge Regel
Wie eines Weibes Laune schmilzt?] (lines 5303–6)

It is clear that the collapse of distinctions between man and woman has everything to do with sexuality because the point at issue is Posa's seduction of the king, a seduction that the king, almost maudlin in his dotage, could not resist because of the irresistibility of the younger man's eyes: "I looked in his eyes" (line 5207).

The Grand Inquisitor's questions are rhetorical, of course. While he argues for the one-sidedness of poison, denying its pharmaceutical power, the reader and the audience know that in this play the Inquisition has con-sistently stood for the manipulation of language and the constant reinter-pretation of deeds based on context. It is, for instance, willing to counte-nance the sexual relationship between the Princess of Eboli and the king for the higher good that their relationship would bring, as the princess points out:

Although you have already proved to me
That cases were possible where the Church
Knew how to use even the *bodies* of her young daughters
For higher purposes.

[Obschon Sie mir bewiesen,
Daß Fälle möglich wären, wo die Kirche
Sogar die Körper ihrer jungen Töchter
Für höhere Zwecke zu gebrauchen wüßte.] (lines 2112–15)

The marquis specifically targets the false virtue of Eboli as someone who does the right thing, but for all the wrong reasons — reasons having to do with the power of the Church. Thus, the Grand Inquisitor's insistence on absolute truths is only evidence for his willingness to manipulate language (and sexuality) to further his means.

To recapitulate, same-sex tensions exist in much of Schiller's work, and the difficulty of interpreting those tensions make them paradigmatic for the pharmakon, the fundamentally undecidable substance that characterizes literature and that is also thematized in his writings. How then do these same-sex tensions play out in *Don Carlos*? Why do Thomas Mann's character Tonio Kröger, Leontine Sagan's *Mädchen in Uniform*, and some of the members of the homosexual emancipation movement in early twentieth-century Germany alight specifically on *Don Carlos* when queering Schiller? If one were to explode the play and pick up the pieces from the floor of the library or the theater, one would find a number of shards and fragments that ring queer bells and strike queer notes. When Carlos and the marquis reminisce about their childhood days together, Carlos remembers Posa's sailor's outfit (line 208), which is the kind of detail that Thomas Mann certainly would remember — Tadzio, for instance, making his first appearance in *Death in Venice* (*Der Tod in Venedig*) in a sailor's outfit. A somber note rings out early in the play, when the Marquise of Mondecar expresses gruesome delight at the prospect of an auto-da-fé in Madrid. This may bring the etymology of "faggot" to the mind of some queer readers. It is an article of faith among many gays and lesbians that the use of faggot to describe gay men derives from the times of the Spanish Inquisition, when sexual deviants were burned like faggots (in the sense of pieces of wood). This belief affects interpretation even though some lexicographers doubt the veracity of this folk etymology.

Regardless of the etymology of faggot, in act one, scene four, the queen sees a blooming hyacinth, a flower that as we have seen in Sachsen-Gotha's *Kyllenion* and Goethe's *Wilhelm Meister* story, brings to mind the story of the mythological male athlete after whom it was named (line 527). Finally, Don Carlos and the Marquis de Posa are repeatedly identified as queer fellows. The king, wondering whether to work with the marquis, calls him a "queer fellow" (*Sonderling*; line 2848). The marquis also uses the same word to refer to himself as the "queer fellow" (line 3387). It is perhaps worth remembering here that Manuela in *Mädchen in Uniform* is also called "queerly sensitive" [*sonderbar empfindlich*]. In any case, the Princess of Eboli, trying to seduce Don Carlos, finds that her heterosexual charms have no effect and uses the same name for him: "all my efforts slide / Off this queer fellow, smooth as a snake" [*All meine Proben gleiten / Von diesem schlangenglatten Sonderling*] (lines 1736–37). She asks him for the key to the "magically locked closet" [*zauberisch verschloßnen Schrank*] (line 1742) that protects him. It is now our job to try to unlock that closet and see if it produces something more than a handful of queer fragments.

While the most obvious male-male erotics of the play *Don Carlos* might seem to be between the prince and the marquis, Tonio Kröger actually concentrates on the king, Philip II, whom he interprets as a lonely man desperately in need of a friend. Mann, of course, knew his Schiller very well. Schiller himself wrote that the dramatic tension of the play had to be in the king and his complicated feelings. Kröger in no way misreads the play when he sees that Philip II is in need of a friend. Indeed, the king pleads to God: "I pray to you for a friend" (line 2811). Carlos, who wants to be that friend and love his father, puts his desires somewhat more effusively than modern readers are used to, rejoicing in "the bliss of this kiss" [*die Wonne dieses Kusses*] (line 1040). The king, however, doesn't want his son, but rather his son's friend. In his superb essay on *Don Carlos*, Kittler writes about the ways in which the play—reversing normal psychoanalysis—recodes the bourgeois family to make comments about politics. Here, Schiller shows his virtuosity with familial constellations by neatly transposing the Oedipal complex: while the son seems to desire his father's bride, the father desires his son's friend.

By the end of the play, the competition between father and son for the friend becomes quite explicit. The king cries: "He had a friend who died / For him—for him!" (lines 5026–27). He wants someone to die for him: "Had he died for me!" (line 5047). The king continues, "I was fond of him, very fond" (line 5048). This competition hinges on the issue of age. At first the king assumes that Carlos is too young to compete with him, but then he comes to realize that he has become too old to be attractive to the knight from Malta:

. . . Not
Philip does he sacrifice to Carlos, only
the old man to the young . . .

[. . . Nicht
Den Philipp opfert er dem Carlos, nur
Den alten Mann dem Jüngling] (lines 5065–67)

Interestingly, Philip is, in the play, about as old as the "sixty-year-old rule" that the Grand Inquisitor asserts has been abandoned in womanly moodiness.

Rejoicing in his youthful attractiveness, Carlos crows that Posa had compromised himself and died for him, not for the king:

. . . to save me, he
Wrote a letter to Orange — O God!
It was the first lie of his life!
To save me, he threw himself at the death
That he suffered.

[. . . Mich zu erretten, schrieb
Er an Oranien den Brief — O Gott!
Es war die erste Lüge seines Lebens!
Mich zu erretten, war er sich dem Tod,
Den er erlitt, entgegen.] (lines 4801–5)

Carlos admits that the marquis might have dallied with the king: "Your scepter was the plaything of his hands" (line 4808). But he is certain that the marquis remains his friend. Both father and son are consciously aware of their rivalry. In these exchanges, the frequent repetition of the verb *buhlen* ("to compete, often sexually; to woo, to have an affair") lends them a physical and lusty nature that allows for a sexual understanding of the reference to the king's "scepter": "You dared to compete [*buhlen*] for his friendship" (line 4814). By the end of the play, the king too uses an unusually frank and physical vocabulary, saying that he is *lüstern* (sexually desirous, lewd) to speak with the spirit of the former king (line 5139). He justifies his attempted relationship with the marquis with a similar expression indicating his physical desire for another person: "Desire arose in me for a human being" [*Mich lüstete nach einem Menschen*] (line 5222). The excitement in this play then would be precisely what Tonio Kröger picks up on: the eruption of physical desire in an older man for another man, a desire that displays itself most dramatically in the issuance from the male of bodily fluids — fluids that happen to be tears.

If the relationship between the king, the marquis, and the prince is a kind of queer reversal of the Oedipal triangle, with the father competing for the son's friend, then is not the relationship between the prince, the queen, and the king a straight Oedipal complex, with the son competing for the father's bride? Not exactly, because the prince is in love with a woman his own age, a woman whom he thought he was going to marry and whom his father has only recently taken in marriage. He is actually in love with a stepmother. His story is strikingly similar to the motif of the lovesick prince, which plays such a prominent role in Goethe's novel of 1796, *Wilhelm Meister's Apprenticeship* (*Wilhelm Meisters Lehrjahre*). In the novel, as we recall, the prince is also in love with and pines for the young bride of his father. The similarities in the constellation of the homosexual and heterosexual triangles that confront both Wilhelm Meister and Don Carlos are striking: just as Wilhelm Meister identifies with the lovesick prince and at the same time clearly goes through homosexual phases, Don Carlos sees himself in the same position as the lovesick prince—in love with the young bride of his father—and will assign his love to a number of men, as we shall see. In addition, Wilhelm's love of the fisherman's boy, first mentioned in the sequel of 1832, *Wilhelm Meister's Journeyman Years* (*Wilhelm Meisters Wanderjahre*), is strongly reminiscent of Carlos's love of Posa, particularly when Wilhelm falls in love with the boy's corpse, just as Carlos does with Posa's "great beautiful death" (line 4796).

The reader of Schiller's play can hardly fault the prince for desiring his stepmother. The play, however, paints this love in the direst terms. Carlos himself tells Posa that his passion for the queen stands in opposition to "the customs of the world, / The order of nature and Rome's laws" (lines 276–77). By his own admission, it is a desperate and evil love: "I love without hope—viciously [*Ich liebe ohne Hoffnung—lasterhaft*]" (line 282). The Princess of Eboli refers to "this strange unnatural behavior" (line 1639). She puts it most exactly in her monologue in act two, scene nine: "So much / Is clear—he loves what he should not" (lines 1890–1). Given the actual facts of the relationship, the play's insistence that such love is unnatural, forbidden, and a crime against nature and humanity seems overstated. This forbidden, hopeless, vicious, unnatural love—who could restrict it merely to the love of a stepmother who was rightfully one's own bride? Is it not more likely that this ostensible love for the queen has, in fact, a slightly different constitution?

The Duke of Alba gives the reader a hint as to the true nature of the unnatural love. He relates that when the queen enters the room in which he and Don Carlos are fighting, the young man's alleged passion for the queen curiously causes him to kiss the duke:

The Queen, upon hearing the din, opens
The room . . .

. . . . . .

His arm freezes—he flies to my neck—
I feel a hot kiss.

[Die Königin auf das Getöse öfnet
Das Zimmer . . .

.   .   .   .   .   .

Sein Arm erstarrt — er fliegt an meinen Hals —
Ich fühle einen heißen Kuß.] (lines 1954-59)

This suggests that the physical part of the prince's relationship with the queen tends to be carried out with men. The vocabulary about "crimes against nature" and "unnatural love" makes sense when one understands that the real object of Carlos's love of the queen is the marquis. Carlos's treatment of the queen immediately after the death of the marquis suggests strongly that the love of the queen was merely a symbolic substitution for the love of the marquis. Now that Posa is dead, he can no longer even befriend her: ". . . I can give to you my friendship / So little as yesterday my love / To another woman" [. . . *Meine Freundschaft kann ich Ihnen / So wenig als noch gestern meine Liebe / Verschenken an ein andres Weib*] (lines 5332-34). As soon as Posa is gone, there turns out to be no need for any love affair to explain Carlos's emotions.

When the queen accuses the marquis of pursuing admiration, using that sexually laden verb *buhlen*, she strikes a blow at him that suggests an undercurrent of erotic jealousy between the two: "Oh, now — now I'm learning to understand you! You were / Only competing for admiration" [*Sie haben / Nur um Bewunderung gebuhlt*] (lines 4385-86). Upon plumbing the depths of the relationship between the men, she decides to give up on men altogether: "Go! / I'll never esteem a man highly again" (lines 4392-93). The marquis, interested only in his all-male world, is delighted: "O God! Life *is* beautiful!" (line 4394). The apparent Oedipal desires of the young prince have turned out to be merely a cover for emotions that really describe the relationship between the two men.

The relation between the prince and the marquis is the most obvious homoerotic love affair in *Don Carlos*. It is the relationship to which Reifegg, for instance, alludes in his essay in *The Exceptional*. Although Tonio Kröger does not specifically refer to this relationship, he reenacts it in his love of Hans Hansen. But the understanding of the possible queerness of the relationship between the two men does not emerge first in the early twentieth century. Schiller seems to be reacting to anxieties about the nature of the relationship in his "Letters on Don Carlos," first published in 1788. The "Third Letter" begins with the notion that passionate friendship is at the root of this tragedy: "You claimed recently to have found in Don Carlos proof that *passionate friendship* [leidenschaftliche Freundschaft] could be just as moving a subject for tragedy as *passionate love* [leidenschaftliche Liebe]" (2: 230). Although the construction of this statement suggests that there is a difference between "friendship" and "love," it is the very same difference that existed in the *Maltese* drama—a difference between simulacrum and original that is in fact indistinguishable. The fact that this friendship is as passionate as love, strengthens the suspicion that there might be something queer in this friendship. Schiller admittedly quickly rejects such a notion that "passionate friendship" is at the center of his tragedy—but perhaps readers should dwell on the question a bit longer.

It turns out that Schiller rejects the centrality of passionate friendship to the play because he claims that the Marquis de Posa is beyond friendship to a mere individual, even as a child: "already here Posa is the colder, the later friend, and his heart already embracing too widely to contract for a single being" (2: 231). Carlos, however, is a different matter altogether. Schiller concedes that the soft young prince does want a passionate relationship of some kind with the marquis. In relation to the marquis, Carlos is "a delicate princely son, with lively feelings, receptive to his [the marquis's] outpourings and voluntarily hurrying toward him" [*ein zart und lebendig fühlender, seiner Ergießungen empfänglicher, ihm freiwillig entgegeneilender Fürstensohn*] (2: 231). Delicate and sensitive, the prince seems to fit a lot of stereotypes about effeminate young men who are forever chasing after strong men, hoping to receive their (bodily?) outpourings. Compliantly and docilely, he clings to the marquis: "the loving Karl snuggled up so submissively, so teachably!" [*Der liebevolle Karl schmiegte sich so unterwürfig, so gelehrig an ihn an!*] (2: 232). So, by Schiller's own argument, even if friendship is not at the center of the drama, the desire for friendship could well be at the center of the character Don Carlos.

Carlos is full of love, pathologically so. His situation is a "state of *leisured enthusiasm, inactive observation*" (2: 232). Schiller's word for "enthusiasm" is *Schwärmerei*, which was a major concern of the psychological physicians of his era. Carlos expends his energy, resulting in "a dark melancholy" (*eine düstere Schwermut*; 2: 232). He is "without energy, without occupation, brooding inwardly, exhausted by heavy fruitless battles, running scared between frightening extremes" (2: 232) and sinks into "a painfully blissful state of *suffering*" (2: 233). In his essay on *Don Carlos*, Kittler has already noted that Posa's awareness of the unnatural red on the prince's pale face and his feverishly trembling lips (lines 148–51) reveal Schiller's medical studies of the effects of illicit sexuality on health. The "Letters" make explicit that Carlos is expending his (sexual) energy in a solipsistic, narcissistic way that would have seriously negative consequences for his health. From these descriptions of Carlos's physical and psychological state, it is clear that something is amiss with his sexuality.

Heterosexual libertinage is apparently not his vice. In a speech to Posa, the young Carlos admits that he has had no sex with women in his twenty-three years:

. . . I am
Still pure, a twenty-three-year-old youth.
That which thousands before me unconscionably
Dribbled away in riotous embraces,
The best part of the spirit, male power,
I saved up for the future ruler.
What could drive you out of my heart,
If women could not do it?

[. . . Ich bin
Noch rein, ein dreiundzwanzigjährger Jüngling.
Was vor mir Tausende gewissenlos
In schwelgenden Umarmungen verpraßten,
Des Geistes beste Hälfte, Männerkraft,
Hab ich dem künftgen Herrscher aufgehoben.
Was könnte dich aus meinem Herzen drängen,
Wenn es nicht Weiber tun?] (lines 970–76)

The Nesselers oddly claim that this speech is "unconsciously" about sex, but it seems in fact quite conscious. Schiller reinforces Carlos's age and innocence when the prince exclaims: "Twenty-three years, / And still nothing done for immortality!" (lines 1147–48). He has not done anything for immortality, because he has not expended his seed fruitfully (i.e., heterosexually). So, despite his pale looks, Carlos has not been wasting his seed—with women, at least. Carlos's lack of sexual interest in women becomes clear again when he has his disastrous encounter with the Princess of Eboli. He puts her off until he hears that she has resisted all the advances of her suitors. Then, upon learning of her asexuality, he becomes delighted with her. In contrast to all this borderline misogyny, Carlos seems to have a positive understanding of masculinity. Calling his seed "the best half of the spirit," he shows an appreciation for the value of the male body and its fluids.

But if Carlos is the weak, fawning prince frightened of female sexuality, desperate for a father figure, and in love with the phallic masculinity of Posa, the marquis is not quite as free of the taint of same-sex desire as Schiller maintains in the "Letters," which, in their allusions to the play, are not—as the editor of the Hanser edition admits—"everywhere exact" (2: 1230). Posa is, after all, a Maltese knight, a member of that organization that Schiller found so fascinating partly because in it male-male love was a surrogate for male-female love. In a letter written on June 13, 1787, to the Hamburg theater director Friedrich Ludwig Schröder, Schiller said that he wanted Posa played by a "lover" (*NA* 24: 100). Throughout the play, Posa is seen as a "sacrifice." There is something sexy about this image of the strong man sacrificing himself for the sake of his friend, weak and pitiable. Carlos triumphs to the king: "The beautiful course of his life was love. Love / For me his great beautiful death" (lines 4793–94). Similar to many of Aschenbach's characters in Thomas Mann's *Death in Venice*, Posa resembles Sebastian, the beautiful male martyr, at the mercy of other men. In Schiller's play he is available not only to the other characters, but also to the audience and the readers.

Posa, of course, cannot help it if others find him attractive, either in his strong or in his weakened state. But there are moments where he reveals that—with all due respect to Schiller in the "Letters"—he is the desiring subject as well as the object of desire. Posa calls Carlos the "favorite of my soul" [*Liebling meiner Seele*] (line 2370) in a discussion about Eboli. And later, he informs the queen that his love for the royal son was a great joy: "To me was granted / A fortune the likes of which is only granted to a few: / I loved a lord's son [*Ich liebte einen Fürstensohn*]" (lines 4253–55). It is significant that these two admissions come in his discussions with these two women, for there are erotic tensions between each of them and him concerning Carlos. I have already mentioned the passages in which Posa and the queen spar jealously. Jealousy is also the best explanation for Posa's reaction to Eboli. Posa's desire to kill the princess in act 4, scene 17, is a serious overreaction, as even he admits: "Desperation / Made me into a Fury, an animal—I set / The dagger to a woman's breast" (lines 4670–73). It is easy to interpret the implication of rape in this image of a dagger at a woman's breast, but one also wonders why Posa says that he was turned into a Fury, an archetypically feminine divinity, at the same time that he is turned into a beast, that is to say, a physical being without consciousness, without those ideals for which the marquis is so famous. This gender-bending at the level of the body suggests that Posa's anger originates in his sexually confused physical response to Carlos. Posa's understanding of the relationship between Carlos and Eboli sounds like that of a lover suffering from self-inflicted wounds: "Abandoned by the only one, you throw / Yourself in the arms of the Princess Eboli— / Unhappy one; in the arms of a devil" [*Verlassen von dem Einzigen, wirfst du / Der Fürstin Eboli dich in die Arme— / Unglücklicher; in eines Teufels Arme*] (lines 4658–60). Here, too, there are odd gender reversals, for Eboli is a masculine "devil": she is a *Teufel*, not a *Teufelin*. Posa's anger at the women involved with the Prince, his blurring of their gender and his own, and his avowed love of the prince all suggest that he too has more at stake at the corporeal level in his love for Carlos than Schiller admitted in the "Letters."

Kittler has the most convincing explanation for Posa's love of the Prince: it is the love of the teacher for his student, a teacher of the kind new to the eighteenth century, a teacher like the Hafis of Goethe's *West-Eastern Divan*, like the teachers in Schiller's own school, the Karlsschule, where teachers worked with youths who were "simultaneously pupils, friends, and beloveds" (265). Given the number of letters in the play, one could argue that Posa teaches Carlos to read and understand the manipulation of signs. But since the sign in its polyvalence is somehow akin to sexuality, one could also remain with the notion that Posa teaches Carlos to love, a theory that Posa himself supports: "my entire direction was / To explain his love to him" (lines 4339–40). Posa discovers that his childhood friend thinks he loves his mother and teaches him to return to the homosocial, if not the homosexual, world. This is the kind of pedagogical love that goes back to Socrates and the *Symposium* and in which Thomas Mann would also delight: the pedagogical love that would always be sexually suspect.

In teaching love, Posa makes clear to Carlos that he, the marquis, was the prince's first love. The prince's first love is an irritant in Schiller's writings. In the "Third Letter" of the "Letters on Don Carlos," which is all about the relationship between the prince and the marquis, Schiller discusses the despondency that afflicts the prince after the two are separated. After a long list of symptoms, Schiller writes: "thus the *first love* finds him [*so findet ihn die* erste Liebe]" (2: 233). One might assume that the queen is meant here— indeed, the queen herself assumes as much when speaking to the prince: "Elizabeth / Was your first love" (lines 790–91). However, in Schiller's letter about the Prince's lovesickness, there is no reference to the queen—only to the separation from the marquis. Subsequently, in the "Eighth Letter," Schiller declares with the same emphasis that a "cheerful humane philosophy" is the prince's "*first love*" (2:252). Some have argued that Schiller is contradicting himself when he at first seems to suggest that Elizabeth is the prince's first love and then asserts that philosophy is the first love (Crawford). But it is odd that Schiller would use so emphatically the same words in letters written a short time apart if he did not mean for there to be a connection. There is less of a contradiction if Elizabeth is *not* the prince's first love. If that first love is the marquis, then this philosophy, which is said to be "a child of friendship" [*eine Geburt der Freundschaft*] (2:252), would be a logical extension of that love. If the marquis is the prince's love—as he is the king's, who exclaims, "He / Was my first love" (lines 5051–52)—then one can fully explain Posa's claim that he taught Carlos the meaning of his love. The marquis first reminds the prince that he is the first love; he then teaches the prince to give up the object of that love and transfer his desire into useful societal channels.

In a letter from October 5, 1785, to the writer Ludwig Ferdinand Huber, Schiller exclaims, "let our hearts join manfully one with the other, enthuse little and feel much, project little and *act* all the more fruitfully" (*NA* 24:25). Male-male bonding in Schiller's world must escape the realm of impotent "enthusing" (*schwärmen*) and become a fruitful act. In order to do so, it must be sublimated. Schiller's queer story does not end in the satisfaction of whatever confused erotic desires connect Don Carlos and the Marquis de Posa. Instead, it ends with the sublimation of those desires for the greater good. Most analyses of the play that argue that it explodes the bourgeois tragedy by forcing its hero to move from the private realm to the public are correct (Klaus-Detlev Müller, for instance); they merely miss the homoerotic twist of private life in *Don Carlos*.

In emphasizing the importance of sublimating homosexual desire, *Don Carlos* plays into a long tradition that is still very evident in the first half of the twentieth century. The renowned psychoanalyst and Goethe expert Kurt Robert Eissler, for instance, argues for the link between sublimated homosexuality and philanthropy in his monumental biography of Goethe. Essentially, Thomas Mann also believes that sublimated homosexuality lies at the root of artistic creativity. Watching a young Argentine tennis player on the court in 1950, Mann contemplates in his diary "this mad and yet passionately maintained enthusiasm, which lies at the basis of everything, for the *incomparable* charm of male youth, *surpassed by nothing in the world*" (*Tagebücher 1949–50* 239). In assuming that his insane enthusiasm for male youth lies at the basis of everything, including his writings, he seems to be arguing for the presence of unsatisfied same-sex desire at the origin of all art. The implicit conclusion of Schiller's play, that male homosexuality must end in a "grand beautiful death" and a commitment to the greater good of humanity, would thus be attractive to Mann.

Mann also surely appreciated the specific way in which Schiller believes that male-male desire becomes sublimated. The "cheerful humane philosophy" that the friendship between the men engenders turns out to have another name: "The bold vision of a new state" [*Das kühne Traumbild eines neuen Staates*] is "the divine child of friendship" [*Der Freundschaft göttliche Geburt*] (lines 4278–79). In the "Letters," Schiller clarifies the nature of this new state: "All principles and favorite feelings of the Marquis circle around *republican* virtue" (2:229). Schiller sees male-male bonding as the cornerstone of modern democracy. When Count Lerma, a Spanish grandee, expresses his condolences and support to the Prince, he links intense friendship with patriotism, which for Schiller would have been an antimonarchical, prorepublican category: "So loves / No friend anymore! All patriots cry / For you" (lines 4932–34). Schiller hereby anticipates the concept of "adhesiveness," " 'manly love' as a governing element of society," that Whitman would advocate (Grier) and that Thomas Mann, Hans Blüher, and many writers for *The Exceptional* would find so appealing.

Homosexuality can be sublimated into writing, as well as politics, as Mann well knew. This is perhaps one reason why sexuality functions so well as a pharmakon. The sublimation of this sexuality appears in the exchanging, writing, and reading of all the letters in the play. When Eboli steals the queen's letter, she practically violates her, forcibly breaking open her locked purse; the king grants Posa the same right when he allows him to have secret access to her purse (Nesseler and Nesseler 133). When Posa asks Carlos for his letters, there is nothing more intimate he could request. When Posa wants a sign of the king's love, he asks for a signature on the secret arrest warrant.

This sublimation of same-sex desire into writing also functions at the real-life level of Schiller writing the play. The friendship between Carlos and Rodrigo and its relation to the greater good was an itch that provoked in Schiller an almost unending scratching of the pen on paper. The play, envisioned in 1782, took five years to complete. The first published version was thousands of lines longer than the edition that Schiller authorized at the end of his life. Schiller shortened the drama several times, sometimes sending directors shortened versions with indications of possible further cuts, suggesting that much of the play was inessential, simply the froth produced by the churning of a writing machine fueled by same-sex desire. As in the case of the *Maltese* project, male-male friendship became a provocation to almost endless writing. In this case, Olga Nesseler, for all her pathologizing, is on to something: "The creative activity of writing can be interpreted as an expression of Schiller's attempts to escape the vicious circle of depression and latent homosexuality" (196). On this issue, a secret sympathy would have existed between Schiller and Mann, who also found suppressed male-male desire to be the wellspring of creativity.

It is appropriate that Tonio Kröger specifically admires the style of *Don Carlos*. If Schiller's obsession with male-male friendship produces reams of poetry that can be cut practically at will, then the reader must assume that style, rather than content, must be Schiller's forte. There are several other elements that tie the short story *Tonio Kröger* closely with *Don Carlos* and show how well Mann appropriates the play for his own queer purposes. Like Carlos, Tonio loves his mother: "Tonio loved his dark and fiery mother" (208). But like Carlos, he really loves another boy, Hans Hansen. Like Carlos, the "queer fellow" (*Sonderling*), Tonio thinks of himself as "queer" (*sonderlich*; 208) because of this love. In the play, Don Carlos is melancholy, soft, and alone, in love with the hard, active, sociable Posa; in the short story, Tonio Kröger suffers and desires painfully, while Hans Hansen is athletic, enjoys life, and has plenty of friends. While the marquis sacrifices himself up for the prince, however, Mann has written a more sobering story in tune with the oppressive nature of the dominant discourses of sexuality and desire in his day. Tonio Kröger must be sacrificed for his friend: "But when a third came, he [Hans] was ashamed of him [Tonio] and sacrificed him" (211). *Tonio Kröger* fantasizes less luridly about the self-sacrifice of strong men for the sensitive men who love them, but the story works within the same universe as *Don Carlos*.

There are other paths that connect Thomas Mann with Schiller via Tonio Kröger. His favorite teacher in school, Dr. Ludwig Bäthke, was a Schiller specialist. Thomas Mann fell in love with Schiller's *Don Carlos*—specifically its beautiful language—when he was a youth of fifteen, as he tells us in his final essay on Schiller. This love relationship between the reader Mann and the text of *Don Carlos* mirrors that between the author Schiller and the text. Schiller's own understanding of his relationship to the text of *Don Carlos* is quite astounding. In a letter to the librarian Wilhelm Friedrich Hermann Reinwald from April 14, 1783, Schiller embeds the play in male-male friendship: "In this splendid breath of morning, I think of *you* friend— and my *Carlos*" (*NA* 23:78). Discussing the protagonist of his play, Schiller confesses that Carlos has replaced a heterosexual love interest for him: "I must admit to you that to a certain extent I have him instead of my girl" [*Ich mus Ihnen gestehen, daß ich ihn gewisermassen statt meines Mädchens habe*] (*NA* 23:81). Interestingly, although Schiller states here that Carlos is his "girl," he has just explained that the author needs to be the "girl" of his character: "The poet must be *less* the *painter* of his hero—he must be *more* his *girl*, his bosom buddy" [*Der Dichter mus weniger der Mahler seines Helden—er mus mehr dessen Mädchen, dessen Busenfreund seyn*] (NA 23:81). This kind of gender blurring lends credence to the interpretations that this chapter presents, as they require a flexible understanding of gender. In addition, the blurring of the boundary between human lovers and fictional characters and works suggests a worldview in which textual constructs are as real as anything else.

Schiller provides further explanation for the love of the author for his characters. He argues: "Every poem is nothing other than an enthusiastic friendship or a platonic love [*eine enthousiastische Freundschaft oder platonische Liebe*] to a creation of the head" (NA 23:79). "Friendship" and "platonic" love may not sound particularly sexual to modern ears, but the pathological adjective "enthusiastic" (*enthousiastisch = schwärmerisch*) preceding friendship makes one wonder how this kind of friendship would differ from nonpathological, that is nonsexual, friendship. In eighteenth-century Germany—as Derks has shown—the adjective "platonic" in no way proved that a love was asexual: it could just as easily suggest that a love was homosexual. Schiller does not in fact seem to want to create strong boundary lines between friendship and love: "And are not all manifestations of friendship and love—from the soft handshake and kiss to the most heartfelt embrace—just so many expressions of a being struggling toward *mixture* [*Vermischung*]" (NA 23:80). For Schiller, the desire of the self to mix with the other grounds both friendship and love. In any case, Schiller clarifies his notion of friendship and platonic love: "But what is friendship or platonic love other than a blissful exchange of being?" [*Aber was ist Freundschaft oder platonische Liebe denn anders, als eine wollüstige Verwechslung der Wesen?*] (NA 23:79). In using the word "blissful" (*wollüstig*), Schiller emphasizes that he is talking about a sensual, lusty, even lascivious exchange of being. Writing about a hero and loving a friend are for him similar activities: "If friendship or platonic love are merely the exchange of a foreign being with our own, merely the passionate desire for his qualities [*eine heftige Begehrung seiner Eigenschaften*], then both are to a certain extent only another effect of the power of poetry" (NA 23:80). Thus the ardent romantic friendship that develops between the characters of *Don Carlos*, *Wallenstein's Death*, and the *Maltese*-fragment is a refraction of the intense desire that Schiller the author feels for his creation.

The other answer Schiller gives to the question, What is friendship or platonic love? is "the contemplation of our self in another mirror" [*die Anschauung unserer Selbst in einem andern Glase*] (NA 23:79). One needs not view this as mere narcissism. For Schiller, both love and writing involve a subjective investment in the other, a blending and a merging of the self with the other that is rooted in desire and borders on the sexual. Although he does not state it explicitly, reading too can perhaps be seen in this way—reading as a kind of rewriting that also involves the loving participation of the reader. Here then we have Schiller's blessing for Mann's reading or rewriting of *Don Carlos* in *Tonio Kröger* and all queer interpretations that are based on the highly subjective involvement of the reader. Schiller understands that any reader-author re-creating a text will do so out of an erotic desire for that text, a desire that leads to a discovery of one's self in the text. Arguing that this creative activity, the lusty blending of the souls, this self-discovery in the other is also a characteristic of passionate friendship, Schiller seems not only to be endorsing queer readings, but also particularly supportive of queer readers.

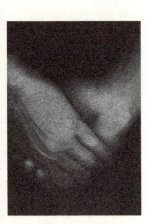

9

LICHTENBERG'S
QUEER FRAGMENTS
Sexuality and the Aphorism

The writings of Georg Christoph Lichtenberg (1742–1799)
occupy a queer place in literature — queer because they
consist either of art criticism, studies on lightning, appeals
for public bathing facilities, or of fragments and aphorisms
that Lichtenberg kept secret from his contemporaries. In
neither case do Lichtenberg's works fall into traditional
categories of literature such as the novel, the poem, or
the drama. Nonetheless, he is one of those authors like
Shakespeare and Pope or Goethe and Heine whose writings are quoted constantly. In the German linguistic realm,
he is said to be the third most frequently cited author,
after Goethe and Schiller, although who knows how such
statistics are determined (Baasner 6). At least in Germany,
literature departments devote whole seminars to his writings, particularly his fragments. If what is queer about
Lichtenberg's position in German literature is that he does
not write the kind of literature usually taught, then perhaps it is time to investigate the queerness of the type of
writing that he offers, the aphorism. Perhaps the queerness
of Lichtenberg's choice of genre is related to another sort
of queerness: that of sexuality.

Queering Lichtenberg is not calling him "gay." In
letters to friends, frequent allusions to girls and women
as the objects of his erotic attention amply demonstrate
his heterosexual side. His love of the flower girl Maria

Dorothea Stechard, who moved in with him shortly after they met when she was eleven and who died five years later in 1782, is well known. Subsequently, he had children with and eventually married his housekeeper, Margarethe Elisabeth Kellner, proving his abilities to beget heterosexually.

One could perhaps think of Lichtenberg—and indeed, many of the eighteenth-century German authors we have been calling "queer"—as bisexual. Bisexuality does indeed queer the binary categories, like male/female and gay/straight, that structure modern life, as Marjorie Garber has argued in her book *Vested Interests*. But the term itself belongs to an era that divides humans up into specific sexual identities—not just two identities, but still a specific number of sexual identities: gay, straight, and bisexual. This book is not interested in ascribing such concrete sexual identities to authors, who lived in a culture that predated those identities anyway. Instead, it seeks to expound upon the ramifications of life in a culture that antedated sexual identity, showing how that life would not have fallen into a default category that looks identical to modern-day straight life. When the possibilities of sexual life in eighteenth-century Germany are fleshed out, the availability of the text for queer reading is enhanced. Thus, as disruptive as the term "bisexual" may be, even it is perhaps more constricting than "queer," which allows for a freer reading.

Queering Lichtenberg does suggest, in any case, that his sexuality disrupted and subverted some of the categories, particularly surrounding gender, that the eighteenth and the nineteenth centuries have constructed. Even critics who assume Lichtenberg's heterosexuality concede that he, "like no other, gave voice to the importance of sexuality for life and particularly intellectual life" (Fricke 72). When he speculates that the "animal" in humanity is responsible for many inventions, he hints that sexuality has an important part to play in much mental activity: "The question remains, who has made the most discoveries, animals or people (or at least the animal in people)" (J 1074; 1:803).[1] In eighteenth-century Germany, the "animal" in people was close to the "sexual" in people.

For Lichtenberg this sexuality is decidedly ambiguous, because it has certain revolutionary tendencies. Sexuality lurks in the realm of the servants, downstairs: "A certain friend whom I knew used to divide his body into three stories, the head, the breast, and the abdomen, and he often wished that the people from the uppermost and the lowermost stories got along better" (B

---

1. Aphorisms cited according to Promies's ennumeration; volume and page numbers are from Promies's edition of Lichtenberg's *Schriften und Briefe*.

334; 1:135–36). In contrast to the head, the seat of rationality, and the heart, seat of sensibility, sexuality dwells in the nonrational body, which sometimes disrupts desires considered rational or sensible.

In the context of the mind-body problem, the identification of sexuality and body is particularly difficult for Lichtenberg because of his own complex relationship to his somewhat misshapen and frequently sick body. He felt that "a bad artist" could have made a better body "in the dark" (quoted by Brinitzer 17). At another point, he describes complete dissociation from his body: "We two, I and my body, have never been so divided as now, at times we scarcely recognize each other, then we run against each other so that neither of us knows where we are" (B 263; 1:115). If the body is associated with sexuality and Lichtenberg does not like or feels alienated from his body, then we begin to understand why Lichtenberg felt more comfortable "upstairs" in his head than "downstairs" in his abdomen.

Lichtenberg's acute awareness of the split between his brilliant mind and his sick body caused him to be one of the bitterest opponents of Johann Kaspar Lavater's physiognomic speculations that were based on mind-body unity. Justifying his claim that he could determine character by examining and interpreting the appearance of others, the Swiss pastor Lavater (1741–1801) poses the question rhetorically: "Shall it be affirmed that mind does not influence body, or that the body does not influence the mind?" (Lavater 1:24). Lichtenberg knew that a beautiful body might not contain a beautiful mind and that a beautiful mind might reside in a less-than-beautiful body. Nonetheless, he did not advocate pure Cartesian dualism. Instead, his thinking on the subject is part of an interesting "reengendering" of mind and body. While, as Schiebinger argues, for centuries mind had been the realm of masculinity and body that of femininity, the second half of the eighteenth century saw a realignment that Lichtenberg expresses when he sets "Man and Woman" and "Body and Soul" as parallel (J 153; 1:676). The reengendering of mind and body has further consequences for Lichtenberg's self-understanding: If he identifies with his rational capacity and distances himself from his body, but sees the soul as female and the body as animalistic and masculine, it becomes interesting to determine where he positions himself on the gender field.

Nowhere is the connection between the loved yet hated body and an unruly sexuality more apparent and concrete than in Lichtenberg's frequent allusions to castration. In this respect, he bears comparison to Jakob Michael Reinhold Lenz, in whose play The Tutor [Der Hofmeister] the protagonist Läuffer castrates himself and whose relationships with other men, like

Goethe, were also somewhat queer (see Graf, "Die Folgen"). Lichtenberg is not below casting aspersions on Lavater's masculinity when he remembers that "you can make a eunuch out of a man, but not a man out of a eunuch" (quoted in Brinitzer 55). The point here is that masculinity is a quality of character, not of body, yet the repetition of the theme of castration in other fragments points to an overall rejection of the male body.

One of his aphorisms has the title "Speech of a person who wants to castrate himself out of desperation because a girl won't listen to him" (B 349; 1:137). This speech is delivered to "Nature," who is described as "mother of us all" and who is said to have gotten the boy's hopes up by promising all kinds of bliss. Lichtenberg leaves open the possibility that it was not nature who made these promises — in which case his desires were unnatural. But apparently he believes that his member is in fact Nature's tongue, which he will cut out by castrating himself. These are the pertinent parts of the aphorism:

When you betray, mother of us all, can you demand virtue from your children? Whose voice was it that called to me, 'this girl will make your earthly happiness.' . . . I believe it was yours, Nature, and was it not? . . . Whom shall I follow if my own drive lies to me shamefully? (He pulls the knife.) Here, flattering liar, quiver! A single cut could silence you forever and make your malicious tongue as quiet as a night in a cemetery. (B 349; 1:137)

Unpacking this fairly long aphorism reveals quite a few of the problems in sexuality that Lichtenberg is analyzing. On the most basic level, it is unruly and difficult, but fortunately corporeal and thus can be cut out. In addition, the hint that his desire is either unnatural or that nature can mislead away from virtue diverges importantly from the nascent bourgeois ideology of the time that liked to see a sexuality carefully delimited around the nuclear family as being the only outgrowth of nature. Finally, in defining his penis as the tongue of female Nature, the mother of us all, he truly confounds gender categories. Thus even though this aphorism allegedly comes from the mouth of a desperate fourteen-year-old embroiled in a hopelessly unrequited love affair with a girl, it disrupts and subverts the underlying assumptions that one tends to associate with that apparently so well-known scene.

Of course, in a certain sense everyone has "problems" with sexuality. Lichtenberg's problems, however, veer in a queer direction. To begin with, Lichtenberg artfully manipulates language to confuse the gender of the women in whom he is interested. Biographers assume that Lichtenberg's "raging passion" for a person to whom he refers as the "comet" was in fact a love for the tailor's daughter, Marie Sachs (Promies 83–84). But he consistently refers to the comet (*der Komet*) as "he." It is particularly striking that in his travel journal of August 14, 1771, he uses the pronoun "he" in English, a language in which, of course, it is not idiomatic to refer to a comet as masculine, especially when the comet is actually a code word for a woman (2:612).

The use of the pronoun "he" to refer to Sachs is perhaps simply a function of Lichtenberg's inadequate English, but the same pattern of turning a woman into a man happens in the great love of Lichtenberg's life, Marie Stechard, the adolescent flower girl. Lichtenberg himself was somewhat embarrassed by his relationship with the eleven-year-old girl, and his biographers continue to have problems explaining his passion. In late eighteenth-century Germany it was in fact, despite the rise of the bourgeois model for the family, not that unusual to consider a girl in her early teens as available for a sexual and erotic relationship — the German Romantic poet Novalis had his twelve-year-old Sophie von Kuhn, whom he courted. But it is not entirely clear that Lichtenberg desired Marie Stechard as a woman. Baasner points out that at least in his self-justification to his friend Gottfried Hieronymus Amelung in early 1783, Lichtenberg does not motivate his relationship with Stechard with desire, love, or sexual attraction, but with pedagogy (78–79). Lichtenberg claims at least that he brought the girl into his house in order to teach her, uplift her — things, in other words, he would also have done with a boy. Indeed, he addressed a letter to her to "Herr Maria Dorothea Stechard" (Brinitzer 136).

In his account of his affair with Stechard, he makes an interesting allusion to the possibility of male-male desire. He writes to Amelung that upon seeing the "handsome girl" selling flowers, he immediately thought about saving her from the Sodom that was Göttingen: "as I knew what sort of a Sodom our nest is, I thought seriously about taking this excellent creature away such a business" (Letter to Amelung, 1783; 4: 489). While August, Duke of Sachsen-Gotha, does not use "Sodom" in his depiction of male-male desire, it does show up in Jean Paul's writing. A man having sex with another man was after all committing the sin of sodomy. So when Lichtenberg decides to take in a girl because he lives in Sodom, one wonders, is he trying to save the girl or himself?

After Stechard's death, Lichtenberg consoled himself by having an affair with his housekeeper, Margarethe Elisabeth Kellner, which resulted in children and eventually even marriage. The parents of the first child born out of wedlock are listed on the birth certificate as being Margarethe Elisabeth Kellner — no hiding her disgrace — and Ludwig Christian Eckhardt, a fictional name consisting of the forenames of Lichtenberg's brother and the maiden name of his mother (Promies 130–31). Despite its fecundity, this relationship does not provide much evidence for Lichtenberg's ability to carry on a relationship with a woman. One biographer sees in it the "sharpest tensions" (Requadt 115). Another biographer writes that about his wife Lichtenberg "records almost nothing but endless violent quarrels" (Stern). Perhaps this relationship manifests Lichtenberg's observation that (hetero)sexuality often turns to violence: "In beating, he had a sort of sexual drive (*Geschlechtstrieb*), he beat only his wife" (J 448; 1:719). Lichtenberg likes his wife, however, when he can turn her into a man. He describes her as someone who affects him "in the many relations of advisor, friend, business companion, bed-comrade, play thing, fun brother (little sister doesn't sound right) [*unter den mannifgaltigsten Relationen von Ratgeber, Freund, Handlungskompagnon, Bettkamerade, Speilsache, lustiger Bruder (Schwester klingt nicht)*]" (2:241). Lichtenberg's emphatic rejection of "sister" (*Schwester*) instead of "brother" (*Bruder*) points out that he has used masculine forms for all of the human roles that his wife plays in his life. It would not be normal to refer to a woman in German as a *Freund* (male friend) rather than a *Freundin* (female friend), but that's how Lichtenberg sees his wife.

While Lichtenberg has problems with the femininity of women, he admires the masculinity of men. Put another way, while he likes his women to be manly, he doesn't like effeminate men. He might use the same linguistic tricks he had used with the women in order to refer to an effeminate man as "it" (*es*; B 204; 1:103), but such a sex-change operation does not become the patient. He speaks contemptuously of man whose only masculine part was hidden from view: "The only thing masculine that he had could not be seen in the name of decency" (B 189: 1:97). Interestingly, Lichtenberg assumes that one cause of femininity in men is found in "the desire to please all girls, which attempts to find its satisfaction in an approach of the masculine nature toward the feminine, and thus in a certain hermaphroditism of the soul [*in einer gewissen Hermaphroditerei in der Seele*]" (B 180; 1:95). The seemingly heterosexual act of womanizing turns out to corrupt masculinity.

Masculinity, pure and unadulterated, is thus what he likes. According to his biographers, the most agreeable way to spend the evening is in a "cell . . . of unpedantic male society" (Mautner, *Lichtenberg*, 160). To a certain extent, this is a textbook case of homosociality, that kind of male-bonding that unites fraternities and patriarchy and that specifically excludes homosexuality. But the distinction between homosociality and homosexuality is vague in the eighteenth century, as Faderman has shown in her discussions of the bluriness of the boundaries of romantic friendship; "sodomites" living in the eighteenth century certainly made use of all the conventions of such homosocial structures as the cult of friendship in order to indicate their interest in each other. That Lichtenberg's misogynist cult of friendship belongs perhaps on the border between homosociality and homosexuality is suggested by the way in which masculinity, which Lichtenberg likes in his friends, is also, as we saw earlier, inextricably bound up with that raw sexuality that he wants to cut out of his life.

The most explicit evidence of the queerness of Lichtenberg's male homosociality comes in the brief autobiographical resume of his love life that begins: "In his 10th year fell in love with a boy named Schmidt (first in the city school), son of a tailor, enjoys hearing about him and talks about him with the other boys, never spoke to him himself, was however delighted to hear that the boy talked about him. Climbed a wall after school in order to see him leaving school" (F 1220; 1:639). Reminiscent of Jean Paul's youthful crush on another schoolboy, this anecdote reminds us that, from the fisherman's son in Goethe's *Wilhelm Meister's Journeyman Years* to Thomas Mann's *Tonio Kröger*, this childhood homosexual infatuation is a mark of the development of the young man in German literature.

In a move that reminds one of Jean-Jacques Rousseau's *Confessions*, Lichtenberg insists that his honesty is more important than any particular sexual mores: "I would be dissatisfied if I were to increase the mistrust of the world through this voluntary confession, but I was a human being and the happiness of the world, if it is ever reached, cannot be found through concealment, in no way; nothing permanent can arise that way" (F 1220; 1:639). To what extent Lichtenberg is completely open about his sexuality remains, nonetheless, a question. Indeed, the pattern of secrecy is quite prominent in his writings. For example, the letter about Stechard, in which Lichtenberg says he took her on because Göttingen was like Sodom, begins with an injunction to secrecy: "*No one* may hear what I tell you" (Letter to Amelung, 1783; 4:489). In another fragment, he wishes he "could publish the history of [his] private life," but he does not do so (quoted in Requadt 40). Except for a few aphorisms, including the one about the schoolboy crush, one finds a lot of secrets that require unraveling in Lichtenberg's aphorisms.

One of the other more open aphorisms is about Jean André Deluc, a friend of Rousseau's whom Lichtenberg met in England. About Deluc Lichtenberg wrote on September 13, 1775: "I have never been in love in a melancholy way, but I have so loved this man that after his departure I now feel in myself something that, judging on the basis of descriptions, is similar to that love" (*RA* 158; 2:683). Intriguingly, the very next aphorism in this collection rejects the ancients, Winckelmann, and Italy, which were all signs of a homoerotic subculture, in favor of Bacon's clearly heterosexual Venus:

Perhaps a time will come, when we see that we are in some ways beyond the ancients, although we now believe ourselves to be behind them. . . . Winckelmann was an enthusiast, a man completely taken in by the ancients, who considered himself blessed when he found himself on classical ground and earth, who trained his taste according to models that he was supposed to judge. Bacon's Venus in Pall Mall could easily stand next to the Venus of the Medicis. (*RA* 159; 2:683)

It is as though Lichtenberg, having come too close to overstepping the boundaries of proper friendship, has to deny any love interest in the masculine (for more on Lichtenberg and Deluc, see Brinitzer 127).

A wave of homoerotic desire also engulfs the Swedish Jöns Matthias Ljungberg, Lichtenberg's most intimate school friend. In a passage thought to be addressed to Ljungberg, Lichtenberg praises that "community of active, intelligent, strong spirits . . . spread out over the whole earth," who are like the Greeks—ostensibly in their cultivation of the mind, but perhaps also in their devotion to Greek love. The full text of the letter to Ljungberg makes clear the connection between the Greeks and the rejection of sexuality with women:

Are women goddesses? Think of the Greeks. The Greeks, not only the wisest and bravest, but also the most sensual people on earth, didn't think women were goddesses, or that association with them was paradise, or that their love was irresistible. They did not even show them the respect one might have expected a free—I won't even say a sensitive—nation would give the sex. They needed them for the production of the raw material from which they themselves could later create heroes, sages, and poets.

Lichtenberg hopes that he, Ljungberg, and like-minded men can re-create such a world in modern times:

But why do I bring the Greeks into it? Does there not exist nowadays a very reasonable nation which is free from the ridiculous, dangerous and mawkish swooning about love, a nation which we must thank for all progress in useful arts, improvement of the human condition and all great ideas. Ljungberg, you know who I mean. It is a community of active, intelligent, strong spirits one finds spread out over the whole earth. (Quoted in Brinitzer 30)

Ljungberg is consistently associated with the world of antiquity. One of the great disappointments of Lichtenberg's life was the shattering of his dream of a trip to Italy, where—despite his anxious rejection of the homoerotic arts of the ancients in the fragment just quoted—he wanted to see such artworks as the Belvedere Apollo. When Ljungberg's petition for a trip was rejected in 1785, Lichtenberg wrote that he was stuck with nothing but "withered hyacinth bulbs" (cited in Promies 95). Given that "hyacinth" was a code word for homosexuality in this era, it is significant that Lichtenberg sees the bulb, the beginning of this passion, destroyed by the inability to travel with the school friend.

Lichtenberg's relationship with his publisher Johann Christian Dietrich was more classically homosocial in that the two bonded through "their," or rather Dietrich's, women. One biographer sympathetically concludes: "for with his secluded life, the rural cleaning women and cooks of Dietrich's house were almost the only beings whom he could approach naturally" (Requardt 116). By his own account he liked Dietrich primarily because of Dietrich's wife Christiane (Mautner, *Lichtenberg*, 75). He seems to have had an affair with another woman from Dietrich's household, the cook Marie (F 1220; 1:639). But this bonding too sometimes breaks its own antisexual bonds. He expresses in the subjunctive—and the role of the subjunctive will prove to be important in these fragments—a desire to kiss Dietrich: "would have kissed Dietrich then" (cited in Mautner 77). At least one critic who does not directly discuss homosexuality seems to betray an awareness of the eroticism of the letters between Dietrich and Lichtenberg when he writes "a stream of manly warmth pours out of them" (Mautner, *Lichtenberg*, 76).

There are other indications of Lichtenberg's not entirely unerotic interest in men as well. He alludes to Volta's good looks (Brinitzer 158). In his "Letters from England" to Heinrich Christian Boie, which were printed in Boie's *German Museum* (*Deutsches Museum*), he reveals his fascination with the body of the actor David Garrick (3:326). His positive allusion to Gleim, the enthusiastic leader of the friendship cult (Mautner, *Lichtenberg*, 50), suggests an affinity for an extremely highly charged homosociality; his references to Winckelmann, which, despite the aphorism quoted above, are generally positive, points to an even more openly sexualized interest in the male body.

Winckelmann returns us to Italy and the Greeks, both of which, as we have seen, were watchwords for entry into the homosexual subcultures of the late eighteenth century. The way in which particularly his friend Ljungberg, with whom he wanted to travel to the Mediterranean, is associated in Lichtenberg's mind with ancient Greece and the "yearning for Italy" comes to mind (Mautner, *Lichtenberg*, 289). Lichtenberg also alludes several times to Socrates, who in the eighteenth century was often a symbol of homosexuality (Derks 62). Lichtenberg does not in any way hide Socrates' desire. Admittedly in one passage he refers to a rare moment of heterosexual eroticism in Socrates' life, when he brushed up against the sister of Kritobolous (B 261; 1:114). But in general he seems quite aware of what his era called "Greek love": "We don't love the poor boys, like the Greeks; when our new era produces a beautiful piece of sculpture, it has to be a maiden" (B 141; 1:84). Like Wieland and Goethe, Lichtenberg seems to accept this Greek love quite objectively, as a matter of changing customs, nothing more. In his attack on physiognomy, he discusses Socrates' attraction for the young Charmides (Schöne 10–11).

Given the era's awareness of the possibilities of Greek and especially Platonic or Socratic love, it is interesting that when the dramatist August von Kotzebue spoofs the enemies of Zimmermann in his play *Doktor Bahrdt with the Iron Forehead. Or: the German Union Against Zimmermann* (1790), he also pillories Lichtenberg, initially as the randy lover of a nymph who finds his lessons in physics boring: "The small horny moon correspondent [*Der kleine geile Mondkorrespondent*] Lichtenberg lies in the ditch and reads experimental physics to a nymph, who however finds his lecture very dry" (Kotzebue 30). As Brinitzer agrees, this is presumably an allusion to Lichtenberg's attempts to teach Maria Stechard (134). But second, Kotzebue makes fun of Lichtenberg as someone into whose mouth Gedike likes to urinate. Friedrich Gedike, the gymnasium director and coeditor of the *Berlin Monthly* (*Berlinische Monatsschrift*), we may recall, is an associate of Karl Philipp Moritz; the librarian Johann Erich Biester, his friend and coeditor of the *Berlin Monthly*, is said to "demonstrate what Greek love is" to Gedike. Subsequently, "the well-trained Gedike considers Lichtenberg's mouth a chamber pot and violently wants to piss in him" (Kotzebue 37). One aphorism suggests that Lichtenberg himself had a certain fascination with urinating with other men: "I have pissed in the same night pots with him for two years, and therefore know pretty well what he's about" (B 272; 1:118).

A series of biographical anecdotes thus suggests that in the confusion of Lichtenberg's sexual desire, one can detect a weakness for men—something usually attributed to women. Just as the crater on the moon named after Lichtenberg is located right at the border between the dark and the light sides (Neumann, *Ideenparadiese*, 86), Lichtenberg himself seems to have stood at the border between the femininity that concerns him and the masculinity that he desires. He writes to a friend that his greatest struggle has been to avoid becoming a woman: "But no one gets put on a pedestal because he heroically prevented himself from becoming—an old woman!" (cited in Requardt 100). His misogyny thus emerges from a projection of what he fears he might become; misogyny becomes an easy answer for a man without a positive vision of male homosexuality.

While critics and biographers have for the most part overlooked Lichtenberg's masculinization of the women in his life and the extreme nature of his homosocial male bonding, they do agree that eros plays a large role in his life and, more particularly, in his writing (Fricke 72). We have already seen how Lichtenberg assumed that the "animal," or the sexual, in humanity was responsible for many inventions, which is to say products of the mind. Sexuality certainly influences Lichtenberg's skeptical response to Kant, who, Lichtenberg felt, placed so much weight on "reason" instead of "passion," simply because he had forgotten what love was like (L 910; 2:523).

Sexuality's importance for Lichtenberg, however, goes beyond his understanding of the content of ideas. Stern writes, "in the puns and curious turns on words, we find him exploiting a direct, more than personal parallel of language to erotic experience" (63). Albrecht Schöne especially has brought out that while Lichtenberg rejected Lavater's physiognomy of the body, he toyed with the notion of a "physiognomy of style [*Physiognomik des Stils*]" (F 802; 1:573), that is to say, a characteristic corporeality on the level of writing itself (7–14). Tellingly, in the same aphorism that mentions the "physiognomy of style," he indicates the kind of corporeal writing he likes: "the masculine prose of Mendelssohn or Feder or Meiners or Garve" (F 802; 1:573). Not only do these writers have a masculine style, but, intriguingly, Christoph Meiners was the classicist from Göttingen who wrote the tract entitled "Observations on the Male Love of the Greeks."

Indeed, it seems that Lichtenberg, more than most authors, gives the reader leeway to translate his physical eroticism into his writing. He indicates the importance of sexuality for his own literary criticism when he writes: "When he finishes a review—so I've heard—he has the most violent erections [*die heftigsten Erektionen*] all the time" (D 75; 1:241). In another aphorism, he compares words to sperm tellingly, using Greek characters: "spermatixoi logoi" (F 446; 1:521). And if the comparison between the act of writing and the act of penetration is not so startling to twentieth-century readers, Lichtenberg's analogy between reading and masturbation still has the power to give one pause: "one should write against reading, as against self-abuse [*Selbstbefleckung*]" (J 1150; 1:815). Thus if a confused sexuality dominates much of Lichtenberg's life, it is clear that it also permeates his writing.

Lichtenberg's *Sudelbücher*, the fragments he jotted down in notebooks, provide the most information on how his queer sexuality affects his writing. On one level, the private nature of his jottings is queer. Lichtenberg could only express aspects of his sexuality in the newly emergent closet, where they remained until they were "outed" posthumously. Lichtenberg apparently intended that these fragments be outed, because he kept them meticulously sorted in separate volumes. The precarious dynamic between something kept secret that was, however, eventually supposed to be revealed reflects the status of the closet where on the one hand a sexuality is hidden but that on the other hand constantly provokes the question, "What's going on in there?"

For their popularity, Lichtenberg's aphorisms rely on their wit and flair, characteristics that have long been attributed to homosexuals. The connection between wit and homosexuality probably became especially strong after Oscar Wilde, himself a successful author of aphorisms. But presumably Oscar Wilde was also working out of a tradition that had already linked the homosexual with witty cleverness. In any case, the aphorism had become synonymous with clever, witty, misogynist remarks at least by the seventeenth and eighteenth centuries, when it was a favorite of the French moralists (Fricke 60). In addition, one of the major links between the golden age of the French moralist writing and the apex of German aphorisms beginning in the late eighteenth century, Nicolas Chamfort (1741–94), was praised both because of his "urbanity" (i.e., wit) and because of his "masculinity" (Mautner, "Der Aphorismus," 45; Neumann, *Ideenparadiese*, 472). This misogynist masculine urbanity might not necessarily be homosexual, but it is a space where history teaches us to look for male homosexual writers.

The queerness of this masculine wit becomes more apparent when one realizes the suspicious kind of masculinity to which this wit is connected: a foppish, citified, prissy masculinity that undermines traditional gender distinctions. Indeed, the queerness of Lichtenberg's aphorisms comes especially to the fore in Lichtenberg's treatment of gender. We have already seen how perplexing the issue was for Lichtenberg. On the one hand, he equated masculinity with the body and with moral turpitude while linking femininity, the soul, and goodness. His preference for his mental facilities over his physical ones seems to be a continuation of this gendered scale of value. On the other hand, he liked men more than women. How does gender fare in Lichtenberg's aphorisms?

An indication of Lichtenberg's interest in gender and his willingness to apply it to categories beyond the biological shows up in aphorism J 740:

"Every male thought found its female. Or the ideas in his head must have been exclusively males or females. For a new one was never produced" (1:758). This fragment reveals a relatively conventional understanding of gender: Male and female belong together. If they don't meet, reproduction will not take place and sterility will result. What is interesting about this aphorism is Lichtenberg's typical sexualization of his thought process. As in some of the aphorisms cited earlier, here too he sees thinking as a clearly gendered and eroticized act.

While the gender conception in J 718 is fairly unsurprising, gender is not always so stable in Lichtenberg's aphoristic world. We recall how deftly Lichtenberg was able to turn women into men, as when he referred to Marie Sachs, his "comet," as "he." Similarly, he turned effeminate men into neuters (Mautner, *Lichtenberg*, 49). This kind of sarcastic critique of effeminate men becomes a degree more serious when he writes: "If only the Mr. Wives were better, the Mrs. Husbands would be acceptable [*Wären nur die Herren Weiber besser, mit den Frau Ehemännern ginge es wohl noch hin*]" (H 4; 2:177). This aphorism is obscure and difficult to translate, but what he seems to be decrying here is a lack of masculinity in society—if the "Mr. Wives" were better (men) then, one could tolerate the "Mrs. Husbands." He therefore tolerates a kind of role reversal as long as masculinity is around.

These gender reversals can become even more complicated. In one fragment, Lichtenberg describes someone (possibly himself) in the following way: "He looked so crumpled, like a girl in men's clothes" (F 314; 1:505). A man looks like a cross-dressed girl—it isn't necessarily a compliment but it does suggest an awareness of the instability of gender categories. It is reminiscent of *Wilhelm Meister*, in which Friedrich dresses up as a woman dressed up as an officer.

While these fragments have a misogynist coloring that excoriates men for being too effeminate, there are other moments where Lichtenberg seems willing to forego that male power that he so admires. In one aphorism he calls for a relinquishing of the male power of the gaze: "Unquestionably masculine beauty has not yet been drawn enough by those hands that alone could draw it, female ones" (F 1086; 1:615). Although he relies on a clearly heterosexual model when he says that "the only hands" that could describe male beauty are female, the aphorism is queer in its glorification of male beauty and its belief that a true appreciation of male beauty could produce many discoveries: "It is always pleasant every time I hear of a new woman poet. If [she] didn't construct after the manner of the men's poems, what couldn't be discovered then?" (F 1086; 1:615). The passive role that the male has in this fantasy is a queer, gender-bending reversal of the usual gender conceptions of late eighteenth-century Germany.

In another fragment, Lichtenberg makes his most comprehensive plea for a reconstruction of gender and an attendant revision of sexuality: "If one could not even recognize gender based on clothing, but even had to guess gender, a new kind of love would arise. This would deserve being treated in a novel with the wisdom and knowledge of the world" (F 320; 1:505). Here Lichtenberg's gender-bending escapes its misogynist tendencies and reaches a truly queer apogee, a position far enough away from Lichtenberg's real world that it transcends the gender barriers that constricted him.

It is important to note the interconnectedness between the reconstruction of gender and that of sexuality. Lichtenberg's utopian world free of gender restrictions produces a new kind of love. He discusses models of love when he compares "Platonic" and "animal" love with, respectively, drinking and intoxication (Mautner, *Lichtenberg*, 70). "Platonic" could easily mean homosexual in the eighteenth century, as we have learned. In another aphorism, significantly about physiognomy and the mind-body problem, he refers to "a mediation between friendship and love" (F 804; 1:574). This conflict between friendship and love is indeed what produces the tension that fill his relationships with women and men: how to be friends with the women for whom he is supposed to feel sexual desire and whether eroticism can play a role in the friendships he has with men.

It is significant that Lichtenberg poses his most radical solution to the problems of gender in the subjunctive and that he proposes a novel to work out the implications of this reengendering of society. As one critic writes, literature becomes for Lichtenberg "a cure for the in many respects unsuccessful experiment of human life" (Schimpf 72). Besides the gender-bending of Lichtenberg's aphorisms, one of the clearest connections between Lichtenberg's sexuality and his writing style is the utopian element of his fragments.

Albrecht Schöne's book *Aufklärung aus dem Geist der Experimentalphysik: Lichtenbergsche Konjunktive* (Enlightenment out of the Spirit of Experimental Physics: Lichtenbergian Subjunctives) is a fascinating study of the importance of the subjunctive in Lichtenberg's fragments. Schöne points out that Lichtenberg uses the subjunctive much more than was normal in the eighteenth century and that he tends to use it for conditional sentences (15–21). The subjunctive thus becomes a "sign of the enlightenment" (45) that allows for thought experiments that can become tremendously productive, in that they produce utopian visions as well as destructive ones, in that they destroy set and established ways of thinking and being. The subjunctive, conditional, utopian nature of Lichtenberg's aphorisms allows his queer sexuality to tear down the barriers in his own life and project new visions of a world that could be.

Lichtenberg's great interest in the travel literature of his era, particularly the writings of Georg Forster on Cook's voyage to, among other places, Tahiti, point to another manifestation of his utopian, escapist side.[2] This interest is not without a specific sexual subtext, because the Orient, especially tropical islands like Tahiti, was increasingly seen in the eighteenth century as a sexual utopia, as we have seen in Jean Paul's writings.

Another of Lichtenberg's aphorisms points in a more theoretical way to his desire to escape this world: "One is never happier than when a strong feeling determines us to live *only* in *this* world. My tragedy is never to exist in *this*, but rather in a plenitude of possible chains of combinations that my fantasy, supported by my conscience, creates" (J 948; 1:786). Lichtenberg's emphasis on the role of his conscience in creating these fantasy worlds has a number of implications. While it seems to stress, somewhat defensively, that Lichtenberg's fantasies are good, it introduces a moral perspective on the issue of hypothetical worlds that is surprising, suggesting that Lichtenberg's hypotheses require a moral judgment. Lichtenberg's confession of his love for his childhood schoolmate suggests that his conscience would in fact support him in producing fantasy worlds that were true to his own spirit. Lichtenberg's description of his predicament as his "tragedy" (*Unglück*) lends his observation a tragic nature, indicating that he is talking about something that affected him very personally—perhaps his sexuality.

In another aphorism, Lichtenberg expounds upon his experimental, utopian thinking:

On Monday the December 10, 1770 I established my slogan of choice, whim. For is it not whim to want to be something in this world that we are supposed to be. We are always something else that depends on the customs of the previous and current world, a tiresome accident of a thing that is not a substance. Is then human nature a thing that has its head in paradise and its tail/penis [*Schwanz*] on the other end of eternity and whose members [*Glieder*] are similar elements of the whole? (B 343; 1:138)

What he whimsically wants is to be what he is supposed to be. What prevents him from living up to his desires is the force of the world before and

2. Neumann, *Ideenparadiese*, 119; Mautner, *Lichtenberg*, 102–6; Brinitzer 108.

around him. All of this fits very nicely with a sexuality struggling to conform with conventional expectations. Sexually he wants to be what he is naturally supposed to be, but cannot do so because of society. Lichtenberg suggests that he is indeed talking about sexuality when he elaborates by asking if our heads have to remain in paradise while our *Schwanz*—either tail or penis—is stuck "on the other end of eternity." The whimsy of Lichtenberg's aphorisms, the utopian, conditional, subjunctive nature of his fragments point back to his concerns about his sexuality.

Neumann argues that "the idea of utopia necessarily belongs to the concept of 'aphoristic' thought" (*Ideenparadiese* 225). If both the utopianism and the gender-bending qualities of Lichtenberg's aphorisms point specifically to the queerness of his sexuality, perhaps something about the aphorism itself is inherently queer—or, more likely, at least traditionally received as queer. Certainly, the aphorism has long been seen not only as utopian, but as a highly erotic form of literature. A German from the 1930s, Arthur-Hermann Fink, writes: "the aphorism is the finest, most spiritualized eroticism [*feinste vergeistigste Erotik*]. The drive to the aphorism is the sex drive of the mind [*der Geschlechtstrieb des Geistes*]."[3] He believes that eros and the aphorism belong together because both unite opposites: "Eros, so reports the saga, lives in the *middle* between the gods and people" (quoted in Margolis 291). Throughout this passage Fink quotes Plato, implying that this kind of eros is "Platonic," which as we have seen often veers into the homosexual. Along these same lines, Fink's discussion of a "spiritualized eroticism" or a "sex drive of the mind" resembles Thomas Mann's reception of Plato, which sees male-male sexuality as primarily an intellectual and artistic phenomenon and male-female sexuality as biologically reproductive.

Gender has of course a central role to play in the sexuality of the aphorism. In his 830-page volume on the fragment, Neumann concludes that gender's complicity in the aphorism goes deeper than the individual circumstances of the author:

Only when one observes the problem of the aphorism in a broader context does it become clear that not only individual circumstances are expressed here but that the thought-form of the aphorism touches something essential: Novalis, Fr. Schlegel and Goethe have connected the conflict between the opposing forms of order that structures the aphorism with the polarity of man and woman, they too attempted to determine this field of tension around the image of erotic relationship. (*Ideenparadiese* 229)

3. Arthur-Herman Fink, *Maxime und Fragmente: Grenzmöglichkeiten einer Kunstform. Zur Morphologie des Aphorismus* (Munich, 1934). Cited by Fricke 2.

With many examples, Neumann shows how all the great aphorists of the German tradition have used gender as a central point for many of their witty aperçus.

Of course, both heterosexuality and homosexuality share a concern with gender. One tradition that suggests this concern with gender has a male homosexual coloring is the aphoristic tradition of misogyny that has been alluded to. This is not to say, of course, that male homosexuality and misogyny are identical — Sachsen-Gotha disproves that generalization with his generous treatment of male and female characters in his novel *Kyllenion: A Year in Arcadia*. But in many cultures male-male love has only been able to express itself in terms of male denigration of women. In other patriarchal cultures — for instance, that of ancient Greece — there seems to have been a kind of male equivalent of the lesbian continuum, in which support for male privilege over women went hand in hand with the love of men.

The misogynist side of the aphorism goes back at least to La Rochefoucauld and the French moralists (Neumann, *Ideenparadiese*, 232), but it really becomes apparent when the Germans start writing aphorisms, as Walter Wehe notes in 1939:

> The aphorism is an emphatically male form of literature; that's why it likes to occupy itself, often in a somewhat superior, unloving way, with woman. Even or especially those men who, for various reasons, stood in a somewhat tense relationship with woman, like Lichtenberg, Schopenhauer, Nietzsche, Oscar Wilde, become talkative here. (133)

The appearance of Wehe's study, Fink's commentary on the "intellectual eroticism" (which is to say, the male-male eroticism) of the aphorism, and Mautner's first essay on the aphorism, which appeared in 1934 and is credited with rehabilitating the aphorism as a genre, in the 1930s is itself revealing. Many German intellectuals were attuned, consciously or not, to the erotic possibilities of the extremes of male bonding offered by the National Socialists.

But if the misogynist tradition of the aphorism received from and gave to male homosexuality a certain impetus, what is truly queer about the aphorism's appeal is the way in which it disrupts, or queers, binarisms of male and female. What Neumann sees as fundamentally linking erotics and the aphorism is the way in which Germans like Schlegel, Goethe, and Nietzsche (and Lichtenberg) deconstruct dichotomies in their aphorisms. Here, Neumann's thesis that the Germans profoundly changed the aphoristic tradition from the inherently conservative, didactic approach of the French moralists to the radical German fragments that question the possibility of knowledge becomes important (Neumann, *Ideenparadiese*, 827). If the French moralists introduced to the aphorism a misogynist understanding of gender that had homosexual possibilities, the Germans, with their radical unmooring of dualities, subvert gender in a way that has queer possibilities.

Nowhere is this radical subversion of dualities more apparent — and more germane to the queer — than in issues of self and other, subjectivity and objectivity. Throughout the last century, critics reading the German aphorists have seen the aphorisms as a genre that breaks down the barrier between the subjectivity of the author and the objectivity of his work. Already Friedrich Schlegel calls for fragmentary literature because "that which is fragmentary in content and form is at the same time subjective and individual and completely objective and like a necessary part of the system."[4] Hofmannsthal wrote Schnitzler a letter on December 29, 1927, after reading his aphorisms: "the rhythm of your thought touches me directly and thereby the true, insoluble mystery of your person" (cited in Neumann, *Ideenparadiese*, 93). Unlike most writing, which is caught in the web of language, the aphorism both reveals the secret of the author's person and touches the reader immediately. Similarly, Robert Musil asserts that the author is directly present in the aphorism: "Important for the aphorism: Who says that? A person, not just the author! Therefore the author as person. Is the aphorism part of first-person novel?"[5] Thus, the aphorism not only disrupts the duality between male and female; it also subverts those carefully laid distinctions between author and work, between author and narrator. Neumann refers to the aphorism's "multiply complicated relationship to the 'I' of the author" (*Ideenparadiese* 37).

In bringing the author more clearly into the text than is usual for literature, the aphorism allows for a greater presence of the author's sexuality. Or, at least, it has been conventionally understood to do this. Here it is so not important whether the aphorism has some inherent connection to the author's sexuality or whether it has simply been used as the appropriate genre for the expression of sexuality. The important point is that it is understood to have this function. At the same time, however, the aphorism does not reveal the author's person or sexuality completely, as Stern perceptively notes: "Its charm hides its antithesis, perfect integrated, issuing from a double-look at a word or an idea. It conceals its autobiographical source, yet displays

---

4. "Athenäums-Fragmente," *Kritische und theoretische Schriften* 85.
5. Cited by Mautner, *Lichtenberg*, frontispiece.

its process of generation. It is self-conscious, yet never exhibits its author's self-consciousness unmodified" (216).

This uncovering and covering of the self is precisely how the homosexual has lived—and how the homosexual author has written—since the development of the closet at the end of the eighteenth century. While he was never to reveal his sexuality, that sexuality was also never to be so completely hidden as to be irrelevant. It would always be important to know that something was going on in that closet. Mautner is on to a similar truth when he sees the two essential elements of the aphorism as the paradox and the act of unmasking (*Lichtenberg* 13). Taken together, these two elements provide a form perfect for the modern Western homosexual, whose life project in the last couple of centuries has been hiding and judiciously revealing his or her existence.

It is worth pausing here to note that the project of queer analysis has, like the aphorism, consistently put the distinction between author and work into question. The narrative breaks in Jean Paul's *Siebenkäs*, in which the author speaks directly to other authors, like Gleim, is one example of this phenomenon of queering the distinction between author and text. Karl Philipp Moritz's autobiographical novel *Anton Reiser*, which also frequently passes on material—such as the friendship with the historical personage Iffland—rather directly from the author's life to his fiction, is another example. Given that the premise of queer theory is to discuss ways in which sexuality affects textuality and vice versa, it is not surprising that in a queer analysis we would find fluid movement between the author's life and his or her writings.

In summary, the aphorism has been received, interpreted, and passed on in ways that make it very accessible to homosexuals. In its misogyny and glorification of masculinity, it allowed a covert expression of male-male desire. More profoundly and universally, in its radical destabilization of dualities it queers the gendered bifurcation of male and female. In blurring the boundary between authorial subject and textual object, it allows the queer author to engender queer texts. All of these conclusions hold for Lichtenberg, whose misogyny bled subtly into desire for men, who clearly tried to inject as much of his personal life, and especially his erotic life, into his writings as possible and who, in those aphoristic writings, envisioned, at moments, a radically different structure of gender and sexuality. Once it is acknowledged how queer they are, Lichtenberg's fragments provide a window for the analysis of the male-bonding in intellectual circles in eighteenth-century Germany and more general observations on the history of the border between male homosociality and homosexuality. They can shed light on subsequent "queer" writers, like Schopenhauer, Nietzsche, Thomas Mann, Musil, and the George Circle, who admired Lichtenberg and wrote aphoristically. The insights that the study of the queer fragments can give demonstrate the value of looking for the queer in literature.

Conclusion

MADE IN GERMANY

Modern Sexuality

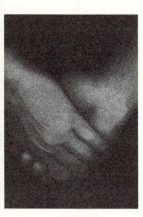

Confronted by efforts of early twentieth-century homosexual literary critics to use sexual categories in interpreting many of the characters and authors of German literature, the poet Stefan George responded with icy aloofness: "We do not ask whether the devotion of Schiller's Don Carlos to Posa, Goethe's Ferdinand to Egmont, the passionate enthusiasm of Jean Paul's Emanuel for Victor or Roquairol for Albano has anything to do with a witch-hunting section of the law or a silly medical category: rather, we have always believed that we find in these relationships an essential, constitutive element of the entire German culture."[1] George's mention of "the witch-hunting section of the law or the silly medical category" refers to the ways in which homosexuality was categorized in the early twentieth century: either as a criminal act or as a pathological state. George not surprisingly rejects both, but he does so by denying the entire concept of sexual identity. In a cynical mode, one might ask whether there were any less-than-noble, self-serving, closeted reasons for the gay George's resistance to a discussion of sexuality and its relationship to literature. It can be very productive, however, to take George seriously and to build on the implications of his argument.

Queer readings need not be limited to the kind

---

1. Cited by Magnus Hirschfeld, *Die Homosexualität des Mannes und des Weibes* (Berlin, 1914), 1022. This citation cited in *Goodbye to Berlin?* 56.

of essentialist labeling, identification, documentation, and pathologizing that George rejects. Instead, they can show how those labeling, identifying, documenting, and pathologizing discourses are, in George's words, a constitutive element in the entirety of German culture. Moreover, one can use literature, which requires attention to language and discourse, to analyze these discourses.

The German literary culture, which George rightly sees as imbued with the various discourses that came to surround male-male friendship, love, eros, and sexuality, has left its mark on modern American culture. Even though few Americans today read works by Goethe, Schiller, or Jean Paul, the characters in their poems, plays, and novels are connected by the web of culture to modern conceptions of sexuality.

In Audre Lorde's "biomythography" *Zami: A New Spelling of My Name*, the African-American narrator struggles with her German as she deals with her sexual identity, eventually receiving good grades in her foreign language course as she begins to come out as a lesbian. Later, Lorde in fact went to Germany to teach for a semester in Berlin, where she became something of a heroine to Afro-German women. She was the inspiration for the groundbreaking anthology of Afro-German writing *Farbe Bekennen* (*Showing Our Colors*), edited by Katharina Oguntoye in 1986, which brings together issues of race and sexuality in Germany. The linkage of "Germanness" and homosexual identity in Lorde's writing is not just a coincidence, for Germany is the forge in which modern sexuality was constructed. The literary, cultural, and medical discourses of eighteenth-century Germany—classicism, orientalism, medicine, faustianism, aphoristic thought, and so on—came together in the nineteenth century with such power as to impose new structures on Western notions of sexuality. This newly structured sexuality has subsequently spread throughout the world, which, as Lorde's biomythography shows, sometimes remembers that modern sexuality has been stamped with that mark of quality, "made in Germany."

The late nineteenth century was more aware of this connection than is our present era. "There is some reason for believing," asserts the English sexologist Havelock Ellis, "that homosexuality is especially prominent in Germany and among Germans" (60). In fact, Ellis writes that "in all classes and in all fields of activity, Germany during the nineteenth century produced a long series of famous or notorious homosexual persons from Alexander von Humboldt to F. A. Krupp" (*Sexual Inversion* 45). "Learning German" is also an important activity in Oscar Wilde's *Importance of Being Earnest*. Commenting on this fact, Eve Sedgwick notes that "Do you speak German?" was a pick-up line for late nineteenth-century French homosexuals. All of this gives a peculiarly Teutonic tone to homosexuality for Sedgwick, a tone that is particularly resonant because, as she points out, the German state was founded in 1871, almost contemporaneous with the establishment of the modern vocabulary of "homosexuality" in 1869 (*Tendencies* and *Epistemology*).

Sedgwick's finds further Germanic signifiers in Wilde's writings, specifically in his references to Nietzsche and Wagner. She sees Nietzsche partly with the hindsight that puts both him and male homosexuality in the vicinity of National Socialism, with all of its homosociality, homophobia, and repressed homosexuality. Less anachronistically, she views Nietzsche in the light of his misogynistic writings about the male-male union of Apollo and Dionysos. In addition, Nietzsche was interested in ancient Greece, decadence, unnaturalness, and Walt Whitman — all shibboleths of late nineteenth-century Euro-American homosexuals.

Sedgwick is interested in the homoerotics surrounding Wagner's works that made him, too, a source of identity for homosexuals in the late nineteenth and early twentieth century. Hans Mayer reports that the French poet Paul Verlaine, scandalously involved with Arthur Rimbaud, idolized Wagner, partly because of the Bavarian King Ludwig II's clearly eroticized admiration and support for the composer (247–50). Hans Fuchs wrote a novel at the turn of the century on the homosexual subculture surrounding the Wagner cult. One of Havelock Ellis's patients also identifies his love of Wagner's music as a constitutive part of his inverted condition (*Sexual Inversion* 131).

Transvestites constituted a special subgroup of this fin-de-siècle queer scene in Germany and Austria. Magnus Hirschfeld, who coined the word "transvestite," wrote an entire book on Berlin cross-dressers. The *Berlin Court Paper* (*Berliner Gerichts-Zeitung*) reported in 1883 that the police had the names of 4,799 men who "are under suspicion of enjoying playing female roles or who have in fact already been caught in female clothes" (*Goodbye to Berlin?* 72). While it is true that male transvestites are often not homosexual, they can be considered queer in the sense of transgressing gender and sexual boundaries. Their strong presence in Berlin at the turn of the century points to the flourishing perverse subculture of Berlin in the late nineteenth century.

Transvestites were only part of the queer scene in Berlin, which became famous as "Eldorado" and attracted homosexuals from around the world (see the catalog *Eldorado*). One of Ellis's patients writes that Berlin was a "revelation," where he discovered "homosexual baths, pensions, restaurants, and hotels, where you can go with one of your own sex at a certain fee per hour" (133). Ellis himself confirms that Berlin is filled with homosexual cafes and bars (60). Exact numbers on these cafes and bars are hard to find, because they did not always identify themselves as such, but there seem to have been about six such establishments in 1896 and around twelve in 1900 (*Goodbye to Berlin?* 71); Mosse adds that there were thirty-eight by 1914. In 1897, a German aristocrat who had spent several years abroad in order to escape the discrimination against male-male love mandated by paragraph 175 of the German basic law wrote to the early homosexual-rights organization the Scientific-Humanitarian Committee that "the life of Urnings in the capital of the fatherland under paragraph 175 is more extensive, less ashamed, and less restricted than in any other place in the Orient or the Occident" (*Goodbye to Berlin?* 70). Mosse reports that "when the French popular playwright Oscar Méténier visited Berlin in 1904, he found a society much more open to homosexuality than that of Paris. He was astounded by the serenity and unself-consciousness of the homosexuals he met at various dances" (90). Hirschfeld even claims that "in Berlin it is not at all unusual for parents to come to terms with the urning nature, and even the homosexual life, of their children" (*Goodbye to Berlin?* 71). Word of the thriving gay culture in Berlin drew many foreigners to the city, including Christopher Isherwood and Stephen Spender, who then passed along their impressions in novels like *Goodbye to Berlin* and *The Temple*.

Part and parcel of this burgeoning queer scene in Berlin was an energetic German-language movement for homosexual rights that was quite remarkable in the nineteenth century. After reading some writings by the early homosexual rights activist Karl Heinrich Ulrichs, Friedrich Engels, tongue in cheek, wrote to Karl Marx that the queers were about to take over: "That was indeed a curious 'urning' whom you sent to me. Those are indeed extremely unnatural revelations. The pederasts [*Päderasten*] are beginning to count themselves and find that they represent a power in the state. Only the organization was lacking, although according to this, it is already beginning to arise in secret" (cited in Derks 172). Engels goes on to paint a dire picture of the future, with the victorious pederasts declaring war on women and demanding tribute from the young men of the future. Interestingly, in the midst of this juvenile humor, Engels declares that such a movement could only emerge from Germany: "Only possible in Germany, by the way, that such a fellow gets up, turns his mess into a theory" (cited in Derks 172). Engles does not mean his remarks positively, but there might be something to his notion about Germany, or at least the German-speaking world being the crucible of queer politics.

Already in the 1830s in Switzerland, Heinrich Hössli published *Eros: The Male Love of the Greeks* (*Eros: Die Männerliebe der Griechen*), his two-volume plea for the just treatment of men who loved men. In 1869, the Hungarian Karl Maria Kertbeny published (under the pseudonym "Benkert") brochures against the Prussian laws pertaining to male-male sex on the books. He assured his place in history by being the first to use the terms *Homosexualist* and *Homosexualität*. These terms therefore are not exclusively medical, as many post-Foucauldians have argued. They emerged first in the political homosexual emancipation movement of nineteenth-century Germany.

Kertbeny had already been in contact with the era's most prominent homosexual rights activist in Germany and indeed the world: Karl Heinrich Ulrichs, who, starting in 1864 under the pseudonym "Numa Numantius," published the *Studies on the Riddle of Male-Male Love* (*Forschungen über das Räthsel der mannmännlichen Liebe*), a series of short monographs that attempted to prove that male-male love was natural and ought to be legalized. Ulrichs did not use Kertbeny's terminology, instead referring to men who loved men as "Urnings" or "uranians" and members of the "third sex," which he saw as consisting of female souls trapped in male bodies. Given the timidity that many gays and lesbians still feel in the late twentieth century when trying to assert their rights, it is downright astonishing to discover that Ulrichs attempted to deliver a speech against the Prussian laws concerning male-male sex at the annual conference of German lawyers on August 29, 1867, an entire century before Stonewall. The protests from the audience prevented him from completing his talk, but his very attempt merits praise to this day.

In 1875, a certain H. Marx published *The Love of Urnings* (*Urningsliebe*), which concluded with a desire "to ground an organisation for the interests of urnings" (*Goodbye to Berlin?* 28). Although it is unclear whether anything came of this call, eventually Germany did produce the world's first organization devoted to homosexual rights. On May 15, 1897, in his apartment in the Charlottenburg neighborhood of Berlin, the sexologist and political activist Magnus Hirschfeld founded the "Scientific-Humanitarian Committee" (Wissenschaftlich-humanitäres Komitee), which was devoted to ending discrimination against homosexuals and promoting their rights. Until the National Socialists came to power in 1933 and drove him into exile in France, Hirschfeld worked tirelessly for gay rights in Germany, allying himself with Social-Democrats and feminist political forces. Anna Ruling and Helene Stöcker were among a number of women who argued for the rights of lesbians in early twentieth-century Germany (see Faderman, *Lesbians in Germany*). Hirschfeld's committee had an institute that maintained a large library on issues of sexuality. Starting in 1899, it published the *Yearbook for Sexual Intermediary Types with Special Attention to Homosexuality* (*Das Jahrbuch für sexuelle Zwischenstufen unter besonderer Berücksichtigung der Homosexualität*), which became one of the first journals devoted to the study of same-sex desire and continued publishing until the the National Socialists came into power. Even before the *Yearbook*'s publication, however, another German-language periodical, *The Exceptional: A Magazine for Male Culture* (*Der Eigene: Ein Blatt für männliche Kultur*), in 1898 shifted its emphasis from anarchist politics to, as one sympathetic reviewer of the time put it, "the artistic representation of homosexuality" (*Goodbye to Berlin?* 49). This journal, under the leadership of Adolf Brand, pursued a more militantly misogynistic and nationalistic approach to homosexuality, as its title, professing exclusivity, indicates. This publication, too, was closed by the National Socialists in 1933.

In 1896, Ellis ascertained that "Germany is the only country in which there is a definite and well-supported movement for the defense and social rehabilitation of inverts" (60). In his review of the history of the American gay movement, Dennis Altman confirms Ellis's observation, describing Germany as "the only country before World War II to develop a large-scale homosexual movement" (111). This political movement emerged partly in response to the increasingly dire legal situation regarding same-sex desire in Germany. The Napoleonic code, based on Enlightenment ideals eager to separate the concepts of sin and vice from that of crime, had decriminalized consensual sexual acts between adults, even adults of the same sex. Napoleon's conquests at the beginning of the nineteenth century brought this code to Germany. Anselm von Feuerbach shored it up in Bavaria in 1813 with a clear statement that it was inappropriate for the state to be involved in male-male sexuality. After Napoleon's defeat, however, the German principalities gradually recriminalized sodomy in the nineteenth century, partly out of nationalistic sentiments that had linked homosexuality with French law. (Similar developments caused the English to retain and sharpen their laws against homosexuality in the nineteenth century, as Crompton documents.) Bavaria—oddly enough, given its late twentieth-century conservativism— was the last state in Germany to recriminalize sodomy and was considered, especially under Ludwig II, a haven for homosexuals. Ulrichs claims in 1864, "Bavaria alone treats male-male love [*mannmännliche Liebe*] completely correctly. It declares the practice completely unpunishable everywhere that the practice of dionic [*dionisch* = heterosexual] love is unpunishable" (Ulrichs, "Vindex," 9).

The nineteenth-century German cultural realm was thus unusual in this time (and perhaps comparable to the United States today) in that it had a broad range of legal responses to same-sex behavior. Queers in one principality could find out relatively easily how their counterparts in neighboring jurisdictions were treated. The very decentralization of the Germanic political landscape in the eighteenth and nineteenth centuries provided an intriguing variety of laboratories in which approaches to sexuality could be developed through legal means, publications, universities, and medical establishments. This had benefit for individuals as well: When a scandal became too hot, as happened to Johannes Müller and Wilhelm August Iffland, the perpetrator could usually find refuge across the border in a nearby German-speaking principality, if he or she were mobile enough.

Since opposition to sodomy had nationalist cachet in Germany (given the leniency toward consensual sex acts among adults in the Napoleonic Code), it is not surprising that sodomy laws made their most spectacular comeback in the new Basic Law, or constitution, of the new German empire of 1871: "For even if one could justify the cessation of legal penalties from the standpoint of medicine . . . the legal convictions of the people regard this act not merely as a vice, but also a crime" (cited in Derks, *Schande*, 168). The new German state, the Second Empire, was grounded in part on the criminalization of sodomy. Tellingly, as it went about recriminalizing sodomy, the new basic law of the land acknowledged both the new medical discourses of the day and the legal distinctions between sin and crime that had emerged in the Enlightenment (the very legal and medical categories that George resists in his discussion of sexuality and literature). Repression generates its own resistance, however: In the very same Germany that was recriminalizing sodomy, Kertbeny, Ulrichs, and Hirschfeld became the first homosexual rights activists to press for the end of such discrimination.

It is worth noting that Germany's experience of decriminalization followed by recriminalization sets it apart from the other European powers, particularly England, which had never decriminalized sodomy, and France, which never recriminalized it. The taste of freedom that the Urnings and homosexuals had enjoyed in the Germanic lands in the early nineteenth century, combined with the variety of legal responses to sodomy with the German world in the mid-nineteenth century, made Germany a fertile political landscape in which the homosexual emancipation movement could take root and grow.

The gay rights movement spread from Germany to many other countries. Henry Gerber, who had been part of the occupation of Germany after World War I in the early 1920s, was impressed enough by the German homosexual emancipation movement to re-create it in Chicago in 1924 as "The Society for Human Rights," the first gay rights organization in the United States. Even today one of the most important organizations devoted to gay rights in the United States is called the Human Rights Campaign Fund, which points to the modern movement's roots in this German-inspired organization. Gerber also published a magazine called *Friendship and Freedom*, the title of which was a direct translation from a German gay magazine of the 1920s, *Freundschaft und Freiheit*.

This political movement was closely related to the medical studies of the German sexologists — so closely, in fact, that many have followed Foucault in arguing that sexological or medical discourses actually created homosexuality. While it is true that these discourses had an important role to play, they were not the exclusive or even the initial founders of the discourse, as witnessed by Kertbeny's politically motivated coinage of the term "homosexual" in 1869. Nonetheless, the early homosexual rights movement worked closely with sexologists to establish a medical grounding for their identity. The English novelist and apologist for homosexual rights, John Addington Symonds, considered Ulrichs "the true founder of the scientific treatment of the phenomenon" of same-sex desire (*Goodbye to Berlin?* 29), granting him a kind of sexological expertise that strengthened his political credibility. The sexologist Gustav Jaeger took over Kertbeny's terminology of "homosexuality" and "heterosexuality" in his sexological treatise *The Discovery of the Soul* (*Die Entdeckung der Seele*), published in 1879. And Magnus Hirschfeld united the positions of activist and sexologist in his own person, using his medical expertise to back up his political efforts.

This medical discourse had a long tradition in Germany, with Johann Ludwig Casper's (1796–1864) studies of pederasts and their characteristics. From a physician's perspective, he argued as a physician for the inborn nature of some homosexual drives. The Berlin psychiatrist Carl Westphal published in 1869 his famous article on "contary sexual feelings" in the *Archive for Psychiatry* (*Archiv für Psychiatrie*), which many, including Foucault, regard as the birth of the modern homosexual. Ellis in any case saw it as the birth of the discussion about homosexuality, a discussion that he says took place "at first exclusively in Germany" (65). For this reason, he believes that "it is in Germany that the foundations of the study of sexual inversion have been laid" (61). Therefore, as he argues, "the scientific and literary publications dealing with homosexuality issued from the German press probably surpass in quality and importance those issued from all countries put together" (60). Ellis himself had to publish his study on sexual inversion in 1896 in Leipzig, Germany, before he published it in England, because the climate in Germany was more accepting of this subject. The cultural historian Edward Westermarck also published his chapter on homosexuality in the German journal *Sexual Problems: Magazine for Sexual Sciences and Sexual Politics* (*Sexual-Probleme: Zeitschrift für Sexualwissenschaft und Sexualpolitik*) in 1908, before publishing it in the English edition of his study on the origin and development of moral concepts.

By the time that Ellis and Westermarck published in Germany, the sexological research was indeed in full swing. According to Hirschfeld, over 1,000 publications on homosexuality appeared between 1898 and 1908 in the German-speaking realm (172; see also Faderman, *Surpassing*, 248). Mosse cites the figure as 320 publications between 1895 and 1905 (24). In addition to Casper, Westphal, and Jaeger, the Berlin physician Albert Moll wrote medical treatises and treated the homosexuality of such patients as Thomas Mann's confidant, the writer Otto Grautoff. Richard Freiherr von Krafft-Ebing was inspired by Ulrich's writings to pursue the subject of same-sex desire and eventually became one of the leading medical voices on the subject. His important *Psychopathia Sexualis* transmitted knowledge of homosexuality and heterosexuality, as well as sadism and masochism, to the entire world, in many editions and translations. Hirschfeld's writings and the essays published in the *Yearbook for Sexual Intermediary Types* are further evidence for the astonishing productivity of the sexological researchers in this era.

Sigmund Freud and his discipline of psychoanalysis were perhaps an even more successful conduit than sexology for the dissemination of knowledge about sexuality. Freud's own writings posit a fascinating, unstable picture of polymorphous, constantly changing sexuality, fundamentally different from the sexological model both in its depth and its resistance to essentialism. In "Three Contributions to Sexuality," he categorically rejects the notion of an essential homosexual identity: "Psychoanalytic research very strongly opposes the attempt to separate homosexuals from other persons as a group of a special nature. . . . All men are capable of homosexual object selection and actually accomplish this in the unconscious" (560). This was a radical deviation from the thinking of the emancipationists and the sexologists, allowing for the sort of constructionist approach to polymorphous sexuality and fluid identity that characterizes the queer.

Freud was at times remarkably nonprescriptive with regard to sexual concerns. In a famous letter to an American woman who wanted her son to be treated for his homosexuality, Freud refused to provide treatment:

Homosexuality is assuredly no advantage, but it is nothing to be ashamed of, no vice, no degradation, it cannot be classified as an illness. . . . Many highly respected individuals of ancient and modern times have been homosexuals, several of the greatest among them (Plato, Michelangelo, Leonardo da Vinci, etc.). It is a great injustice to persecute homosexuality as a crime, and cruelty too. If you do not believe me, read the books of Havelock Ellis. (Cited by Fuss 27)

Despite Freud's resistance to pathologizing and essentializing views of the sexologists, he nonetheless regards Plato, Michelangelo, and Leonardo da Vinci all as "homosexuals," without showing any understanding of the historically constructed nature of this category. Moreover, to prove his point, he cites a sexologist, who would also have believed in historically constant sexual categories. Freud probably understands that in the pragmatic world of parents concerned about their son's sexuality, socially constructed categories are quite real and active.

Freud's pragmatism teaches us an important lesson. While this book's premise is that sexuality is historically constructed, it also takes seriously the notion that historical constructs function as reality. Since we live in a world of social constructions, it is necessary to try to build something with these constructed identities. Nietzsche's statement in his essay "On Truth and Lying in an Extramoral Sense" is relevant here:

In this respect man can probably be admired as a mighty architectural genius who succeeds in building an infinitely complicated conceptual cathedral on foundations that move like flowing water; of course, in order to anchor itself to such a foundation, the building must be light as gossamer — delicate enough to be carried along by the wave, yet strong enough not to be blown apart by the wind.

The foundations of sexual identity may be fluid, but the conceptual cathedral built upon those foundations still rises imperiously in our society.

Freud's occasionally pragmatic acceptance of the concept of the homosexual allowed conventional psychoanalysis, especially when it reached American shores, to revert to a sexological understanding of homosexuality as a perversion that could be cured. Even today, and even among the most progessive psychoanalysts, one frequently encounters an odd kind of de facto essentialism that dooms everyone to the same relationships with the father, the mother, the paternal, the maternal, the symbolic, the imaginary, the phallus, and so forth—all of which seems to result in a reinscribed essentialism.

Sexology and psychoanalysis drew customers from throughout the world to the German-speaking countries. The vocabulary of the sexologists (homosexuality, heterosexuality, sadism, masochism) as well as the conceptual framework of psychoanalysis (repression, latency, Oedipus, and so forth) soon became the most influential models for understanding the psyche.

Perhaps the flowering of sexological and psychoanalytical thinking on sexuality in Germany in the late nineteenth century was partly a result of the German university system that had been restructured under Wilhelm von Humboldt in the early 1800s to foster and encourage research. While England and France had set up separate medical schools that effectively segregated the medical community from the more philosophical and speculative faculties, the German medical school system produced academics who were interested in such theoretical topics as the nature of homosexuality, because medicine remained within the fold of the university. Thus German sexologists had the time, resources, and motivation to analyze sexual perversions from an academic medical perspective.

It is also significant that in the wake of Humboldt's late eighteenth-century educational reforms, German universities maintained classics departments at a high standard, allowing for extensive research in ancient culture that continually brought German intellectuals in contact with notions and narratives of same-sex desire. Classicists could not help but produce essays like "Observations on the Male Love of the Greeks" (1775), by Christoph Meiners. Joan DeJean has made a strong case for the importance of these early nineteenth-century German academic discussions of Greek same-sex desire for the eventual contours of the medical and legal definition of homosexuality. Such academic discussions moved into more general circulation via the writings of such philosophers as Arthur Schopenhauer, who attached a lengthy discussion of pederasty to the third edition of his *World as Will and Representation* (*Die Welt als Wille und Vorstellung*) of 1859. Ulrichs, incidentally, gratefully cites Schopenhauer frequently and at length in his *Studies on the Riddle of Male-Male Love.*

Additionally, Mosse argues cogently for the significance of this neo-classicism in the establishment of new ideals of masculinity that took root in the eighteenth century and persist to the present day. In a manner pleasing to those steeped in the paradoxes of queer theory, the sexually dissident Winckelmann would, by this theory, be establishing the sexually notorious Greeks as the standard bearers for the new, presumptively straight, masculinity. Winckelmann's adulation of Greek youth represents a flowering of the ideal of "Bildung" promulgated by eighteenth-century Germans. Bildung, in this interpretation, becomes the creation of a new man, well rounded, personally stable, and socially productive. Moritz, Wieland, Jean Paul, Schiller, and of course Goethe — most of the authors addressed in this book — are invested in the concept of Bildung, and by now it should be clear that most can be seen as integrally concerned with issues of sexuality.

The homosexual emancipation movement, sexology, psychoanalysis, and academic discourses such as classics and the ideology of Bildung are phenomena that share strong roots in German culture, history, and literature and could have helped create and spread Germanic notions of sexuality throughout the rest of the world. Another path by which the German concept of homosexuality has reached the rest of the world, specifically the United States, is the film industry, which thrived in Germany at the beginning of the twentieth century and made its significant exodus to America with the ascent of the Nazis in the 1930s. Before the Nazis took over, "Germany was clearly in the forefront of film realism and compassion" with regard to homosexuality, writes film historian Boze Hadleigh (18). German film was successful worldwide throughout the 1920s. Once the National Socialists came to power, many of those who woven issues of sexuality into their films moved to the United States.

Considered the earliest film on male homosexuality, *Different from the Others* (*Anders als die anderen*) was directed by Richard Oswald in 1919. Its story is a plea for relaxing the legal prohibitions against homosexuality in order to reduce the dangers of blackmail. *Anders* showed to sold-out audiences until the Germans reintroduced a film censorship committee in 1921. Leontine Sagan's film *Mädchen in Uniform* (1931), one of the all-time classics on lesbians, also emerges out of the highly developed queer culture of Weimar Berlin (Rich). The diplomat and art collector Harry Graf Kessler noted in his journal that this film was selling out in cinemas for over nineteen weeks in Paris (727). Still, *Mädchen* was not the first film with a full-fledged lesbian character; that honor goes to the original German version of G. W.

Pabst's *Pandora's Box* (*Die Büchse der Pandora*), in which the Countess Geschwitz is a lesbian. In the non-German releases of the film, her character is made more obscure by censorship.

Conrad Veidt, who starred in *Different from the Others,* was one of many queer German actors to emigrate to Hollywood once the National Socialists took over. Leontine Sagan shows up in Klaus Mann's diaries as part of the émigré scene also. Marlene Dietrich was perhaps the most prominent example of the many artists who brought to the States a certain sexual queerness of a peculiarly Teutonic stamp. Her male attire and the famous lesbian kiss in *Morocco* perpetuated the Germanic aura of same-sex desire to an entire world via film.

Hand in hand with the cinematic culture was the glorification of the body that with the nudist movement and the *Wandervögel* (the back-to-nature movement for young Germans) became a characteristic part of Germanic culture by the end of the nineteenth century. Pondering in his diary entry of August 26, 1932, the "almost pathological interest in Germany" that the world had in the early 1930s, Kessler cites the nudist movement and the revaluation of morals in German youth in connection with "the amusement bars with pretty boys instead of girls" (726). Elsewhere he notes repeatedly and positively the emergence of a body culture Germany: "Nudity, light, air, sun, the worship of life, of bodily perfection, of the sense, without false modesty, without prudery. It is also astonishing how the bodies, the bodily reality in the young generation, obeys this drive, how much more beautiful the young people are today than before the war" (July 14, 1930; 674). Again, on October 2, 1930, Kessler writes: "In the twelve years since the revolution, we have—and it's almost a miracle—created a new beauty that is in harmony with the worker's democracy, indeed produced even more beautiful people, finer, thinner, more glowing; today's youth is, especially when naked, more beautiful than the youth before the war" (681). In France on August 28, 1932, Kessler notes the contrast between Germany and other cultures: "The contrast to Germany is remarkable. At home, young people come together on Sundays and hike, play, bathe; one doesn't see a trace of bourgeois Sunday best, but rather beautiful, strong bodies, unclothed or half-clothed. Here, however, the petit bourgeois style of clothing and Sunday pleasures still rules supreme" (729). Kessler is just one source, but he points to the emergence of a body culture in Germany in the first half of the twentieth century that because of its openness to bodily desire is closely related to the simultaneous flowering of queer culture.

Another source corroborating Kessler's observations is Thomas Mann.

He regrets that American films did not show as much beefcake as their German counterparts:

German films give me something which those of other nationalities scarcely offer: pleasure in youthful bodies, particularly male ones, in their nakedness. This is connected with German "homosexuality" and is lacking in the attractions of French and also American products: the showing of young male nudity in flattering, indeed loving photographic lighting whenever the opportunity presents itself. . . . The Germans, or the German Jews, that do this are certainly right: there is basically nothing "more beautiful." (February 2, 1934; 33–34:309)

The quotation marks around "homosexuality" and "more beautiful" suggest that Mann regards both sexuality and beauty as constructed notions. Mann's identification of the construct of "homosexuality" as a German product reinforces the Teutonic origins of modern notions of sexuality. Mann's qualification about the "German Jews" is odd—one thinks of Leni Riefenstahl's highly eroticized male bodies filmed in the context of anti-Semitic German nationalism. Mann, it seems, is displacing his awareness of the queerness of this interest in the nude male body from a sexual to an ethnic category, following perhaps the same urge that compelled him to set the homosexual seduction of Gustav von Aschenbach in *Death in Venice* in Italy.

Some of the roots of the specifically German interest in images of masculinity may be found in Wilhelm von Gloeden's nineteenth-century photographs of Italian boys, which are still sold today as gay kitsch. Speculations about the rise of the body culture and its manifestations in German popular culture lead to another arbiter of modern American gender construction with roots in Germany: Barbie, the doll with the stereotypically perfect female body and beauty, began as a German doll. Having imprinted her image as the standard of beauty on the minds of generations of young Americans, she has gone on to be appropriated by gays and lesbians in such books as *Barbie's Queer Accessories*. In any case, Barbie suggests that the ways in which German gender and sexual constructions reached America were many and varied from academic to popular culture.

This queer culture moved by a variety of direct and indirect routes to the rest of the Western world, and specifically to the United States, even before the National Socialist regime in Germany. The National-Socialist takeover of Germany in the 1930s accelerated this transmission of the new culture to the United States. Many homosexuals fled the country, pressured by the threat of incrimination and even concentration camps. Leaders and innovators from the most modern artistic fields and most technologically up-to-date professions also left Germany when the political system began to turn fascist. The sexologist and activist Hirschfeld went to France as soon as the National Socialists took over; his final work was published in French and English translations before it appeared in German. Freud flew to London when the Germans annexed Austria. At the same time many queer, Jewish, and socialist academics left the country, some of whom eventually found jobs at American universities. On many levels, therefore, a forced transfer of German culture to other Western lands, particularly the United States, took place.

In the film world, directors like Leontine Sagan, Fritz Lang, and F. W. Murnau joined stars like Veidt and Dietrich in moving to Hollywood. Some, like Veidt and Dietrich, embodied in themselves the queer culture that was being transmitted. Murnau, who is said to have died in an embarrassing situation with his chauffeur, is a director who belongs in this group. Other transmitted queerness in a more distanced way. The German presence in the film world added a touch of pre-Nazi German sexual freedom to the American cinematic experience. The German-born Billy Wilder, for instance, came to the States, worked with Dietrich, and directed *Some Like It Hot*, a remake of an earlier Germany film *Fanfares of Love* (*Fanfaren der Liebe*, 1951), which, with its transvestism, worked toward loosening up American attitudes toward cross-dressing and gender-bending in 1959. Other films inspired by pre–World War II Germany that made it big in America were *Cabaret*, based on Isherwood's *Goodbye to Berlin*, and *Victor/Victoria*, based on a 1931 German film by the name of *Viktor/Viktoria*.

After World War II, one of the cofounders of the Mattachine Society, a direct antecedant of the gay rights organizations of the 1960s and 1970s, was Rudi Gernreich, the fashion designer and then-lover of Harry Hayes, the early American gay rights pioneer. Gernreich was born in Vienna and his family had fled the Nazis. While Gernreich was too young to have taken part in the homosexual emancipation movement of the German-speaking realm, he may well have been influenced by that tradition in re-creating the movement in the United States. In Canada, on the masthead of the gay newspaper *Body Politic* stood the words of Kurt Hiller, the gay German activist from the Weimar Republic: "The liberation of homosexuals can only be the work of homosexuals themselves" (Altman 18). Once again, we see cuttings of the German gay movement from the first half of the twentieth century taking root in the New World.

Despite the liberatory side of the German influence on American culture, there is also the impact of fascist elements in the modern entertainment industry, as Horkheimer and Adorno discuss. Scholars working in their tradition, like Rickels, have been able to argue cogently that even today there is a peculiar link between early twentieth-century Germany and late twentieth-century California. In *The Case of California*, Rickels has suggests that much of this heritage runs over queer lines that emphasize the androgyny, the gender-bending, and the hard body of the boy-woman.

This culture that transfered by whatever means to the United States and other Western lands was rooted in the texts of the late eighteenth century. Unlike other Western European nations, Germany had seen its own culture emerge comparatively late, in the eighteenth century, not anything more ancient. Although the Romantics would look back to medieval German culture, Germany does not have cultural legacies from the early modern era who bear comparison with Shakespeare in England, or Montaigne, Molière, and Racine in France. Winckelmann, Wieland, Moritz, Goethe, Schiller, Jean Paul, and Lichtenberg constituted the tradition of German Bildung.

The German late nineteenth- and early twentieth-century homosexual community cited these authors frequently and German sexologists also referred frequently to the classical authors of the age of Goethe. Gustav Jaeger's chapter on homosexuality refers specifically to Goethe's "To the Moon" ("An den Mond") as an example of intense, possibly erotic, male-male friendship. It further cites Frederick the Great, Winckelmann, Johannes von Müller, August Wilhelm Schlegel, and Wilhelm August Iffland as alleged homosexuals from the age of Goethe. Freud in particular relied on Goethe in establishing psychoanalysis, as Eissler, Ronell (*Dictations*), and Prokhoris have shown, positing a direct link between the authors of late eighteenth-century Germany and the modern understanding of the psyche. The German film industry also began with a much more decisive bent toward "high culture" than did Hollywood, attempting to produce cinematic versions of German classics, such as Murnau's *Faust*, in order to gain respectability.

Via the paths of popular culture, film, psychoanalysis, sexology, and the homosexual emancipation movement, as well as by countless other routes, German notions of sexuality entered the United States, whence they subsequently went on to influence the rest of the world, eventually making their way back to Germany where the gay movement now looks to the United States for inspiration. The theme of this reimportation of a gay rights movement from the United States was central to the 1997 exhibit at the Academy of the Arts (Akademie der Künste), "Goodbye to Berlin?" on the history of the homosexual rights movement. Rosa von Praunheim's 1997 film on San Francisco, *In Love with a Tattooed Penis* (*Verliebt in einen tatowierten Schwanz*) is a good example of this modern German reimportation of American concepts of sexuality. In a series of other films, he shows American queer communities as positive models for the German gay and lesbian world: *Army of Lovers or Revolt of the Perverts* (*Armee der Liebenden oder Aufstand der Perversen*, 1979), *My New York* (*Mein New York*, 1982), *Silence = Death* (1990). Monika Treut's films similarly view the United States as a positive queer alternative to stuffy Germany. In her first film, *Seduction: The Cruel Woman* (*Verführung: Die grausame Frau*, 1985), an American girl comes to learn and then master a sadomasochistic relationship. In *Virgin Machine* (*Die Jungfrauenmaschine*, 1988) and *My Father Is Coming* (1991), uptight Germans come to the United States to learn about queer sexuality from American personalities like Suzie Sexpert and Annie Sprinkle.

The text of modern sexuality, which seems like much else in the world to be so dominated by the English language and American culture, is actually woven from an inordinately diverse and complex variety of German threads; it is a cloak knitted with a lot of German yarn. Perhaps now, having looked at the panic in Weimar, at the queerness in eighteenth-century German texts, we can understand more clearly why they would interest a late twentieth-century reader. We see how these texts document the coalescing of a multitude of discourses around male-male desire, prefiguring a gay identity. At the same time, they explain why discursive identity will necessarily be pharamaceutical, in the sense of being both itself and another. They point therefore to the queerness of identity in general, to the instability and polyvalence that inhere in identity because of identity's discursive nature. Paraphrasing the eighteenth-century notion that sodomy was both in and against nature, these texts are about, for, and against sexual identity. Our interest in them turns out to be a look backward at the texts constructing our own identity. Given their importance in the constitution of modern American culture, they should help many discover more about the construction of their identity as well.

BIBLIOGRAPHY

Adelung, Johann Christoph. *Grammatisch-kritisches Wörterbuch der Hochdeutschen Mundart*. Vienna: Pichler, 1807.

Aldrich, Robert. *The Seduction of the Mediterranean: Writing, Art, and Homosexual Fantasy*. London: Routledge, 1993.

———. "Weiße und farbige Männer. Reisen, Kolonialismus und Homosexualität zwischen den Rassen in der Literatur." *Forum Homosexualität und Literatur* 7 (1989): 5–24.

Altman, Dennis. *The Homosexualization of America, the Americanization of the Homosexual*. New York: St. Martin's, 1982.

Angier, Natalie. "Theory Tested on Why Body's Defenses Go Haywire in AIDS." *New York Times* (May 5, 1994): B6.

Arnold, Thomas. *Beobachtung über die Natur, Arten, Ursachen und Verhütung des Wahnsinns oder der Tollheit*. Translated by J. Chr. G. Ackermann. 2 vols. Leipzig: Friedrich Gotthold Jacobäer und Sohn, 1784.

Ashton, Rosemary. "Plots and Plotters." *Times Literary Supplement* (Sept. 11, 1992): 18.

Aurnhammer, Achim. *Androgynie: Studien zu einem Motiv in der europäischen Literatur*. Cologne: Böhlau, 1986.

Außerordentliches Beispiel der großen Verdorbenheit der Sitten in England. Reprinted in *Capri. Zeitschrift für schwule Geschichte* 22 (August 1996): 31–33.

Austen, Roger. "Stoddard's Little Tales in *South Sea Idyls*." In *Literary Visions of Homosexuality*, edited by Stuart Kellogg, 73–82. New York: Haworth Press, 1983.

Baasner, Rainer. *Lichtenberg: Das große Ganze. Ein Essay*. Paderborn: Schönigh, 1992.

Baird-Lange, Lorrayne Y. "Victim Criminalized: Iconographic Traditions and Peacham's Ganymede." In *Traditions and Innovations: Essays on British Literature of the Middle Ages and the Renaissance*, edited by D. G. Allen and R. A. White, 231–50. Newark: University of Delaware Press, 1990.

Bakshi, Parminder Kaur. "Homosexuality and Orientalism: Edward Carpenter's Journey to the East." In *Edward Carpenter and Late Victorian Radicalism*, edited by Tony Brown. London: Frank Cass, 1990.

Barkan, Leonard. *Transuming Passion: Ganymede and the Erotics of Humanism*. Stanford: Stanford University Press, 1991.

Barthes, Roland. *The Fashion System*. Translated by Matthew Ward and Richard Howard. New York: Hill and Wang, 1983.

————. *Mythologies*. Translated by Annette Lavers. New York: Hill and Wang, 1972.

Batley, Edward M. "Zur Problematik der Glaubwürdigkeit der Geschichte. Mit besonderer Berücksichtung der Marquis-Posa-Figur in Schillers 'Don Karlos' und der 'Malteser'-Fragment." In *Friedrich Schiller. Angebot und Diskurs. Zügange, Dichtung, Zeitgenossenschaft*, edited by Helmut Brandt, 250–75. Berlin: Aufbau, 1987.

Baudrillard, Jean. *Seduction*. Translated by Brian Singer. New York: St. Martin's, 1990.

Beck, Gad. *Und Gad ging zu David: Die Erinnerungen des Gad Beck, 1923 bis 1945*. Edited by Frank Heibert. Berlin: Edition dia, 1995.

Bennett, Benjamin. *Goethe's Theory of Poetry: "Faust" and the Regeneration of Language*. Ithaca: Cornell University Press, 1986.

Bennett, Jane. "'How Is It, Then, That We Still Remain Barbarians?' Foucault, Schiller, and the Aestheticization of Politics." *Political Theory* 24.4 (1996): 653–73.

Berlant, Lauren, and Michael Warner. "What Does Queer Theory Teach Us About X?" *PMLA* 110.3 (May 1995): 343–49.

Berman, Marshall. *All that Is Solid Melts into Air: The Experience of Modernity*. New York: Simon and Schuster, 1982.

Boone, Joseph A. "Mappings of Male Desire in Durrell's *Alexandria Quartet*." *South Atlantic Quarterly* 88.1 (Winter 1989): 73–106.

Borchmeyer, Dieter. *Die Weimarer Klassik. Eine Einführung*. Königstein: Athenäum, 1980.

Bornemann, John. "AIDS in Two Berlins." *October* 43 (Winter 1987): 233–34.

Boswell, John. *Same-Sex Unions in Premodern Europe*. New York: Villard, 1994.

Boulby, Mark. *Karl Philipp Moritz: At the Fringe of Genius*. Toronto: University of Toronto Press, 1979.

Boyle, Nicholas. *Goethe: The Poet and the Age*. 2 vols. Oxford: Clarendon, 1991.

Bray, Alan. *Homosexuality in Renaissance England*. London: Gay Men's Press, 1982.

Bredbeck, Gregory W. "Milton's Ganymede: Negotiations of the Homoerotic Tradition in *Paradise Regained*." *PMLA* 106 (1991): 262–76.

Brinitzer, Carl. *A Reasonable Rebel: Georg Christoph Lichtenberg*. New York: Macmillan, 1960.

Brown, Jane K. "Faust." In *European Romanticism: Literary Cross-Currents, Modes and Models*, edited by Gerhart Hoffmeister, 181–96. Detroit: Wayne State University Press, 1990.

Bullough, Vern. *Sexual Variance in Society and History*. New York: Wiley, 1970.

————, ed. *An Annotated Bibliography of Homosexuality*. 2 vols. New York: Garland, 1976.

Büsching, Anton Friedrich. *Character Friedrichs des Zweytens*. 2nd ed. Halle: Witwe, 1788.

Butler, Judith. *Bodies that Matter: On the Discursive Limits of "Sex."* New York: Routledge, 1993.

————. *Gender Trouble: Feminism and the Subversion of Identity*. New York: Routledge, 1990.

Campe, Joachim, ed. *Andere Lieben. Homosexualität in der deutschen Literatur. Ein Lesebuch*. Suhrkamp Taschenbuch 1451. Frankfurt a/M: Suhrkamp, 1988.

Casanova, Jacques. *Histoire de ma Vie*. Wiesbaden: Brockhaus, 1961. Volumes 7–8.

Conrady, Otto Conrad. "Ganymed." In *Die deutsche Lyrik. Form und Geschichte. Interpretationen vom Mittelalter zur Frühromantik*, edited by Benno von Wiese, 227–36. Düsseldorf: Bagel, 1964.

Crawford, Ronald L. "Don Carlos and Marquis Posa: The Eternal Friendship." *Germanic Review* 43.3 (1983): 97–105.

Crompton, Louis. *Byron and Greek Love: Homophobia in Nineteenth-Century England*. Berkeley: University of California Press, 1985.

Daly, Mary. *Gyn/Ecology: The Metaethics of Radical Feminism*. Reprint of 1978 edition. Boston: Beacon Press, 1990.

de Jean, Joan. "Sex and Philology. Sappho and the Rise of German Nationalism." *Representations* 27 (Summer 1989): 148–71.

de Lauretis, Teresa. "Introduction," *Differences* 3.2 (1991): iii–xviii.

Deleuze, Gilles. *The Logic of Sense*. Translated by Mark Lester. Edited by Constantin Boundas. New York: Columbia University Press, 1990.

D'Emilio, John. *Making Trouble: Essays on Gay History, Politics, and the University*. New York: Routledge, 1992.

Derks, Paul. *"Die Schande der heiligen Päderastie": Homosexualität und Öffentlichkeit in der deutschen Literatur 1750–1850*. Berlin: Rosa Winkel, 1990.

———. "Nachwort" to *Kyllenion: Ein Jahr in Arkadien*, by August von Sachsen-Gotha. Berlin: Rosa Winkel, 1985.

Derrida, Jacques. *Disseminations*. Translated by Barbara Johnson. Chicago: University of Chicago Press, 1981.

———. *Of Grammatology*. Translated by Gayatri Chakravorty Spivak. Baltimore: Johns Hopkins University Press, 1976.

———. *The Politics of Friendship*. Translated by George Collins. New York: Verso, 1997.

Detering, Heinrich. *Das offene Geheimnis: Zur literarischen Produktivität eines Tabus von Winckelmann bis zu Thomas Mann*. Göttingen: Wallstein, 1995.

———. " 'Zur Sprache kommen': Eine homoerotische (Auto-)Biographie 1789." Reprint of "Nachricht von einer seltsamen Irrung eines menschlichen Triebes." *Beiträge zur Beruhigung und Aufklärung über dieeinige Dinge, die dem Menschen unangenehm sind oder sein können, und zur näheren Kenntniß der leidenden Menschheit*, 2nd part. Leipzig: Weidmann, 1789. In *Grenzüberschreitungen. Friedenspädagogik, Geschlechter-Diskurs, Literatur—Sprache—Didaktik. Festschrift für Wolfgang Popp zum 60. Geburtstag*. Essen: Blaue Eule, 1995.

Deutsches Wörterbuch von Jacob Grimm und Wilhelm Grimm. 16 vols. Leipzig: Hirzol, 1954.

Diener, Gottfried. *Goethe's "Lila": Heilung eines "Wahnsinns" durch "psychische Kur."* Frankfurt a/M: Athenäum, 1971.

Dietrich, Hans [= Hans Dietrich Hellbach]. *Die Freundesliebe in der deutschen Literatur. Nachdruck der Ausgabe Leipzig 1931*. Homosexualität und Literatur, 9. Berlin: Rosa Winkel, 1996.

Dolan, Jill. "Gender Impersonation Onstage: Destroying or Maintaining the Mirror of Gender Roles?" In *Gender in Performance: The Presentation of Difference in the Performing Arts*, edited by Laurence Senelick, 4–13. Hanover, N.H.: University Press of New England, 1992.

Drux, Rudolf. "Dichter und Titan. Der poetologische Bezug auf den Prometheus. Mythos in der Lyrik von Goethe bis Heine." *Heine-Jahrbuch* 25 (1986): 11–26.

Dyer, Richard. *Now You See It: Studies on Lesbian and Gay Film*. New York: Routledge, 1990.

Edelman, Lee. *Homographesis: Essays in Gay Literary and Cultural Theory*. New York: Routledge, 1994.

Eissler, Kurt Robert. *Goethe: A Psychoanalytic Study, 1775–1786*. 2 vols. Detroit: Wayne State University Press, 1963.

Eldorado: Homosexuelle Frauen und Männer in Berlin, 1850–1950: Geschichte, Alltag und Kultur. Berlin: Frolich & Kaufman, 1984.

Ellis, Havelock. "Sexual Inversion." In *Studies in the Psychology of Sex*. 2 vols. New York: Random House, 1905.

Faderman, Lillian. *Surpassing the Love of Men: Romantic Friendship and Love Between Women from the Renaissance to the Present*. New York: Morrow, 1981.

Faderman, Lillian, and Brigitte Eriksson. *Lesbians in Germany: 1890s-1920s*. 2nd ed. Tallahassee, Fla.: Naiad Press, 1990.

Femmel, Gerhard, ed. *Corpus der Goethezeichnungen*. 3 vols. Leipzig: Seeman, 1965.

Femmel, Gerhard, and Christoph Meckel, eds. *Die Erotika und Priapea aus den Sammlungen Goethes*. Frankfurt a/M: Insel, 1990.

Fenichel, Otto. *The Collected Papers of Otto Fenichel: First Series*. New York: Norton, 1953.

Ferris, Lesley. "Goethe, Goldoni and Women-Hating." In *Acting Women: Images of Women in Theater*, edited by Lesley Ferris, 47–64. New York: New York University Press, 1989.

———. "The Legacy of Goethe's Mimetic Stance." In *Crossing the Stage: Controversies on Cross-Dressing*, edited by Lesley Ferris, 51–57. New York: Routledge, 1993.

Fink, Arthur-Hermann. *Maxime und Fragmente: Grenzmöglichkeiten einer Kunstform. Zur Morphologie des Aphorismus*. Munich, 1934.

Flaherty, Gloria. "Sex and Shamanism in the Eighteenth Century." In *Sexual Underworlds of the Enlightenment*, edited by G. S. Rousseau and Roy Porter, 261–80. Manchester: Manchester University Press, 1987.

———. *Shamanism and the Eighteenth Century*. Princeton: Princeton University Press, 1992.

———. "The Stage-Struck Wilhelm Meister and Eighteenth-Century Psychiatric Medicine." *MLN* 110 (1986): 493–515.

Fone, Byrne S. "The Other Eden: Arcadia and the Homosexual Imagination." In *Literary Views of Homosexuality*, edited by Stuart Kellogg, 13–34. New York: Haworth Press, 1983.

Fortis, Alberto. *Travels into Dalmatia*. New York: Arno Press, 1971.

Foucault, Michel. *The History of Sexuality*. 3 vols. Translated by Robert Hurley. New York: Random House, 1978–86.

———. *The Order of Things: An Archaeology of the Human Sciences*. New York: Pantheon, 1970.

———. *Wahnsinn und Gesellschaft: Eine Geschichte des Wahns im Zeitalter der Vernunft*. Translated by Ulrich Köppen. Frankfurt a/M: Suhrkamp, 1969.

Freud, Sigmund. *Basic Writings*. Translated by A. A. Brill. New York: Modern, 1938.

Fricke, Harald. *Aphorismus*. Stuttgart: Metzler, 1984.

Friedel, Johann. *Briefe über die Galanterien von Berlin auf einer Reise gesammelt von einem österreichischen Offizier 1782*. Edited by Sonja Schnitzler. Berlin: Eulenspiegel, 1987.

Friedenthal, Richard. *Goethe. Sein Leben und seine Zeit*. Munich: 1963.

Frye, Marilyn. *The Politics of Reality: Essays in Feminist Theory*. Trumansburg, N.Y.: Crossing Press, 1983.

Fuss, Diana. "Pink Freud." *GLQ* 2.1–2 (1995): 1–10.

Gallagher, Bob, and Alexander Wilson. "Michel Foucault: An Interview." *Edinburgh Review* (1986): 52–59.

Garber, Marjorie. *Vested Interests: Cross-Dressing and Cultural Anxiety*. New York: Routledge, 1992.

———. *Vice Versa: Bisexuality and Eroticism in Everyday Life*. New York: Simon & Schuster, 1995.

Gilman, Sander L. "AIDS and Syphilis: The Iconography of Disease." *October* 43 (Winter 1987): 86–107.

———. *The Case of Sigmund Freud: Medicine and Identity at the Fin de Siècle*. Baltimore: Johns Hopkins University Press, 1993.

———. *Sexuality: An Illustrated History. Representing the Sexual in Medicine and Culture from the Middle Ages to the Age of AIDS*. New York: Wiley, 1989.

Goethe, Johann Wolfgang von. *Erotische Gedichte. Gedichte, Skizzen und Fragmente*. Edited by Andreas Ammer. Frankfurt a/M: Insel, 1991.

———. *Faust 1 & 2*. Edited and translated by Stuart Atkins. Goethe's Collected Works, 2. Boston: Suhrkamp/Insel, 1984.

———. *Gedenkausgabe der Werke, Briefe, Gespräche, 29 August 1949*. 25 vols. Edited by Ernst Beutler. Zurich: Artemis, 1948.

———. *Goethes Werke: Hamburger Ausgabe in 14 Bänden*. Edited by Erich Trunz. 11th ed. Munich: Beck, 1981.

———. *Goethes Werke: Herausgegeben im Auftrage der Großherzogin Sophie von Sachsen*. 143 vols. Tokyo: Sansyusya, 1975. Reprint. Munich: DTV, 1987.

———. *Sämtliche Werke nach Epochen seines Schaffens, Münchner Ausgabe*. Edited by Karl Richter and Gerhard Sauder. Munich: Hanser, 1985.

———. *The West-Eastern Divan — West-östlicher Diwan*. Translated by J. Whaley. London: Wolff, 1974.

Goldberg, Jonathan. *Sodometries: Renaissance Texts, Modern Sexualities*. Stanford: Stanford University Press, 1992.

Goldoni, Carlo. *Three Comedies*. Oxford: Oxford University Press, 1961.

Goodbye to Berlin? 100 Jahre Schwulenbewegung. Eine Ausstellung des Schwulen Museums und der Akademie der Künste, 17 Mai bis 17. August 1997. Berlin: Rosa Winkel, 1997.

Graf, Roman. " 'Die Folgen des ehelossen Standes der Herren Soldaten': Male Homosocial Desire in Lenz's *Die Soldaten*." In *Space to Act: The Theater of J. M. R. Lenz*, edited by Alan C. Leidner and Helga S. Madland, 35–45. Columbia, S.C.: Camden House, 1993.

———. "The Homosexual, the Prostitute, and the Castrati: A Closet of Male Desire in J. M. R. Lenz." In *Outing Goethe and His Age*, edited by Alice Kuzniar, 77–93. Stanford: Stanford University Press, 1996.

Greenberg, David F. *The Construction of Homosexuality*. Chicago: University of Chicago Press, 1988.

Greif, Martin. *The Gay Book of Days*. Secaucus, N.J.: Mainstreet Press, 1982.

Grier, Edward. "Walt Whitman." In *The Encyclopedia of Homosexuality*, edited by Wayne R. Dyers, 2:1389. New York: Garland, 1990.

Guldin, Rainer. *"Lieber ist mir ein Bursch . . ." Zur Sozialgeschichte der Homosexualität im Spiegel der Literatur*. Homosexualität und Literatur, 8. Berlin: Rosa Winkel, 1995.

Guy, Basel. "*Ad majorem Societatis gloriam*: Jesuit Perspectives on Chinese Mores in the Seventeenth and Eighteenth Centuries." In *Exoticism in the Enlightenment*, edited by G. S. Rousseau and Roy Porter, 66–85. Manchester: Manchester University Press, 1990.

Hadleigh, Boze. *The Lavender Screen. The Gay and Lesbian Films: Their Stars, Makers, Characters, and Critics*. New York: Citadel Press, 1993.

Hahnemann, Samuel. *Organon of Homoeopathic Medicine*. 4th American ed. New York: Radde, 1860.

Hammer, Stephanie Barbe. "Schiller, Time and Again." *German Quarterly* 62.2 (1994): 153–72.

Hanson, Ellis. "Undead." In *inside/out: Lesbian Theories, Gay Theories*, edited by Diana Fuss, 324–40. New York: Routledge, 1991.

Hausen, Karin. "Family and Role-Division: The Polarisation of Sexual Stereotypes in the Nineteenth-Century: An Aspect of the Dissociation of Work and Family Life." In *The German Family: Essays in the Social History of the Family in Nineteenth- and Twentieth-Century Germany*, edited by Richard Evans and W. Robert Lee, 51–83. Totowa, N.J.: Barnes & Noble, 1981.

Heilbut, Anthony. *Thomas Mann: Eros and Literature*. New York: Knopf, 1996.

Heller, Erich. "From Love to Love: Goethe's *Pandora* and Wedekind-Alban Berg's *Pandora-Lulu*." *Salamagundi* 84 (Fall 1989): 100.

Heuser, Magdalene. " 'Das beständige Andenken vertritt die Stelle der Gegenwart': Frauen und Freundschaft in Briefen der Frühaufklärung und Empfindsamkeit." In *Frauenfreundschaft—Männerfreundschaft: Literarische Diskurse im 18. Jahrhundert*, edited by Wolfram Mauser and Barbara Becker-Cantarino, 141–65. Tübingen: Niemeyer, 1991.

Heyne, Moris. *Deutsches Wörterbuch*. Leipzig: Hirzel, 1905.

Hirsch, Marianne. "Spiritual 'Bildung': The Beautiful Soul as Paradigm." In *The Voyage In: Fictions of Female Development*, edited by Elizabeth Abel, Marianne Hirsch, and Elizabeth Langland, 23–48. Hanover, N.H.: University Press of New England, 1983.

Hirschfeld, Magnus. *Geschlechtsverirrungen*. Flenburg: Stephenson, 1994.

Hohmann, Joachim S., ed. *Der unterdruckte Sexus. Historische Texte und Kommentare zur Homosexualität*. Lollar: Aschenbach, 1977.

Horkheimer, Max, and Theodor Adorno. *Dialectic of Englightenment*. Translated by John Cumming. New York: Continuum, 1990.

Hössli, Heinrich. *Eros. Die Männerliebe der Griechen.* 3 vols. Berlin: Rosa Winkel, 1996.

Howard, Jean. "Cross-Dressing, the Theatre, and Gender Struggle in Early Modern England." *Shakespeare Quarterly* 39.4 (1988): 418–40.

Hufeland, Christoph Wilhelm. *Die Kunst, das menschliche Leben zu verlängern.* Jena, 1797.

Hull, Isabel. *Sexuality, State, and Civil Society in German, 1700–1815.* Ithaca: Cornell University Press, 1996.

Huussen, Arend H., Jr. "Sodomy in the Dutch Republic During the Eighteenth Century." In *Hidden from History: Reclaiming the Gay and Lesbian Past*, edited by Martin Duberman, Martha Vicinus, and George Chauncey, Jr., 141–59. New York: Penguin, 1989.

Hyam, Ronald. *Empire and Sexuality: The British Experience.* Manchester: Manchester University Press, 1990.

Irigaray, Luce. *This Sex Which Is Not One.* Translated by Catherine Porter. Ithaca: Cornell University Press, 1985.

Jacobs, Friedrich. *Friedrich Jacobs akademische Reden und Abhandlungen. Erste Abteilung. Vermischte Schriften von Friedrich Jacobs. Teil 3. Leben und Kunst der Alten. Teil 2.* Leipzig: Dyck, 1829.

Jaeger, Gustav. "Ein bisher ungedrücktes Kapitel über Homosexualität aus der Entdeckung der Seele. (Original 1879)." *Jahrbuch für sexuelle Zwischenstufen, unter besonderer Berücksichtigung der Homosexualität* 1 (1899): 53–125.

Jenisch, Daniel. *Ueber die hervorstechendsten Eigenthümlichkeiten von Meisters Lehrjahren.* Berlin: 1797.

Jones, James W. "Discourse on and of AIDS in Western German, 1986–90." In *Forbidden History: The State, Society, and the Regulation of Sexuality in Modern Europe*, edited by John C. Fout, 261–90. Chicago: University of Chicago Press, 1993.

Kalveram, Maria, and Wolfgang Popp, eds. *Homosexualitäten—literarisch.* Amsterdam: Blaue Eule, 1991.

Kant, Immanuel. "Träume eines Geistersehers, erläutert durch Träume der Metaphysik." *Kants Werke in zwölf Bänden: Theorie Werkausgabe.* Vol. 2. Frankfurt a/M: Suhrkamp, 1968.

Karsch, Ferdinand. "Heinrich Hössli (1784–1864)." *Jahrbuch für sexuelle Zwischenstufen* 5.1 (1903): 449–556. Reprinted in Hössli, vol. 3.

Kates, Gary. "D'Eon Returns to France: Gender and Power in 1777." In *Body Guards: The Cultural Politics of Gender Ambiguity*, edited by Julia Epstein and Kristina Straub, 167–94. New York: Routledge, 1991.

Kaus, Rainer J. *Der Fall Goethe: ein deutscher Fall. Eine psychoanalytische Studie.* Heidelberg: Winter, 1994.

Keilsen-Lauritz, Marita. "Maske und Signal—Textstrategien der Homoerotik." In *Homosexualitäten—literarisch*, edited by Maria Kalveram and Wolfgang Popp. Amsterdam: Blaue Eule, 1991.

Keppel-Kriems, Karin. *Mignon und Harfner in Goethes "Wilhelm Meister": Eine geschichtsphilosophische und kunsttheoretische Untersuchung zu Begriff und Gestalt des Naiven.* New York: Peter Lang, 1986.

Kershner, Sybille. "'Aus Furcht, zu zerspringen': Grenzen der Selbsterkenntnis, Krankheit und Geschlecht in popularphilosophischen Texten von Weikard, Pockels und Moritz." *Das achtzehnte Jahrhundert. Mitteilungen der Deutschen Gesellschaft für die Erforschung des achtzehnten Jahrhunderts* 16.2 (1992): 120–36.

Kessler, Harry Graf. *Tagebücher, 1918–1937.* Edited by Wolfgang Pfeiffer-Belli. Frankfurt a/M: Insel, 1996.

Kimball, Roger. "'Heterotexuality' and Other Literary Matters." *Wall Street Journal* (December 31, 1992): 31.

Kittler, Friedrich A. "Carlos als Carlsschüler. Ein Familiengemälde in einem fürstlichen Haus." In *Unser Commercium. Goethe und Schillers Literaturpolitik,* edited by Wilfred Barner, Eberhard Lammert, and Norbert Oellers, 241–74. Stuttgart: Cotta, 1984.

———. "Über die Sozialisation Wilhelm Meisters." In *Dichtung als Sozialisationsspiel,* edited by Friedrich A. Kittler and Gerhard Kaiser. Göttingen: Vandenhoeck & Ruprecht, 1978.

Klinger, Friedrich Maximilian. *Klingers Werke in zwei Bänden.* Edited by Hans Jürgen Geerdts. Berlin and Weimar: Aufbau, 1981.

Klischnig, Karl Friedrich. *Mein Freund Anton Reiser. Aus dem Leben des Karl Philipp Moritz.* Edited by Heide Hollmer and Kirsten Erwentraut. Berlin: Gatza, 1993.

Koestenbaum, Wayne. *The Queen's Throat: Opera, Homosexuality, and the Mystery of Desire.* New York: Vintage, 1993.

———. "Wilde's Hard Labor and the Birth of Gay Reading." In *Engendering Men: The Question of Male Feminist Criticism,* edited by Joseph A. Boone and Michael Cadden, 176–89. New York: Routledge, 1990.

Kotzebue, August von. *Doktor Bahrdt mit der eisernen Stirn. Oder: die deutsche Union gegen Zimmermann. Ein Schauspiel in vier Aufzügen von Freyherrn von Knigge.* 1790.

Kuzniar, Alice. "Titanism and Narcissism: The Lure of the Transparent Sign in Jean Paul." *Deutsche Vierteljahresschrift* 60 (1986): 440–58.

La Mettrie, Julien Offray de. *Man a Machine: French-English: Including Frederick the Great's "Eulogy" on La Mettrie and Extracts from La Mettrie's "The Natural History of the Soul."* Compiled Gertrude Carman Bussey. Chicago: Open Court, 1912.

Laqueur, Thomas. *Making Sex: Body and Gender from the Greeks to Freud.* Cambridge, Mass.: Harvard University Press, 1990.

Lavater, Johann Kaspar. *Essays on Physiognomy for the Promotion of Knowledge and the Love of Mankind.* 3 vols. Translated by Thomas Holcroft. London, 1789.

Lehnert, Gertrud. "Weiblichkeit als Maskarade: Zur Inszenierung der Geschlechterrollen bei Christoph Martin Wieland und Radclyffe Hall." *Forum: Homosexualität und Literatur* 28 (1996): 7–28.

Lichtenberg, Georg Christoph. *Schriften und Briefe.* 4 vols. and 2 vols. commentary. Edited by Wolfgang Promies. Munich: Hanser, 1968.

Lugowski, Clemens. "Goethe: Ganymed." In *Gedicht und Gedanke. Auslegungen deutscher Gedichte,* edited by Heinz Otto Burger, 102–18. Halle: Niemeyer, 1942.

Luhmann, Niklas. *Liebe als Passion: Zur Codierung von Intimität.* Frankfurt a/M: Suhrkamp, 1994.

MacLeod, Catriona. *Embodying Ambiguity: Androgyny and Aesthetics from Winckelmann to Keller*. Detroit: Wayne State University Press, 1998.

———. "The 'Third Sex' in an Age of Difference: Androgeny and Homosexuality in Winckelmann, Friedrich Schlegel, and Kleist." In *Outing Goethe and His Age*, edited by Alice Kuzniar, 194–214. Stanford: Stanford University Press, 1996.

Mandelkow, Karl Robert, ed. *Briefe an Goethe*. 2nd ed. 2 vols. Munich: Beck, 1982.

Mann, Klaus. *Tagebücher, 1931 bis 1933*. Edited by Joachim Heimannsberg, Peter Laemmle and Wilfred F. Schoeller. Munich: Spangenberg, 1989.

Mann, Thomas. *Die Erzählungen. Erster Band*. Frankfurt a/M: Fischer, 1967.

———. *Leiden und Grösse der Meister*. Frankfurt a/M: Fischer, 1982.

———. *Tagebücher, 1933–34*. Edited by Peter de Mendelssohn. Frankfurt a/M: Fischer, 1977.

———. *Tagebücher, 1949–1950*. Edited by Inge Jens. Frankfurt a/M: Fischer, 1991.

Margolis, Hans. "System und Aphorismus." In *Der Aphorismus: Zur Geschichte, zu den Formen und Möglichkeiten einer literarischen Gattung*, edited by Gerhard Neumann, 280–92. Darmstadt: Wissenschaftliche Buchgesellschaft, 1976.

Mauchart, Immanuel D., ed. *Allgemeines Repertorium für empirische Psychologie und verwandte Wissenschaften*. Nuremberg: Felsecker, 1792–98.

Mautner, Franz H. "Der Aphorismus als literarische Gattung." In *Der Aphorismus: Zur Geschichte, zu den Formen und Möglichkeit einer literarischen Gattung*, edited by Gerhard Neumann, 19–74. Darmstadt: Wissenschaftliche Buchgesellschaft, 1976.

———. *Lichtenberg: Geschichte seines Geistes*. Berlin: De Gruyter, 1968.

Mayer, Hans. *Outsiders*. Translated by Dennis Sweet. Cambridge, Mass.: MIT Press, 1982.

Meiners, Christoph. *Vermischte philosophische Schriften. Part I*. Leipzig: Weygand, 1775.

Meyer-Krentler, Eckhardt. *Der Bürger als Freund. Ein sozialethisches Programm und seine Kritik in der neueren deutschen Erzählliteratur*. Munich: Fink, 1984.

Minder, Robert. *Glaube, Skepsis und Rationalismus. Dargestellt aufgrund der autobiographischen Schriften in Karl Philip Moritz*. Frankfurt a/M, 1974.

Mirabeau, Honore Gabriel de Riqueti. *Histoire secrete de la cour de Berlin. Ou Correspondance d'un voyageur francois, depuis le mois de Juillet 1786 jusqu'au 9 Janvier 1787*. N.p.: 1789.

Mitter, Partha. *Much Maligned Monsters: History of European Reactions to Indian Art*. Oxford: Clarendon Press, 1977.

Moritz, Karl Phillip. *Anton Reiser. Ein psychologischer Roman*. Leipzig: Insel, 1959.

———, ed. *Das Magazin für Erfahrungsseelenkunde*. Facsimile edition, 1783–92. Edited by Anke Bennholdt-Thomsen and Alfredo Guzzoni. Lindau: Antiqua, 1979.

Mosse, George. *The Image of Man: The Creation of Modern Masculinity*. New York: Oxford University Press, 1996.

Müller, Friedrich. *Goethes Unterhaltungen mit dem Kanzler Müller*. Edited by Albrecht Knaus. Munich, 1950.

Müller, Johann Valentin. "Entwurf der gerichtlichen Arzneywissenschaft. 1796." In

Der unterdruckte Sexus, edited by Joachim S. Hohmann, 211–24. Lollar: Aschenbach, 1977.

Müller, Johannes von. *Allgemeine Aussicht über die Bundesrepublik in Schweizerland. Deutsche Fassung. 1776–1777. Erstausgabe.* Edited by Doris Walser-Wilhelm and Peter Walser-Wilhelm. Zurich: Amman, 1991.

———. *Sämtliche Werke.* Edited by Johann Müller. Tübingen: Cotta, 1811–15.

Müller, Klaus. *Aber in meinem Herzen sprach eine Stimme so laut. Homosexuelle Autobiographien und medizinische Pathographien im neunzehnten Jahrhundert.* Berlin: Rosa Winkel, 1991.

Müller, Klaus-Detlev. "Die Aufhebung des bürgerlichen Trauerspiels in Schillers 'Don Karlos.'" In *Friedrich Schiller. Angebot und Diskurs. Zügange, Dichtung, Zeitgenossenschaft*, edited by Helmut Brandt, 218–34. Berlin: Aufbau, 1987.

Müller, Lothar. *Die kranke Seele und das Licht der Erkenntnis: Karl Philipp Moritz' "Anton Reiser."* Frankfurt a/M: Athenäum, 1987.

Müller-Sievers, Helmut. "Writing Off: Goethe and the Meantime of Erotic Poetry." *MLN* 108 (1993): 427–45.

Nessller, Olga, and Thomas Nesseler. *Auf des Messers Schneide. Zur Funktionsbestimmung literarischer Kreativität bei Schiller und Goethe. Eine psychoanalytische Studie.* Freiburger literaturpsycholgische Studien, 3. Würzburg: Könighausen und Neumann, 1994.

Neumann, Gerhard. "'Ich bin gebildet genug, um zu lieben und trauern': Die Erziehung zur Liebe in Goethes *Wilhelm Meister.*" In *Liebesroman—Liebe im Roman*, edited by Titus Heydenreich and Egert Pohlmann. Erlangen: Univeritätsbibliothek Erlangen-Nürnberg, 1987.

———. *Ideenparadiese. Untersuchungen zur Aphoristik von Lichtenberg, Novalis, Friedrich Schlegel und Goethe.* Munich: Fink, 1976.

Nicolai, Ernst Anton. *Gedancken von den Würkungen der Einbildungskraft in den menschlichen Körper.* 2nd ed. Halle: Hemmerde, 1751.

Nietzsche, Friedrich. *On the Genealogy of Morals.* Translated by Walter Kaufmann and R. J. Hollingdale. New York: Random House, 1967.

———. "On Truth and Lie in an Extramoral Sense." In *Friedrich Nietzsche on Rhetoric and Language*, edited by Sander L. Gilman, Carole Blaire, and David Parent. New York: Oxford University Press, 1989.

Nunokawa, Jeff. "'All the Sad Young Men': AIDS and the Work of Mourning." In *inside/out: Lesbian Theories, Gay Theories*, edited by Diana Fuss. New York: Routledge, 1991.

Och, Gunnar. "'. . . und beschenkten sogar mehr als Moses.' Jean Paul und sein jüdischer Freund Emmanuel Osmund." *Jahrbuch der Jean-Paul-Gesellschaft* 21 (1986): 123–47.

Oguntoye, Katharina, May Opitz, and Dagmar Schultz, eds. *Farbe bekennen. Afrodeutsche Frauen auf den Spuren ihrer Geschichte.* Frankfurt a/M: Suhrkamp, 1992.

Oosterhuis, Harry, ed. *Homosexuality and Male Bonding in Pre-Nazi Germany: The Youth Movement, the Gay Movement, and Male Bonding Before Hitler's Rise. Original Transcript from "Der Eigene," the First Gay Journal in the World.* Translated by Hubert Kennedy. New York: Harrington Park, 1991.

Ortheil, Hanns-Josef. *Jean Paul.* Rowohlts Monographien 329. Reibek bei Hamburg: Rowohlt, 1984.

Orton, Graham. *Schiller: Don Carlos.* London: Arnold, 1967.

Panofsky, Erwin. *Studies in Iconography.* New York: Harper & Row, 1962.

Peters, Jürgen. "Eine Lücke in Moritzens Geschichten." *Forum: Homosexualität und Literatur* 28 (1997): 19–29.

Pfeiffer, Joachim. "Friendship and Gender: The Aesthetic Construction of Subjectivity in Kleist's Letters and Literature." Translated by Robert Tobin. In *Outing Goethe and His Age*, edited by Alice Kuzniar, 214–27. Stanford: Stanford University Press, 1996.

———. " 'Jegliches Mitleid verwischt der Regen': Tod und Aids in der deutschsprachigen Literatur." *Forum Homosexualität und Literatur* 19 (1993): 11–26.

Pietzcker, Carl. *Einführung in die Psychoanalyse des literarischen Kunstwerks am Beispiel von Jean Pauls "Rede des toten Christus."* Würzburg: Königshausen and Neuman, 1983.

———. *Trauma, Wunsch und Abwehr. Psychoanaltyische Studien zu Goethe, Jean Paul, Brecht, zur Atomliteratur und zur literarischen Form.* Würzburg: Königshaus & Neumann, 1985.

Pizer, John. "Gadamer's Reading of Goethe." *Philosophy and Literature* 15 (1991): 268–77.

Platen, August von. *Memorandum meines Lebens: Eine Auswahl aus den Tagebüchern.* Edited by Gert Mattenklott and Hansgeorg Schmidt-Bergmann. Frankfurt a/M: Insel, 1996.

Plato. *The Collected Dialogues of Plato.* Translated by Huntington Cairns. Edited by Edith Hamilton and Huntington Cairns. New York: Pantheon, 1961.

Pockels, Karl. *Versuch einer Charakteristik des weiblichen Geschlechtes.* 5 vols. Hannover, 1799–1802.

Popp, Wolfgang. " 'Weibliches Schreiben' — 'männliches Schreiben': Geschlechtsidentität und literarische Authentizität am Beispiel von Christa Wolf, Hans Henny Jahnn und Hubert Fichte." In *Homosexualitäten—literarisch*, edited by Maria Kalveram and Wolfgang Popp, 123–32. Amsterdam: Blaue Eule, 1991.

Porter, Roy. "The Exotic as Erotic: Captain Cook in Tahiti." In *Exoticism in the Enlightenment*, edited by G. S. Rousseau and Roy Porter, 117–44. Manchester: Manchester University Press, 1990.

Poubelle, Blanche. "Loose Lips: The Apples of Sodom." *The Guide* 14.3 (March 1994): 7.

Praetorius, Numa [= Eugen Wilhelm]. "Die strafrechtliche Bestimmung gegen den gleichgeschlechtlichen Verkehr, historisch und kritisch dargestellt." *Jahrbuch für sexuelle Zwischenstufen, unter besonderer Berücksichtigung der Homosexualität* 1 (1899): 97–158.

Prokhoris, Sabine. *The Witch's Kitchen: Freud, Faust, and the Transference.* Translated by G. M. Goshgarian. Ithaca: Cornell University Press, 1995.

Promies, Wolfgang. *Georg Christoph Lichtenberg.* Hamburg: Rowohlt, 1964.

Pruys, Karl Hugo. *Die Liebeskosungen des Tigers: Eine erotische Goethe Biographie.* Berlin: Edition q, 1997.

Ragusa, Isa. "Goethe's 'Women Parts Played by Men in the Roman Theater.' " In

Crossing the Stage: Controversies on Cross-Dressing, edited by Lesley Ferris, 47–57. New York: Routledge, 1993.

Rahmdohr, Friedrich Wilhelm Basileus. *Venus Urania: Ueber die Natur der Liebe, über ihre Veredlung und Verschönerung*. 3 parts. Leipzig: Goschen, 1798.

Rand, Erica. *Barbie's Queer Accessories*. Durham, N.C.: Duke University Press, 1995.

Requadt, Paul. *Lichtenberg*. 2nd ed. Stuttgart: Kohlhammer, 1964.

Rey, Michel. "Police and Sodomy in Eighteenth-Century Paris: From Sin to Disorder." In *The Pursuit of Sodomy: Male Homosexuality in Renaissance and Enlightenment Europe*, edited by Kent Gerard and Gert Hekma, 129–46. New York: Harrington Park, 1989.

Rich, B. Ruby. "From Repressive Tolerance to Erotic Liberation: *Mädchen in Uniform*." In *Out in Culture: Gay, Lesbian, and Queer Essays on Popular Culture*, edited by Corey R. Creekmur and Alexander Doty, 136–68. Durham, N.C.: Duke University Press, 1995.

Richter, Johann Paul Friedrich [= Jean Paul]. *Jean Paul. Werke in drei Bänden*. Edited by Norbert Miller. Vol. 1. Munich: Hanser, 1969.

Richter, Simon. "Winckelmann's Progeny: Homosocial Networking in the Eighteenth Century." In *Outing Goethe and His Age*, edited by Alice Kuzniar, 33–46. Stanford: Stanford University Press, 1996.

Rickels, Laurence A. *The Case of California*. Baltimore: Johns Hopkins University Press, 1991.

Ronell, Avital. *Crack Wars: Literature, Addiction, Mania*. Lincoln: University of Nebraska Press, 1992.

———. *Dictations: On Haunted Writing*. Bloomington: Indiana University Press, 1986.

———. "The Worst Neighborhoods of the Real: Philosophy–Telephone–Contamination." *Diacritics* 1.1 (1989): 125–45.

Rothschuh, Karl Eduard. "Leibniz, die prästabilierte Harmonie und die Ärzte seiner Zeit." In *Akten des internationalen Leibniz-Kongresses Hannover, 14–19 November 1966*, 2:231–54. 5 vols. Studia Leibnitiana Supplementa, 2. Wiesbaden: Franz Steiner, 1969.

Rousseau, George Sebastian. *Perilous Enlightenment: Pre- and Post-Modern Discourses: Sexual, Historical*. Manchester: Manchester University Press, 1991.

Rousseau, George Sebastian, and Roy Porter. Preface. In *Exoticism in the Enlightenment*, edited by G. S. Rousseau and Roy Porter, vi–x. Manchester: Manchester University Press, 1990.

Rowse, A. L. *Homosexuals in History*. New York: Macmillan, 1977.

Ruas, Charles. "An Interview with Michel Foucault." In *Death and the Labyrinth: The World of Raymond Roussel*, by Michel Foucault. Translated by Charles Ruas. New York: Doubleday, 1986.

Sachsen-Gotha, August Herzog von. *Ein Jahr in Arkadien. Kyllenion. Nachdruck der Ausgabe von 1805*. Edited by Paul Derks. Berlin: Rosa Winkel, 1985.

Said, Edward. *Orientalism*. New York: Random House, 1978.

Saslow, James. *Ganymede in the Renaissance: Homosexuality in Art and Society*. New Haven: Yale University Press, 1986.

Schenck, Ernst von, ed. *Briefe der Freunde. Das Zeitalter Goethes im Spiegel der Freundschaft.* 1937.

Schidlof, Berthold. *Das Sexualleben der Naturvölker. Band 1. Das Sexualleben der Australier und Ozeanier.* Leipzig: Leipziger, 1911.

Schiebinger, Londa. *The Mind Has No Sex? Women in the Origins of Modern Science.* Cambridge, Mass.: Harvard University Press, 1989.

Schiller, Friedrich. *Sämtliche Werke.* 5 vols. Edited by Gerhard Fricke and Herbert G. Göpfert. Munich: Hanser, 1965.

———. *Werke. Nationalausgabe.* Edited by Julius Petersen and Gerhard Fricke. Weimar: Bohlaus, 1942.

Schimpf, Wolfgang. " 'In des Witzes letzten Zeilen': Lichtenberg als Literaturkritiker." *Georg Christoph Lichtenberg, Text und Kritik* 114 (April 1992): 64–75.

Schings, Hans-Jürgen. "Agathon—Anton Reiser—Wilhelm Meister: Zur Parthogenese des modernen Subjekts im Bildungsroman." In *Goethe im Kontext: Kunst und Humanität, Naturwissenschaft und Politik von der Aufklärung bis zur Restauration: Ein Symposium,* edited by Wolfgang Wittkowski, 42–68. Tübingen: Niemeyer, 1984.

———. "Der anthropologische Roman: Seine Entstehung und Krise im Zeitalter der Spätaufklärung." In *Deutschlands kulturelle Entfaltung: Die Neubestimmung des Menschen,* edited by Bernhard Fabian, Wilhelm Schmidt-Biggemann, and Rudolf Vierhaus, 247–75. Munich: Kraus, 1983.

Schlegel, Friedrich. "Athenäums-Fragmente." *Kritische und theoretische Schriften.* Edited by Andreas Huyssen. Stuttgart: Reclam, 1978.

Schöne, Albrecht. *Aufklärung aus dem Geist der Experimentalphysik: Lichtenbergsche Konjunktive.* Munich: Beck, 1982.

Schwanitz, Hans Joachim. *Homöopathie und Brownianismus. Zwei wissenschaftstheoretische Fallstudien aus der praktischen Medizin.* Medizin in Geschichte und Kultur 15. New York and Stuttgart: Fischer, 1983.

Sedgwick, Eve Kosofsky. *Between Men: English Literature and Male Homosocial Desire.* New York: Columbia University Press, 1985.

———. *The Epistemology of the Closet.* Berkeley: University of California Press, 1990.

———. *Tendencies.* Durham, N.C.: Duke University Press, 1993.

Seidel, Siegfried, ed. *Briefwechsel zwischen Friedrich Schiller und Wilhelm von Humboldt.* 2 vols. Berlin: Aufbau, 1962.

Selden, Daniel L. " 'Just When You Thought It Was Safe to Go Back in the Water . . .' " In *The Lesbian and Gay Studies Reader,* edited by Henry Abelove, Michèle Aina Barale, and David M. Halperin, 221–23. New York: Routledge, 1993.

Shelley, Percy Bysshe. *The Selected Poetry and Prose of Percy Bysshe Shelley.* Edited by Carlos Baker. New York: Random House, 1951.

Siegel, Linda. "The Piano Cycles of Schumann and the Novels of Jean Paul Richter." *Piano Quarterly* (Fall 1969): 16–22.

Sontag, Susan. *AIDS and Its Metaphors.* New York: Farrar, Straus and Giroux, 1988.

Stahl, Georg Ernst. *Über den mannigfaltigen Einfluß von Gemütsbewegungen auf den menschlichen Körper (Halle, 1695). Über die Bedeutung des synergischen Prinzips für die Heilkunde (Halle 1695). Über den Unterschied zwischen Organismus und Mechanismus (1714). Überlegungen zum ärztlichen Hausbesuch (Halle 1703).* In

Sudhoffs Klassiker der Medizin 36. Translated by B. Josef Gottlieb. Leipzig: J. A. Barth, 1961.

Steakley, James. "Iconography of a Scandal: Political Cartoons and the Eulenberg Affair in Wilhelmine Germany." In *Hidden from History: Reclaiming the Gay and Lesbian Past*, edited by Martin Duberman, Martha Vicinus, and George Chauncey, Jr., 233–63. New York: New American Library, 1989.

———. "Sodomy in Enlightenment Prussia." In *The Pursuit of Sodomy: Male Homosexuality in Renaissance and Enlightenment Europe*, edited by Kent Gerard and Gert Hekma, 163–75. New York: Harrington Park, 1989.

Stern, J. P. *Lichtenberg: A Doctrine for Scattered Occasions. Reconstructed from His Aphorisms and Reflections*. Bloomington: Indiana University Press, 1959.

Stockinger, Jacob. "Homosexuality and the French Enlightenment." In *Homosexualities and French Literature: Cultural Contexts/Critical Texts*, edited by George Stambolian and Elaine Marks, 161–85. Ithaca, N.Y.: Cornell University Press, 1990.

Stone, Lawrence. *The Family, Sex and Marriage in England, 1500–1800*. New York: Harper & Row, 1979.

Straub, Kristina. "The Guilty Pleasures of Female Theatrical Cross-Dressing and the Autobiography of Charlotte Clarke." In *Body Guards: The Cultural Politics of Gender Ambiguity*, edited by Julia Epstein and Kristina Straub, 142–66. New York: Routledge, 1991.

Sucher, C. Bernd. "Faust, der Prahlheinz—Faust, der Zweifler." *Süddeutsche Zeitung* (October 12, 1992): 14.

Sweet, Dennis. "The Personal, the Political, and the Aesthetic: Johann Hoachim Winckelmann's German Enlightenment Life." In *The Pursuit of Sodomy: Male Homosexuality in Renaissance and Enlightenment Europe*, edited by Kent Gerard and Gert Hekma, 147–62. New York: Harrington Park, 1989.

Tissot, Samuel. *Versuch von denen Krankheiten, welche aus der Selbstbefleckung entstehen*. Translated from the Latin. Frankfurt: Fleischer, 1771.

Treichler, Paul. "AIDS, Homophobia, and Biomedical Discourse: An Epidemic of Signification." *October* 43 (Winter 1987: 31–70).

Trumbach, Randolph. "The Birth of the Queen: Sodomy and the Emergence of Gender Equality in Modern Culture, 1660–1750." In *Hidden from History: Reclaiming the Gay and Lesbian Past*, edited by Martin Duberman, Martha Vicinus, and George Chauncey, Jr., 129–40. New York: Penguin, 1989.

———. "London's Sapphists: From Three Sexes to Four Genders in the Making of Modern Culture." In *Body Guards: The Cultural Politics of Gender Ambiguity*, edited by Julia Epstein and Kristina Straub, 112–41. New York: Routledge, 1991.

———. "London's Sodomites: Homosexual Behavior and Western Culture in the Eighteenth Century." *Journal of Social History* 11 (1977): 1–33.

Tyler, Carole-Anne. "Boys Will Be Girls: The Politics of Gay Drag." In *inside/out: Lesbian Theories, Gay Theories*, edited by Diana Fuss, 32–70. New York: Routledge, 1991.

Ulrichs, Karl Heinrich. *Forschung über das Räthsel der mannmännlichen Liebe*. 4 vols. Berlin: Rosa Winkel, 1994.

Vaget, Hans Rudolf. *Goethe—Der Mann von 60 Jahren. Mit einem Anhang über Thomas Mann.* Königstein: Athenäum, 1982.

van der Meer, Theo. "The Persecutions of Sodomites in Eighteenth-Century Amsterdam: Changing Perceptions of Sodomy." In *The Pursuit of Sodomy: Male Homosexuality in Renaissance and Enlightenment Europe*, edited by Kent Gerard and Gert Hekma, 263–307. New York: Harrington Park, 1989.

Vicinus, Martha. " 'They Wonder to Which Sex I Belong': The Historical Roots of Modern Lesbian Identity." In *The Lesbian and Gay Studies Reader*, edited by Henry Abelove, Michèle Aina Barale, and David Halperin, 436–37. New York: Routledge, 1993.

Vollhaber, Tomas. *Das Nichts, die Angst, die Erfahrung: Untersuchung zur zeitgenoössischen schwulen Literatur.* Berlin: Rosa Winkel, 1987.

Vondung, Klaus. " 'Wilhelmine Meister?' Männliche Identität als psychologisches, gesellschaftliches und ästhetisches Problem im Bildungsprozeß." In *Grenzüberschreitungen, Friedenspädagogik, Geschlechter-Diskurs, Literatur—Sprache—Didaktik*, 279–95. Essen: Blaue Eule, 1995.

Wagnitz, H. B. *Historische Nachrichten und Bemerkungen über die merkwürdigsten Zuchthäuser in Deutschland. Nebst einem Anhange über die zweckmäßigste Einrichtung der Gefängnisse und Irrenanstalten.* 2 vols. Halle: Gebauer, 1791–94.

Waldecke, St. Ch. "Jean Paul Friedrich Richter." *Der Eigene* (1921–22): 168–72.

Wangenheim, Wolfgang von. " 'Daß aus seinem Munde die deutsche Jugend zuerst von griechischer Liebe gehört': Wilhelm Heinse in einer Briefanthologie der Dreißiger Jahre." *Forum: Homosexualität und Literatur* 14 (1992): 89–104.

Weeks, Jeffrey. "Discourse, Desire and Sexual Deviance: Some Problems in a History of Homosexuality." In *The Making of the Modern Homosexual*, edited by Kenneth Plummer, 76–111. London: Hutchinson, 1981.

Wehe, Walter. "Geist und From des deutschen Aphorismus." In *Der Aphorismus: Zur Geschichte, zu den Formen und Möglichkeiten einer literarischen Gattung*, edited by Gerhard Neumann, 130–43. Darmstadt: Wissenschaftliche Buchgesellschaft, 1976.

Westermarck, Edward. "Homosexualität." Translated by L. Katscher. *Sexual-Probleme: Zeitschrift für Sexualwissenschaft und Sexualpolitik* 4 (1908): 248–79.

Westphal, Carl. "Die conträre Sexualempfindung." *Archiv für Psychiatrie und Nervenkrankheiten* 2.1 (1869).

Wieland, Christoph Martin. *Werke.* 5 vols. Edited by Fritz Martini and R. Döhl. Munich: Hanser, 1964.

Wittkowski, Wolfgang, ed. *Friedrich Schiller: Kunst, Humanität und Politik in der späten Aufklärung. Ein Symposium.* Tübingen: Niemeyer, 1982.

Wolff, Eugen. *Mignon: Ein Betrag zur Geschichte des Wilhelm Meister.* Munich: Beck, 1909.

Zacchia, Paulus. "Zu Fragen der gerichtlichen Medizin: Über die Knabenschändung." In *Der unterdruckte Sexus. Historische Texte und Kommentare zur Homosexualität*, edited by Joachim S. Hohmann, 205–9. Lollar: Aschenbach, 1977.

Zantrop, Susanne. "Dialectics and Colonialism: The Underside of the Enlightenment." In *Impure Reason: Dialectic of Enlightenment in Germany*, edited by

W. Daniel Wilson and Robert C. Holub, 301–21. Detroit: Wayne State University Press, 1993.

Zimmermann, Johann Georg. *Fragmente über Friedrich den Großen: Zur Geschichte seines Lebens, seiner Regierung, und seines Charakters.* Leipzig, 1790.

———. *Über die Einsamkeit.* 4 vols. Leipzig, 1785.

———. *Über Friedrich den Großen und meine Unterredungen mit ihm kurz vor seinem Tod.* Leipzig, 1788.

———. *Von der Erfahrung in der Arzneykunst.* New edition. Zurich: Orell, Geßner, und Füeßli, 1777.

Zimmermann, Rolf Christian. *Das Weltbild des jungen Goethe. Studien zur hermetischen Tradition des deutschen 18. Jahrhunderts.* 2 vols. Munich: Fink, 1969.

ACKNOWLEDGMENTS

Parts of Chapter 4, "Literary Cures in Wieland and Moritz," appeared in "Healthy Families: Medicine, Patriarchy and Heterosexuality in Eighteenth-Century German Novels," in W. Daniel Wilson and Robert C. Holub, eds., *Impure Reason: Dialectic of Enlightenment in Germany* (Detroit: Wayne State University Press, 1993).

Earlier versions of parts of Chapter 5, "Pederasty and Pharmaka in Goethe's Works," were published as "'In and Against Nature': Goethe on Homosexuality and Heterotextuality," in *Outing Goethe and His Age*, edited by Alice A. Kuzniar; used with the permission of the publishers, Stanford University Press. Copyright 1996 by the Board of Trustees of the Leland Stanford Junior University.

Parts of Chapter 7, "Male Members: Ganymede, Prometheus, Faust," appeared in "Faust's Membership in Male Society: Prometheus and Ganymede as Models," in Jane K. Brown, Meredith Lee, and Thomas Saine, with Paul Hernandi and Cyrus Hamlin, eds., *Interpreting Goethe's Faust Today* (Columbia, S.C.: Camden House, 1994).

Parts of Chapter 8, "Thomas Mann's Queer Schiller," appeared under the same title in *Queering the Canon: Defying Sights in German Literatures and Culture*, ed. Chris Lorey (Columbia, S.C.: Camden House, 1999).

My thanks to Stanford University Press, Wayne State University Press, and Camden House for permission to reprint.

I would also like to express my gratitude to Whitman College and its trustees for generously funding several semester-long sabbaticals for this research. The college also provided money for the preparation of the manuscript. The Institute of European Studies also helped me by placing me as a Faculty Associate at Humboldt University in Berlin during the summer of 1997 when I was preparing this book. Barbara Gügold, Katrin Arendt, and Katharina Schwinges were a constant source of help during that time.

Over the years, many people have read these chapters and provided valuable insights and feedback. Stanley Corngold introduced me to the heady combination of eighteenth-century German literature and twentieth-century literary criticism. Sander Gilman, Todd Kontje, Jane Brown, Alice Kuzniar, Chris Lorey, Joachim Pfeiffer, and Dan Wilson have all offered feedback on one or more of the chapters in this book. Jim Soden, my colleague at Whitman, has read most of my work and always offered specific, helpful criticism in a kind and gentle way. Jürgen Lemke and Rosa von Praunheim helped connect me with knowledgeable people in Berlin while I was finishing the manuscript. My student Analiese Sand van den Dikkenberg helped in some of the research and manuscript preparation, as part of a scholarship funded by Whitman College. Throughout the development of the book, my partner Ivan Raykoff has been a wonderful reader and an inspirational conversationalist. This book is dedicated to him.

INDEX

de Pauw, Cornelius, 54

Der Eigene. See *The Exceptional*

Derks, Paul, 4, 14, 16n, 31, 32, 40, 74, 75, 86, 96, 101n, 124, 147, 149, 155, 158, 172, 182, 197, 200

Derrida, Jacques: on formalism, 40; on friendship, 19–20, 22, 38, 48–50; on the pharmakon, 99–101, 158

Der teutsche Merkur. See *The German Mercury*

Desgouttes, Franz (murderer), 22, 75

Detering, Heinrich, 4, 13, 16, 17, 31, 70, 80

de Troilius, Uno (travel writer), 56

Deutsches Museum, 182

Diderot, Denis, 57, 71

Die Büchse der Pandora, 206

Die Horen, 106

Diener, Gottfried, 72, 95

Dietrich, Hans [=Hans Dietrich Hellbach], 36

Dietrich, Johann Christian (friend of Lichtenberg), 182

Dietrich, Marlene, 206, 208

Die Zeit, ix

Different from the Others (*Anders als die anderen*), 205, 206

Dionysos, 196

Dolan, Jill, 119

Don Quixote, 74, 78, 88

Drag, 62, 119, 130. *See also* Berdache; Cross-dressing; Mahhus; Queens; Transvestites

Drux, Rudolf, 133, 134n

Duras, Marguerite, 144

Edelman, Lee, 8

Egypt, 53

Ehrlich, Lothar, ix

Eissler, Kurt Robert, 96, 97, 98, 107, 113, 114, 120, 131n, 169, 209

Eldorado, 63, 81, 196

Ellis, Havelock: on Germanness of homosexuality, 195, 196, 197, 199, 201, 202; and orientalism, 52–53, 58; and transvestism, 129; on Wordsworth's reaction to *Wilhelm Meister*, 109

Engels, Friedrich, 197

Enlightenment, dialectic of, 66, 88

Erasistratus (ancient physician), 113

Erections, 184

Erxleben, Dorothea (physician), 72

"The eternal feminine," 132, 144

Euryalus and Nissus, 15

The Exceptional (*Der Eigene*), 45, 149, 164, 170, 199

Extraordinary Example of the Great Decay of Morals in England (*Außerordentliches Beispiel der großen Verdorbenheit der Sitten in England*), 14

Faderman, Lillian, 68, 127, 179, 199, 202

Family: history and etymology of word, 8–10; and the Bildungsroman, 73. *See also* Bourgeoisie, family structures

Fanfares of Love (*Fanfaren der Liebe*), 208

Fashion, 5, 39

Faust, historical figure, 137–38. *See also* Goethe. Works: *Faust*

Faust, Wolfgang Max, 93

Faustianism, 195

Feinberg, David, 92

Female body, 67

Female impersonation, 87, 137

Female orgasm, 68

Female sexuality, 77, 88, 110–11

Femmel, Gerhard, 101n, 102

Fenichel, Otto, 120

Ferris, Lesley, 119, 120

Feuerbach, Anselm von (jurist), 199

Film, 205, 207

Fink, Arthur-Hermann, 189

Firbank, Ronald, 40

Flaherty, Gloria, 53, 54, 64, 111

Flaubert, Gustave, 53

Flimm, Jürgen, 144

Forster, Georg (explorer), 57, 188

Fortis, Alberto (travel writer), 58

Foucault, Michel: and "birth of man," 6; and "birth" of the homosexual, 5, 11, 200; on Faust, 100; and friendship, 35, 87; and hysteria and hypochondria, 67; and sodomy, 28

Franklin, Benjamin, 64

Frederick the Great (king of Prussia): and Berlin, 81; and classicism, 30; and medicine, 67, 70; misogyny, 29; and orientalism, 54; rumored to be sexually interested in men, 15–17, 82, 101, 209; scandalous interpretations of the Bible, 136, 209

Gray, Thomas (poet), 20
Greece: boundary between friendship and love in, 37–38; in Jean Paul, 60; for Lichtenberg, 181, 182; and male bonding, 190; marker for male-male desire, 29–34, 196; proximity to the Orient, 58; in Schiller, 156–57; in Wieland, 76; for Winckelmann, 19
Greek love, 36, 49, 81; Iffland accused of, 86; Lichtenberg aware of, 183; Moritz accused of, 81–83; allegedly introduced to Germany by Wieland, 74. *See also* Homosexuality; Pederasty; Sodomy
Greenberg, David, 68, 70
Greif, Martin, viii, 20
Grier, Edward, 170
Grimm, Jacob and Wilhelm, 8, 10, 40, 103, 144
Guilbert, Hervé, 93
Guldin, Rainer, 4
Gustafson, Susan, 4
Guy, Basel, 54
Guyon, Madame de (pietist), 87
Gymnasia, 33

Hackett, Phillip (artist), 97
Hadleigh, Boze, 205
Hadrian, 17
Hafis (Persian poet), 102, 168
Hahnemann, Samuel (physician), 72
Hamann, Johann Georg (philosopher), 32, 34, 76
Hammer, Stephanie, 155
Hansen, Ellis, 92
Happiness, 70–71
Hardenberg, Friderich von (= Novalis), 178
Hartenberg, Fritz von (takes advantage of Müller), 22
Hausen, Karen, 72
Hayes, Harry, 208
Hays, Dennis, 52
Heilbut, Anthony, 148
Heine, Heinrich, 174
Heinrich (prince of Prussia, brother of Frederick the Great), 16
Heinse, Wilhelm (novelist), 34, 136
Helen, 99
Heliogabolus (emperor of Rome), 59
Heller, Erich, 133n, 139

Henri III (king of France), 42
Henry IV, 101
Herder, Johann Gottfried, 10, 21, 32, 34, 76, 134
Hermaphrodites, 52, 142; in Lichtenberg, 179
Herz, Henriette (salon hostess), 84
Herz, Marcus (physician), 79, 84
Heterosexuality: "compulsory," 61; undermined by cross-dressing, 122; medical support of, 72
Heyne, Morris (lexicographer), 9, 10
Hiller, Kurt, 208
Hirschfeld, Magnus, 194n; on homosexuality in Germany, 196, 197, 198, 199, 200, 201, 202, 208; "Panic in Weimar," vi, vii, viii; on Schiller, 149, 158; the third sex, 122
Hoffmann, Friedrich (physician), 66, 67
Hofmannsthal, Hugo von, 191
Homeopathy, 72, 73, 84, 111, 112, 117, 131
Hom(m)osexuality, 50, 111
Homosexual emancipation movement, 198, 199, 200, 205
Homosexuality: linked to blackness, 91; economic factors in development of, 6; history of, 5, 50, 198, 200; and language, 104; and medicine, 69, 87, 198, 200; and National Socialism, 196; sublimated, at the root of art, 169, 170, 171; youthful crushes as part of normal development, 180. *See also* Greek love; Pederasty; Sodomy
Homosociality, male, 29, 50, 111, 155, 179–80, 196. *See also* Male bonding
Horace, 32
Horkheimer, Max, 66, 209
Hössli, Heinrich: on classicism, 30, 33; development of discourse of homosexuality, 198; on friendship, 36, 38, 98; and lovesick prince, 113; on orientalism, 35, 54; and Wieland, 75
Howard, Jean, 128
Huber, Ludwig Ferdinand (correspondent of Schiller), 74, 169
Hufeland, Christoph Wilhelm (physician), 70, 71, 95
Hull, Isabel, 14
Humboldt, Alexander von, 55, 195
Humboldt, Wilhelm von, 32, 33, 76, 157, 204
Huussen, Arend, 13
Hyacinth, 30, 40, 58, 77, 114, 160, 182

Platonic love, 82, 183, 187
Pockels, Karl (editor), 50
Pope, Alexander, 62, 174
Popp, Wolfgang, 1
Population control, 71
Portig, G. (early homosexual rights author), 148
Praunheim, Rosa von (filmmaker), 42, 92, 209–10
Prokhoris, Sabine, 209
Prometheus, 132–37
Promies, Wolfgang, 175n, 179, 182
Proust, Marcel, 28
Pruys, Karl Hugo, ix
Psychoanalysis: and knowledge of homosexuality, 202–4, 205; and literature, 153
Purchas, Samuel (explorer), 53
Purple prose, 40

Queens, 40. *See also* Berdache; Cross-dressing; Drag; Mahhus; Transvestites
Queer: as critique of identity, 3; etymology and translation of, 2
Queer reading, 2, 4, 38, 194–95; of Goethe's *Faust*, 132; and history, 2, 3, 37; sanctioned by Schiller, 173
Queer theory: and eighteenth century, 1; and language, 2; as rhetorical analysis, 24; and role of the author, 192

Racine, Jean (French playwright), 209
Ragusa, Isa, 117
Ramdohr, Friedrich Wilhelm Basileus: on friendship, 35, 38, 50; and gender binarisms, 11; on gymnasia, 34; on misogyny, 33; and orientalism, 54, 55; and same-sex desire, 14, 70–71, 98; rejected by Schiller, 147, 156; and universities, 79–80; and Winckelmann, 18
Reichert, Stefan, 93
Reifegg. *See* Kiefer, Otto
Reil, Johann Christian (physician), 95
Reinhard, Karl Friedrich Graf (correspondent of Goethe), 22
Reinwald, Wilhelm Friedrich Hermann (librarian), 171
Reiske, Ernestine Christiane (practitioner of "pious fraud"), 72

Religion, 45
"Report on a Strange Deviation" ("Nachricht von einer seltsamen Irrung"), 31, 70, 81
Requadt, Paul, 179, 180, 182, 183
Rey, Michel, 13, 14
Ricci, Matteo (explorer), 54
Rich, B. Ruby, 205
Richter, Johann Paul Friedrich (=Jean Paul), 36, 44–64, 81, 178, 188, 194, 195, 205, 209; biography, 45; on friendship, 48; decision to use pseudonym, 46; and religion 45; youthful crush, 180. Works: *Hesperus*, 48; *Siebenkäs*, 46–64, 106, 192; "Speech of the Dead Christ" (*Rede des toten Christus*), 45
Richter, Simon, viii, 4, 14, 20, 37
Rickels, Laurence, 4, 48, 209
Riefenstahl, Leni (filmmaker), 207
Riggs, Marlon (filmmaker and poet), 63, 92
Rimbeau, Arthur (poet), 196
Roberts, David, 110
Ronell, Avital, 89, 100, 101, 144, 209
Rothschuh, Karl Eduard, 66
Rousseau, George Sebastian, 8, 12–13, 16n, 18, 53, 65, 97
Rousseau, Jean-Jacques, 100, 114, 180
Rubbing, as sexual activitiy, 68, 114
Ruling, Anna (early German feminist), 198

Saadi (Persian poet), 104
Sachs, Marie (Lichtenberg's beloved), 177, 186
Sachsen-Gotha and Altenburg, August, Duke. *See* August (duke of Sachsen-Gotha and Altenburg)
Sade, Marquis de, 21, 100
Safe sex, 90
Sagan, Leontine (filmmaker), 149–50, 160, 205, 206, 208
Said, Edward, 52, 58, 63
Samuel, Emmanuel (=Emmanuel Osmund, friend of Jean Paul), 46, 62
Sappho, 68–69
Sarduy, Severo, 126
Saslow, James, 135n
Satire, 61
Sauer, Martin (explorer), 53
Schelling, Caroline Böhmer Schlegel (salonist), 74